# Crime and Justice in Japan and China

# Crime and Justice in Japan and China

## A Comparative View

L. Craig Parker

CAROLINA ACADEMIC PRESS

Durham, North Carolina

Library of Congress Cataloging-in-Publication Data

Parker, L. Craig.
  Crime and justice in Japan and China : a comparative view / L. Craig Parker.
    p. cm.
  Includes bibliographical references and index.
  ISBN 978-1-61163-086-2 (alk. paper)
  1. Crime--Japan. 2. Crime--China. 3. Criminal justice, Administration of--
Japan. 4. Criminal justice, Administration of--China. I. Title.

  HV7110.5.P37 2012
  364.951--dc23

                     2012025992

CAROLINA ACADEMIC PRESS
700 Kent Street
Durham, North Carolina 27701
Telephone (919) 489-7486
Fax (919) 493-5668
www.cap-press.com

Printed in the United States of America

*For Meg and Daniel Frost,*
*my grandchildren and future scholars*

# Contents

# Preface

My first visit to Japan, in 1980, provided the most exciting and perhaps frustrating year of my professional life. Unacquainted with Japanese culture and language, I was like a bull in a china shop. I was the only researcher that year that was not a Japanologist—that is, a person knowledgeable in the culture and language of Japan. The National Police Agency had sent a short note to the Fulbright office in Tokyo stating, "we can give Professor Parker about one week for his research," as they were very busy at the time. I had arrived for a year on a jointly funded Fulbright Research Fellowship that was supported by both the United States and Japanese governments. I believed that given this support I would be welcomed by the National Police Agency. Obviously I was wrong and my ignorance of Japanese customs played into this misunderstanding. Fortunately, a day later, at a glittering party for Japanese Fulbrighters headed for America, I met a prominent Japanese constitutional law scholar who introduced me to some colleagues and high-ranking justice officials. While it took about six weeks of a variety of intense and frustrating meetings, I eventually was given full access to the police for research purposes.

As I noted in my book on the Japanese police system, "A Japanese businessman will not approach a fellow businessman or a bureaucrat without a proper introduction if he expects to be successful in his endeavors. Often the initiating party will ask a former classmate or an acquaintance to arrange the meeting. This go-between may be able to lay the groundwork or actually arrange an introduction. The Japanese have a word for this: *nemawashi*, meaning 'to lay the groundwork for obtaining one's objective'" (Parker, 2001).

Fellow scholars and criminal justice professionals helped immensely in my understanding of Japanese culture and I was blessed with two young wonderful interpreters. Mari Kanai had studied at a variety of international schools (learning English) during overseas trips with her family. Her father had worked as a Japanese ambassador in countries around the world. Susumu Kitaidai was a student at the International Christian University and was fluent in English. He had lived in New York City and Washington, D.C., for a number of years during the period in which his father worked for the Tokyo Broadcasting System.

Interpreters are important as they do more than translate words between English and Japanese. They represent you and their interpersonal skills are critical to the researcher. Approaching the Japanese National Police Agency for a research project by an American Fulbright Scholar proved to be a daunting task. Police in general are reluctant to have outside researchers come in for purposes of study. Japan is a very insular nation and *gaijin*, or "foreigners," are often viewed with suspicion.

One element that worked to my advantage, despite having to draw on interpreters for many of my meetings, was that some Japanese police and justice officials spoke English. Many of them learn English starting in junior high school and some are eager to practice their English. Others, however, are uncomfortable in speaking English, and many Japanese lack opportunities to speak English once they have left secondary school. I focused on and became friends with a number of Japanese police and justice officials who spoke English.

My introduction to China had an interesting Japanese twist. In 1985, after returning to the University of New Haven from sabbatical, I received a fascinating letter from a Chinese woman scholar, Zhang Yun Yi. She was an instructor at the Police Officers University outside of Beijing, teaching comparative criminal justice. She asked for my assistance and stated, "I know you from your book on the Japanese police system. Would you be kind enough to send me some books on the history of the American criminal justice system? I'm sorry I don't have any Western currency, but perhaps there is something you would like from China?" She also commented that she had a masters degree from Nanjing University. I immediately responded to her request and stated that I did not desire to have any money or gifts from her, but would like to engage in correspondence. I was curious about her life and work as a professor at this law enforcement institution of higher learning. She proved to be a very open and expressive person and she shared some of the most personal and searing moments of her life, including her experiences with the Red Guards. Red Guards were young teenagers that Mao unleashed on many establishment figures in the population. They had harassed her father and ultimately he died in a prison during the infamous Cultural Revolution. While he was still alive, family members were required to participate in what the Chinese called "struggle sessions" of verbal attack and abuse directed at her father. He had been a prominent economist in the Communist Party, but like many establishment figures, was subjected to the assaults unleashed by teenage Red Guards supporting Mao's directives to maintain the revolution. Hundreds of thousands, if not millions, of Chinese, died during this horrific period between 1966 and 1976. The emotional scars of this traumatic era, when Zhang Yun Yi was merely a teenager, were clearly evident when I finally met her during my one-month lecture tour in Beijing a year later.

Other Chinese friends have subsequently added their own tales of pain and misfortune from this dark period of Chinese history. Zhang Yun Yi arranged, through colleagues of her deceased father—who incidentally was still highly regarded by his colleagues—my visit to China in the Summer of 1986. Officially, I was invited by Vice-President Zhu Sen of the Police Officers University, and the experience was both educational and very exciting. A year later, I sponsored Zhang Yun Yi for a master's degree in criminal justice at Northeastern University in Boston. In the Fall of 1987, I arranged a follow-up visit of two professors and two administrators, including Vice-President Zhu Sen, to the United States for a month-long lecture tour. They met with faculty from the University of New Haven, the University of New Hampshire, Northeastern University, Mercy College, and C.W. Post College of Long Island. A final exchange of scholars took place in 1988, which allowed American scholars from the above named universities to visit China as part of a reverse exchange that I arranged. This was a year prior to the infamous Tiananmen Square Massacre in which an unknown large number of private citizens and students were gunned down by police and the military. Contacts were frozen with the staff of the Police Officers University and never resumed. However, my interest in Chinese criminal justice and Chinese culture continued unabated. I developed friendships with a number of Chinese scholars. One Chinese Fulbright Scholar, Hou Wei Rei, arrived at Yale to pursue his scholarly studies in English literature and we stayed friends until his death in 1999. Since 2006, I have enjoyed sitting in on many lectures at the Yale China Law Center, which were offered by China legal experts and social scientists from both China and the United States.

There are many exciting and revealing changes taking place in the justice systems of Japan and China—the nations covered in this book. Many of these changes reflect the fascinating cultural and historical foundations of the countries. While sharing some interesting similarities, there are vast differences in how the criminal justice systems operate in each country. One of the major themes of this work is how each society's culture influences crime. In fact, it is evident that the social and cultural make-up of each of the two countries has a far more profound effect on the crime rates than any efficiencies that can be produced by the criminal justice agencies.

The Japanese and Chinese justice systems are vastly different in how they have evolved. Significant developments continue to emerge in both Japan and China. For example, in Japan the jury system has returned after an absence of more than 50 years. Not since the American occupation of Japan in the late 1940s, and the end of World War II, have Japanese citizens been required to participate in a process that many of them approached with anxiety. General MacArthur and his staff attempted to transplant some of the key features of the American democratic experience on to the authoritarian landscape of Japan. While some concepts took root, others were tossed aside after a brief experiment. For example, the police were decentralized under MacArthur, but were organized into the current national structure a few years later.

China's government is still communist in its political structure, but its wide-open economic system mirrors in many respects capitalistic countries around the world. Chinese officials call it "market forces." Students of international or comparative criminal justice will enjoy the many comparisons offered with the United States system. Some of the approaches and concepts illustrated in this text may intrigue American students of criminal justice, and indeed some approaches may be implemented in the United States. Many, however, cannot be transplanted because of their unique cultural character.

My wide and extensive experience as a criminal justice scholar—with two acclaimed books on Japan—provides the reader with a penetrating and in-depth look at the justice systems of both Japan and China. Unlike many comparative analyses offered to students and scholars, I offer a strong critique of each nation's justice systems based in part on personal experiences. In addition, this work offers insight into how these rival nations approach the problem of crime and how this may play out in the future. Finally, I shed light on how both countries interact with each other in what is often a complex and intriguing dance—at times cooperative and at times competitive. The legacy of Japan's invasion and brutal assaults on Chinese private citizens during World War II is echoed in today's relationships between the nations. By 2011, China had overtaken Japan as the second largest economy in the world and this powerful economic machine has recast the relationship. China's gross domestic product during the first decade of the twenty-first century has far outstripped Japan's. On average, it has been 8–10 percent in China compared to 2–4 percent in Japan. The later has been in and out of recession for more than 20 years.

It is difficult to draw comparisons between crime reports from Japan and the United States because the different levels of public confidence in police effectiveness in these countries result in different rates of reporting crime. Many crimes go unreported in all three nations. Descriptive terms for crimes—even after making allowances for the possible inaccuracy of translation—may have different meanings in each country, further confusing the issue. Japanese people report a larger percentage of crime than Americans do. In China, citizens are often reluctant to report crime, as the police—called "public security"—are not respected by many citizens, and are often viewed skeptically as corrupt tools of the state. Because of the unreliability of data issued in the *Uniform Crime Reports* of the Federal Bureau of Investigation (F.B.I.), the U.S. Department of Justice began direct household surveys of crime a number of years ago. This approach revealed, not surprisingly, a significantly higher incidence of actual crime than that reported by citizens to police. Reports to police, similar to the *Uniform Crime Reports* of the F.B.I., are also relied upon in Japan and China.

Police departments in many countries are tempted to manipulate crime statistics to make their department or agency look good. In the United States, there are various grants available from the federal government to police departments, and presenting a particular department in a favorable light may assist in the successful application for these funds. In Japan and China, unlike the United States, the systems are fundamentally national in character. Although Japan has 47 prefectural police agencies, which have limited autonomy, they fundamentally operate in a top-down national fashion. By employing national systems, the Japanese and Chinese have the luxury of creating standardized systems of policies and practices. However, Chinese law enforcement practices and personnel policies are still modernizing and are of lower quality than those in the United States and Japan. Professional training programs and education of police in China are making strides but remain far behind those found in Japan and the United States. In talking with police officers in the United States about their experiences in interacting with other law enforcement agencies, one becomes aware of a great variety of responses that spring from ignorance to jealousy to outright hostility. The one U.S. national agency—the Federal Bureau of Investigation—operates very independently and its relationships with American police forces vary a great deal. Occasionally there are joint task forces that are organized to fight gangs or illegal drugs. The F.B.I. becomes involved with local police when bank robberies occur as they are required by law to respond to such crimes. On many occasions, the agencies don't interact. Relationships are often tied to the personal skills of the actors.

The structure of police activities in the United States is so decentralized and fragmented that potential terror attacks in the wake of the September 11 devastation of the World Trade Center and other targets have continued to create serious gaps in the Homeland Security system of detection and prevention. Local police departments in the United States are often left to their own devices to create systems of crime detection and apprehension of criminals. In the United States, there is still no fully integrated system to defend against terrorism, but this is linked to the nature of the separate local, county, and statewide police agencies.

On the bright side, some middle-ranking police officers are offered opportunities to attend the F.B.I. training academy and often praise these educational opportunities, but overall, the number who attend is a small portion of local police nationwide.

# About the Author

L. Craig Parker is a psychologist and professor emeritus at the Henry C. Lee College of Criminal Justice at the University of New Haven. He has studied criminal justice systems in a variety of foreign countries including Great Britain, Canada, Denmark, The Netherlands, Sweden, Iceland, Finland, and Japan. The author recieved Fulbright Research Fellowships in both Japan and Finland. Previously he was a professor at the University of Wisconsin-Milwaukee and the University of Alberta. The author was also a Visiting Scholar at Columbia Law School and a Visiting Faculty Fellow at Yale University. He continues to teach forensic psychology and global criminal justice at the University of New Haven.

# Acknowledgments

I received critical assistance from two people who helped me prepare the manuscript before Tim Colton and the wonderful staff at Carolina Academic Press took over. Janet Giarratano, of Yale University, has worked with me on a number of my books and does an excellent job taking my messy, handwritten material and converting it on her word processor. I am also grateful to Steve Hopkins, who did a thorough job editing my manuscript. I learned the hard way that having a good editor is essential and I appreciate his work on this project.

# Crime and Justice in
# Japan and China

# 1

# Crime in Japan

## Overview

In the United States, starting in the early 1980s, awareness of Japan increased, largely due to what was perceived as a growing economic threat. With economic anxiety, however, came a certain amount of cross-cultural curiosity. One issue was Japan's surprisingly low crime rate. In recent decades, from around 1990, the Japanese economy has been deeply mired in recession. During a brief period, around 2010 and early 2011, there was a brightening of the economic landscape, but the giant earthquake and tsunami in the spring of 2011 wreaked havoc on whatever economic prosperity that had started to emerge. However, in typical Japanese fashion, the country pulled together with citizens helping each other and supporting each other in the rebuilding process. The Japanese are famous for employing the group. Youngsters, unlike in America, are socialized to put the group first. Indirectly the role of the group has an impact on crime in many different ways. Individualism, so prized in the United States, is often considered selfishness in Japan.

Michael Wines (2011), writing for the *New York Times*, commented that "to an outsider, much is striking about Japan's response to two weeks of serial disasters: the stoicism and self-sacrifice; the quiet bravery in the face of tragedy that seems almost woven into the national character." He continued that in the town of Rikuzentakata, hard hit by catastrophe, "evacuees here live in a place that can kennel your dog, charge your cell phone, fix your dentures and even provide that nonnegotiable necessity of life, a steamy soak in a hot tub of water." This approach reflects the Japanese penchant for organization and order. Reports continued to be filed by foreign correspondents in which they expressed amazement at the lack of crime and thievery during this turbulent period of the spring of 2011.

Economically, the data, as was noted in *The Economist* (2011), showed that while industrial production had plunged by 15.5 percent in the immediate aftermath of the crisis, by February and March of 2011, economists were anticipating a pickup within three months. Long term, experts were positive. Alan Wheatley observed, "but out of this crisis affecting a large part of the population, a sense of 'public morality' is building up" (*Globe and Mail*, 2011).

Notwithstanding the historical Japanese ability to cope with various crises, including the nuclear attacks of the 1940s, the overall experience was very sobering. Routines, including the punctual arrivals and departures of trains and subways, were all impacted. Although the coastal area, more than 150 miles above Tokyo, was the hardest hit area, Tokyo and other regions nationwide were impacted. The bright lights of the famed Ginza shopping and dining area of Tokyo were dimmed as the Fukushima Daiichi nuclear power plants melted down and electricity output was broadly diminished. Japanese were humbled by the experience, and interviews with storekeepers noted a decline in the sale of high-end brand-name products. Japanese are famous for their appetite for top brand products like Tiffany, Hermès, Burberry, and Gucci. The scale of the earthquake, with the loss of over 25,000 lives, did impact national confidence. While Japanese have a reputation for *gaman* or "endurance," the trauma experienced by survivors who lost loved ones and homes continued to play out in the following three months, and this trauma will last for years. Psychologist Susumu Hirakawa, who specialized in post-traumatic stress, stated, "In the tsunami they could see loved ones dying right in front of them" (Belson, 2011). Most observers believe it will take years for the nation to fully recover.

A much different factor that has the potential for an even greater long-term impact on Japanese life is linked to the population decline. First brought to my attention by my colleague Professor Isshu Takahashi of Hosei University Law School in 1999, the Japanese birthrate was already in decline (Takahashi, 1999). Marriage and fertility rates have dropped substantially and demographers estimate that by 2030, one-third of the population will be older than 64. The fertility rate of 1.37 was down from 2.13 in 1970, as Japanese are not replacing themselves, according to Lindsay Whipp (*Financial Times*, 2010). The government has tried to encourage couples to have more children, but the financial incentives have not borne fruit. One dimension of the problem is that women have gradually become more independent financially and exist in much greater numbers in the workforce since the 1980s. This has also resulted in a greater willingness to marry later and postpone having children. Historically strong *conformity* pressures insured that when a woman entered the workplace she would be expected to leave by the time she married or reached child-bearing age.

Today a small minority of women forgo marriage entirely. Despite these changes, in speaking of conformity, the Japanese are fond of the expression "the nail that sticks up gets hammered down."

# Crime in Japan

In my various visits to Japan in 1980, 1983, and 1999, I always felt comfortable strolling the streets of cities like Tokyo, Kyoto, Kobe, Yokohama, and Sapporo. I never felt threatened and would walk through Ueno Park in the heart of Tokyo at midnight without fear of being robbed or assaulted. I rode buses and trains that were not defaced with graffiti and generally experienced a sense of serenity associated with the very low crime rates in Japan. I acknowledge that this took some time to adjust to. In the apartment next door to mine, in a section of Tokyo called Higashi-Koenji, I would often witness a young girl of around 10 years of age with her little backpack (common to most school-age children) hop on a subway by herself on the way to school. I thought it was remarkable, but couldn't overcome a sense of anxiety about her safety. While acknowledging the problems of engaging in comparisons of crime between Japan and the United States, what do the numbers look like? The Japanese population was 127.9 million in 2009 and the United States population was 308.8 million (more than double that of Japan). The incidence of crime was much greater in the United States. Japan lives up to its reputation as a densely populated nation with 339.2 people per square kilometer. The United States has a population of just 32.9 individuals per square kilometer. China falls between the two, with a population of 139.7 citizens per square kilometer (*The Economist*, 2011b).

In Japan in 2009, there were a total 1,703,044 penal code offenses reported to the police. The police cleared (that is, solved or resolved) 544,699 penal code offenses—a decrease of 5.0 percent from the previous year (National Police Agency of Japan, 2011). There has been a trend in the decline of most crimes in Japan over a number of years. For example, from 2006 until 2009, the decline of "felonious offenses" went from 10,124 to 8,314. Murder declined from 1,309 to 1,094 over the same period. Robbery, always considered important to criminologists as a symbol of serious and violent crime, fell from 5,108 cases in 2006 to 4,512 in 2009. The Japanese authorities note that there is an erosion in the willingness of citizens to step forward and report crime and they view it as a gradual weakening in the cohesiveness of Japanese society. Industrialized nations around the world seem to be experiencing a similar phenomenon. Japanese still report crime to police at a relatively high level

Table 1.1  Violent Offenses in Japan and the United States, 2009

|           | Japan  | United States |
|-----------|--------|---------------|
| Murder    | 1,094  | 15,241        |
| Robbery   | 4,512  | 408,217       |
| Rape      | 1,402  | 88,097        |
| *Assault  | 56,102 | 806,843       |

* Assault in Japan includes both "assault" and "bodily injured" in Table 1.1. Assault in the United States is defined as "aggravated assault."
*Source:* National Police Agency of Japan, 2011 and United States Department of Justice, *Uniform Crime Reports*, 2011.

compared to citizens in the United States. Witnesses are said to be less cooperative when police contact them.

The total number of murders, robberies, rapes, and assaults in Japan during 2009 numbered 36,646. In the United States for 2009, the comparable numbers of murders, robberies, rapes, and assaults amounted to 1,115,168. A breakdown by categories is offered in Table 1.1. As is clearly evident from this portrayal, the proportion of violent crime is much greater in American society than in Japan, notwithstanding the fact that the United States has more than double the population. Of course, it always must be noted that rape is an underreported offense in most countries, and I suspect that it is seriously underreported in Japan given the overall lack of willingness of the Japanese to report domestic violence. Returning to the subject of clearances, the following data are offered for both countries: murder (98% Japan; 66% U.S.), robbery (65% Japan; 28% U.S.), rape (83% Japan; 41% U.S.), assault (72% Japan; 57% U.S.).

Although clearance rates may be declining in Japan, they are significantly higher than in the United States. There is a greater willingness on the part of Japanese citizens to cooperate with police and criminal investigators. In reviewing trends in crime data for both nations, it is evident that both countries experienced significant declines from 2006 to 2009. In fact, these trends have been going on for a much longer period of time in both countries. In Japan, murders declined from 1,309 in 2006 to 1,094 in 2009, and the trend was similar for the same time span in the United States. Murders declined from 17,318 in 2006 to 5,241 in 2009. Robberies in Japan dropped from 5,108 to 4,512, while in the United States for the same years the numbers went from 449,803 to 408,217. The statistics on rape in Japan went from 1,948 to 1,402 during this period and in the United States between 2006 and 2009, the numbers went from 94,782 to 88,097. Therefore, in examining these particular categories for violent crimes, the pattern of decline is consistent on both Japan and the United States. How can one account for these dramatic differences in two of the most industrialized countries in the world? By examining this issue, for both Japan and China, I hope to shed light on our own crime problem. As will be evident later in this book, when China's crime situation is examined, there are fascinating comparisons to be offered between the two Asian giants and America.

One of the problems that Japan must face—particularly in light of the 2011 earthquake, tsunami, and nuclear disaster—is that they must import much of their energy. Japan looked to develop nuclear energy because of its lack of natural energy resources like coal, oil, and natural gas.

## Reasons for Low Crime Rates

One key reason for low crime rates in Japan is tied to the homogenous nature of Japanese society. Approximately 97 percent of the entire population of Japan is made up of individuals who are similar racially and ethnically and in their customs and religious practices. Unlike in the United States and China, there are few racial or cultural tensions in the country. Few minorities exist, with Koreans representing the largest share—upwards of 700,000 in the overall population of 127.9 million individuals. Many Koreans, although born in Japan, are not citizens. I occasionally would meet a Korean and would discover that he or she carried an alien registration card like myself. It is very difficult for a foreigner to obtain citizenship and the applicant must be fluent in Japanese. Many lifelong Korean residents are unable to attain this citizenship status. As Herbert (1996) noted, there are second- and third-generation descendants who, after the annexation of Korea as a de facto colony in 1910, were deported to Japan as child laborers. Herbert's doctoral dissertation also shed light on how prejudice played a role in the way foreign criminality has been portrayed by the media—including both print and electronic versions.

Another group that has been identified as a minority, but in reality is ethnically and racially Japanese, is the *burakumin*—historically called *eta*, meaning "very filthy," a word that has been banished from discourse. Most Japanese do not use the word. These are individuals who, for more than a century, have been outcasts in Japanese society. They were "very filthy" by standards of Shinto religion because they had blood on their hands. They were butchers, gravedig-gers, and those who dealt with animal skins. In the modern world, they have operated shoe stores and have lived in ghettos throughout Japan. Due to the extensive registration of all citizens, a family could hire a private detective and check to see if a future son-in-law or daughter-in-law was from the *buraku-min* community. Some parents disown their offspring if a son or daughter made a conscious choice to marry a *burakumin*. Historically, Japanese corpo-rations blacklisted *burakumin* to avoid hiring them. Still, some are now "pass-ing" for mainstream Japanese and pockets of society have eased their hostility, contempt, and blatant discriminatory practices toward them. In recent years, as Nicholas Kristof pointed out, almost two-thirds of *burakumin* claimed in opin-ion polls that they had never been subject to direct discrimination (*New York Times*, 1995). While the problem appears to have lessened, there is still dis-crimination. Approximately 3 million *burakumin*, or a bit more than two per-cent of the population, reside in Japan. Although rarely suffering overt discrimination, they have disproportionate levels of poverty, crime, and home-lessness (Kristof, 1995). Therefore, they are more accurately described as an oc-cupational minority, not a racial one. Officially, these outcasts were emancipated in 1871, and the current Japanese constitution forbids all discriminatory prac-tices. Some inter-marriage now exists and gradually some non-*burakumin* are allowing their children to marry *burakumin*. *Burakumin* is a euphemism mean-ing "village people," and the media are not allowed to discuss the subject. A fellow American scholar, in a manuscript prepared on Japanese police prac-tices, included a discussion of these "outcasts" and a prominent Japanese pub-lishing house refused to publish the manuscript due to passages that discussed this problem. Crime rates are higher among this minority group. Both Kore-ans and *burakumin* suffer higher unemployment, but they also dominate crim-inal groups of *yakuza*, or organized crime.

As in the case of some African-American youth growing up in inner cities with high crime rates, *burakumin* youngsters view the fancy homes and cars of *burakumin yakuza* bosses and become attracted to this life of crime (Kristof, 1995). Of course, some have risen to high political office or have become doc-tors, lawyers, and other professionals. Educationally, *burakumin* are begin-ning to approach the high-school graduation rates of their peers, but overall, Japanese society sets a higher bar for this minority group to succeed in this highly homogenous nation.

By the beginning of the twenty-first century, greater numbers of foreigners, particularly Chinese, were of concern to Japanese justice officials. Some were legal but some were illegal and committing crimes. Japan has always expressed concern about *gaijin*, or foreigners. The word *gaijin* also means "outsiders."

The media has often characterized foreigners as individuals to be treated with skepticism. Surveys of Japanese citizens have revealed that most Japanese do not wish to become "closer" to foreigners. One Japan scholar friend once joked that non-Japanese are viewed as less than human. Suspicion of foreigners can be traced to Commodore Perry of the United States and his arrival in the seventeenth century. In the current period, despite the nation's need for an increased labor supply, foreigners as permanent citizens are still unwelcome.

Approximately 2 million foreigners live legally in Japan, but the justice ministry claimed there were 91,778 illegal residents during 2010 (*The Economist*, 2010). However, some experts claim it is much higher—boosted by the cheap Chinese labor pool. Jorge Bustamante, the UN's specialist on migrants rights, complained that both legal and illegal migrants faced "racism, discrimination, exploitation, and a tendency by the judiciary and the police to ignore their rights" (*The Economist*, 2010).

Tabuchi reported on the deportation of Brazilians of Japanese ancestry during 2009. The Japanese government was paying thousands of dollars to fly these guest workers back to their native land. In one instance, Mrs. Rita Yamako, who lost her factory job, said she and her husband were given "an offer she could not refuse." The agreement included the stipulation that she and her husband agree to never seek work in Japan again. This Japanese policy was extended to hundreds of thousands of blue-collar Latin American immigrants in an attempt to ease the problem of the decades-long recession in Japan (Tabuchi, 2009). The policy of encouraging foreign labor commenced around 1990 with the industrial labor shortage that existed at that time. Approximately 366,000 Brazilians and Peruvians arrived, and they became the largest group of foreign guest workers. Like guest workers in many countries, they filled jobs that were *kitsui, kitanai,* and *kiken* (hard, dirty, and dangerous) (Tabuchi, 2009).

However, when the industrial sector went into decline, these workers were expendable. The Japanese term *nikkei* was applied to the special visas granted to these immigrants of Japanese ancestry. In China, unlike in Japan, Spanish immigrants were allowed to reclaim their residency and work visas after three years. The Japanese working-age population is expected to fall by a third by 2050, which will exacerbate the problem of economic decline.

In the case of Chinese labor, the Japanese feared but continued to need the help of this foreign pool of labor. By 2006, the overall foreign workforce had climbed to more than 1 million from less than 700,000 in 1996. In one rural Japanese community of 4,000—Kawakami—615 temporary Chinese workers were hired to do agricultural seasonal work due to the lack of Japanese farming labor (Onishi, 2008). The Japanese government has used various loopholes, including the categories of "students," "temporary workers," and "foreign trainees" to fill the void. Many of these temporary workers have been paid less than the minimum wage. Advocates for the Chinese foreign workers claim that they have suffered abuses and restrictions on their movements. Some of the Chinese workers in Kawakami were told to go home by 8 P.M. and not to ride bicycles except for work. Some claimed they had been instructed not to talk with young Japanese women (Onishi, 2006).

Illegal immigrants can face hardship and abuse at the hands of Japanese authorities. One Ghanaian, Abubakar Awudu Suraj, was found dead after an Egyptian flight from Tokyo to Cairo (*The Economist*, 2010). Having lived in Japan illegally, he was forced onto a plane in handcuffs with a towel gagging him and knotted to restrain him. He was found dead later and an autopsy failed to determine a cause of death. His spouse claimed that she observed facial injuries when she identified the body. Perhaps surprisingly in the case of Mr. Suraj, he had lived in Japan for 22 years, was fluent in Japanese and was married to a Japanese citizen. His application for a "special residency permit" had been denied. He fell into a legal abyss after he was arrested for overstaying his visa. Additionally, two detainees in 2010 committed suicide, and 70 inmates staged a hunger strike demanding better treatment.

Interestingly enough, it is not just foreigners who have problems living and working in Japan. There are many stories and reports of Japanese adults and their families struggling to adjust upon returning to Japan from overseas work and educational assignments. Returning Japanese are scrutinized for being tainted by their Western experiences. Some Japanese hesitate to accept foreign opportunities as they fear they will be out of step upon returning to their native land. A number of years ago, Howard French wrote about several examples of individuals struggling to adjust after returning from overseas experiences (*New York Times*, 2000). In one case, Ayako Shuna returned after spending several years attending high school in South America. She felt confident and took pleasure in her ability to make decisions and express opinions openly in classrooms, whereas her fellow Japanese students rarely seemed to offer opinions. Fellow students, however, began to shun her and it became hard for her to make friends. After a while, she began biting her tongue rather than speaking out. In a country famous for keeping foreigners at arm's length, returning Japanese claim that the "taint of foreign cultures" is often enough for them to be regarded as somehow not fully Japanese (French, 2000).

Some Japanese are no longer willing to suffer this hostile reception back in their native land. Sociologists have called it the "U-turn phenomenon," and the problem affects all human relationships and the flow of everyday life.

Strangely, some Japanese claim that the readjustment in returning to Japan was more stressful than the original adjustment to the foreign country. Opinion polls conducted around 1999 demonstrate that many Japanese expatriates were happier overseas than back in Japan (French, 2000). Returning school-age youngsters are often taunted and called *gaijin* in a derogatory tone. Eye contact and touching are much less common in Japan compared with many countries. Corporate managers become concerned that someone who experienced higher education in a foreign country may find it difficult to fit in with the group harmony expected from their employees. Sometimes managers sent overseas are assigned back-office jobs upon returning until their superiors are convinced that their "foreign ways have dissipated" (French, 2000). Often, returning parents will send their children to international schools to assist them in the adjustment process.

A second factor explaining low crime rates is the role of groups. Group life in all areas—work, play, school—predominates. Unlike in the United States and other Western cultures that prize individualism, group consensus becomes critical to Japanese decision-making. Japanese strongly identify with the group and are taught to fit in and not stand out. Youngsters are socialized into this practice at a very early age.

Ms. Okada, director of a program for returning overseas students at International Christian University, a prominent private university outside of Tokyo, noted, "I was always uncomfortable with groupism in Japan, but as I have matured, I find what bothers me most is the non-egalitarian ways of this society" (French, 2000). Ms. Okada went on to observe that since Japan was a much more male-oriented society, she felt she had to constantly tone down her views and opinions and work hard to not intimidate her peers. While women have made significant advances in the workplace since 1984, and since the first edition of my book on the Japanese police (Parker, 1984), they still have second-class status.

A third consideration is the emphasis Japanese place on the importance of interpersonal harmony. Japanese try to solve interpersonal issues without resorting to conflict. An ability to get along with others is linked to the emphasis on groups, as I reported in an article I wrote for the *Japan Times* newspaper and mentioned in the second edition of my book on Japanese policing: "Japanese rarely act on feelings of hostility in public. A shove will not bring retaliation in a physical way, or probably even a verbal way. In Chicago, an obscene gesture could possibly result in your summary execution by the offended party. A shove in a New York subway might conceivably result in a knife between your ribs" (Parker, 2001).

Japanese are very disciplined and assist each other in a variety of ways. For example, police occasionally assist a drunk during the late evening hours when many groups of men have been out socializing, but colleagues are more likely to help out. In general, aggressive and hostile behavior is frowned on, and Japanese try to avoid direct confrontations in their interpersonal relations whenever possible.

A fourth reason for the low crime rate is tied to the economy. Economic consideration must be included, notwithstanding the fact that the nation has been in and out of recessions over the past 30 years. Japanese, in any number of surveys over the years, refer to themselves as middle class and there is much truth to this assertion. While greater numbers of citizens have fallen into poverty in the last two decades and elderly criminality has increased, the unemployment rates are still in the 4–5 percent range. For example, *The Economist* (2011) reported unemployment at just 4 percent for the year 2008. A smaller wealthy class exists in Japan compared with the United States. Unlike in the United States and China, where large gaps exist between the haves and have-nots, reports on Japanese business leaders have noted that their executives have salaries and incomes that are much greater than those of their employees, but not hundreds of times greater, as in the case of American executives.

In Wilkinson and Pickett's fine book *The Spirit Level: Why Greater Equality Makes Societies Stronger* (2009), the authors point to a variety of problems that are far more damaging in the United States than in Japan, where the gap between the upper and lower income levels is much less. The authors link the homicide rates of a number of countries to the disparity in incomes and there are strong correlations for the more than 20 countries analyzed. In general, the authors claim that inequality linked to violence is even better established and accepted than the other effects of inequality. Other factors included overall health, poverty, and suicide rates. In presenting data on 23 different nations around the world, the authors demonstrate that the United States has the second largest gap between the richest 20 percent of citizens compared to the poorest 20 percent. Japan has the lowest discrepancy (Wilkinson & Pickett, 2009).

A fifth consideration explaining low crime rates in Japan has to do with some important values that many Japanese ascribe to and actively practice in daily life. These include the pressure to conform and fit in with others. I mentioned this value earlier in the context of the changing role of women in the workplace. This value of conformity interacts with the importance of groups. Avoiding shame has a major impact on Japanese life and individuals strive to avoid bringing shame on their families. This cultural value alone contributes to what sociologists call social control, and it definitely contributes to the low crime rates that have existed for many decades.

A sixth consideration is the value of conflict resolution through non-adversarial methods. While litigation has increased in Japan over recent decades, and the government is actively seeking to increase the number of lawyers and legal functionaries, there is still support in society to use non-legal means to resolve conflicts. Disputes over backyard boundaries, which may result in an American hiring a lawyer, will draw a different response in Japan. The parties will often seek to sort out the dispute amicably and the desire for interpersonal harmony will kick in.

A seventh factor, which carries considerable weight, is the broad respect that Japanese have for legal and governmental institutions, which is stronger than in the United States. Working for a governmental agency in Japan often carries more prestige than working for a private company—the reverse of the situation in the United States. Whereas in America the police are kept at a distance and often viewed with suspicion, they enjoy the respect and trust of most Japanese citizens.

Another important factor that contributes to low crime rates is the strong gun-control laws in Japan. The National Police Agency of Japan (1998) described the policy concerning firearms and swords:

> In Japan, in principle, possession of firearms and swords is prohibited under the Firearms and Swords Control Law. The Law's intent is to prevent danger and to secure the public safety. To possess firearms, one must obtain a license from the Prefectural Public Safety Commission. No firearms license is granted to persons under age 18 (or under 20 for a hunting gun), persons suffering from mental disorder, persons addicted to drugs, persons with no fixed residence, persons having a criminal record (particularly in violation of the Firearms and Swords Control Law), and persons, like *Boryokudan* members, who are justifiably feared as a threat to public safety. Gun licenses must be renewed every three years. As of 1996, approximately 440,000 hunting guns and air guns were licensed. Handgun regulations are the most restrictive. Handgun possession is almost totally banned, except for legally permitted police officers and Self Defense Forces personnel only while on duty, and a limited number of sport pistol shooters permitted by the prefectural Public Safety Commission. Possession of a toy gun is also prohibited as long as the gun falls under the category of "imitation gun." Whether a toy gun is regarded as an "imitation

### Table 1.2  Firearms Related Crimes

|                              | 2005 | 2006 | 2007 | 2008 | 2009 |
|------------------------------|------|------|------|------|------|
| Number of incidents          | 389  | 325  | 324  | 275  | 253  |
| Handgun-related incidents    | 200  | 182  | 183  | 139  | 162  |
| Homicide                     | 24   | 23   | 34   | 19   | 14   |
| Handgun-related homicide     | 21   | 21   | 27   | 19   | 12   |
| Robbery                      | 111  | 111  | 94   | 75   | 100  |
| Handgun-related robbery      | 91   | 96   | 79   | 67   | 95   |
| Others                       | 254  | 191  | 196  | 181  | 139  |
| Other handgun-related        | 88   | 65   | 77   | 53   | 55   |

*Source:* National Police Agency of Japan, 2011.

gun" depends on its resemblance to a genuine one in appearance, mechanism, or function. (35)

In 2009, there were just 253 firearm related crimes in Japan, 162 of which involved handguns. Twelve handgun-related homicides were recorded (see Table 1.2). Japanese friends and colleagues are amazed at Americans' obsession with firearms and are astonished at the weak regulations in this country. However, it must be noted that since Japan is a small island country, it is easier to implement the strong gun-control laws that are on the books. There were just four cases that involved the smuggling of firearms into Japan in 2009. Some of the seized handguns in Japan involved organized crime, or *boryoku-dan*. Japanese officials no longer use the term *yakuza*, which has a more romanticized meaning from an earlier era. In 2009, 148 weapons were linked to *boryokudan*, with 259 weapons associated with other persons (National Police Agency of Japan, 2011).

# 2

# Japanese Historical and Legal Background

As already noted, Japanese have often embraced non-adversarial means of justice and seek out mediation to resolve conflict, relying on the courts as a last resort. Legal disputes have been an anathema to the Japanese in searching for the resolution of problems that often lead to litigation in the West. In the 1963, Kawashima observed:

> Litigation presupposes and admits the existence of a dispute and leads to a decision which makes clear who is right or wrong in accordance with standards that are independent of the wills of the disputants. Furthermore, judicial decisions emphasize the conflict between the parties, deprive them of participation in the settlement, and assign a moral fault which can be avoided in a compromise solution. (p. 43)

During the period of modernization and the opening up of Japan, referred to as the *Meiji era*, the Japanese looked to Europe for everything from beer making to justice institutions. Japan moved from the feudal period to formalized criminal justice agencies that resembled those in the West, albeit with a strong Japanese flavor. Both French and German models were reflected in the social and political reforms that were instituted. Tanabe's (1963) comments reflected the unease in which Japanese viewed litigation:

> Under the long tradition of unusually strong governmental control and community pressure, the rights consciousness of the Japanese people was very low. Strong social and psychological pressures discouraged the filing of lawsuits, and manifold out-of-control resolution, techniques and mechanisms, such as mediation by relatives, court marshals, or local leaders, were commonly used. The compromise of civil disputes was generally regarded as the most desirable solution. In farming villages and small towns, suit against a neighbor was even a moral wrong. (p. 77)

While less common today, some agreements are still reached orally, without the benefit of an attorney. Individuals may prepare a brief written agreement themselves.

One primary feature of the Japanese police system is the widespread availability of mini-police stations called *koban*. More about these operations will be offered later. While they serve many functions, they also allow citizens to contact the police *(koban)* officers for counseling on low-level conflicts. Referred to as *komarigoto sodan*, it is a service that would be foreign to Western police agencies.

Historically there have always been efforts to sort out conflicts without the formalized legal machinery of the courts. Gibney's 1975 comments are apropos to this:

> To the Japanese, the law is not a norm but a framework for discussion. The good Japanese judge is the man who can arrange and settle the most compromises out of court. When an American calls his lawyer, he is confident and happy to rely on the strength of his whole social system, the rule of law. When a Japanese calls his lawyer, he is sadly admitting that, in this case, his social system has broken down. (p. 82)

Notwithstanding these historical notes, Japanese society is clearly becoming much more litigious as the twenty-first century unfolds. One major piece of evidence to support this view is the creation of the over 68 new law schools that parallel the U.S. legal-education system (Fuyuno, 2004). Prior to this major change, the Japanese system relied on graduating all its legal functionaries from the two-year Legal and Research Training Institute. It graduated around 500 individuals per year. Effectively, that meant that all the prosecutors, judges, and private lawyers emerged from this one institution. However, as various experts have noted, the Japanese government has rigidly kept the lid on the total number of lawyers they are allowing into the system. The projection for Japanese legal personnel, including lawyers, prosecutors, and judges, is targeted at 50,000 by 2018, while currently the numbers are at approximately 30,000. In contrast, the United States has around 1 million lawyers and many are currently unemployed in legal work. Of course there are no restrictions on the numbers that are allowed into the system based on law school enrollments or those passing the bar exam. As far back as the mid 1970s, Auerbach (1976) wrote an article, entitled "A Plague of Lawyers," in which he commented that the ratio of Americans to lawyers was 1100 to 1.

Lee (2011) offered data concerning the employment rate for U.S. law school graduates in recent years. Significant numbers of graduates, even after having completed law school nine months earlier, remained unemployed.

Given the downturn for new graduates, American law schools are revising their curriculum to meet the needs of law firms. More actual case work and clin-

Figure 2.1 The Employment Rate for Law-School Graduates,
Nine Months After a Typical May Graduation for United States Graduates

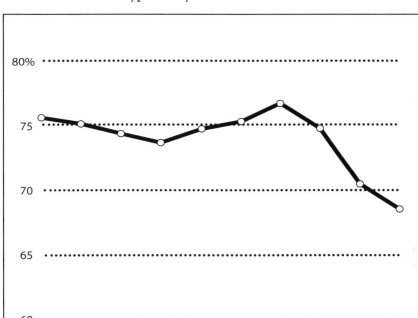

*Source:* National Association for Law Placement.

ical training that emphasizes interpersonal skills is being added by even prominent law schools such as Harvard and Stanford. Dean Larry Kramer of Stanford Law School stated, "law firms are saying you're not sending us people who are in a position to do anything useful for clients." For example, in 2010 there were more than double as many individuals who passed the bar exam as there were legal job openings.

While Japanese law graduates are increasing at a rapid clip, the government to date is still keeping a lid on those allowed to pass the bar exam (Fuyuno, 2004). They have been keeping that number at around 3,000 annually. This expansion of attorneys is not the result of a growth in crime rates—those continue to go down—but due to shifts in the corporate culture. Up until very recent years, the Japanese government has rigidly controlled business activity within the private sector and lawsuits were rare. In the twenty-first century, Japan has deregulated and opened up markets and a great variety of litigation has emerged. This includes everything from employee lawsuits to intellectual property rights matters. Court cases escalated and jumped to 544,000 civil suits in 2002. This represented an increase of over 140 percent from 1990 (Fuyuno, 2004). Even foreign lawyers have a greater opportunity to practice under the more liberal Japanese governmental policies.

In the system that operated in the preceding few years, applicants needed to pass the bar exam, but just 3 percent of those who took the exam passed. In the current system of law schools, students take a standardized test, to be followed by an admissions test for a particular law school. The legal education system looks somewhat American—case studies taught by practicing judges and lawyers and classes on oral and legal skills. When the new law schools started to open large numbers of applicants quickly applied to these schools. In 2002, there were six applicants for every opening at the country's most famous university—Tokyo University. A prestigious private university, Waseda, had 15 applicants for every opening (Fuyuno, 2004). Critics believed, though, that until the government ends or changes its policy of allowing just 3,000 to pass the bar exam each year, fundamental legal reform will be inhibited.

In returning to a discussion of social relationships and the role of groups, relationships have been both "particularistic" and "functionally diffusing." By that, I mean that citizens in the same community, who enjoy equal status relationships, are supposed to be close, and the roles are defined vaguely and flexibly so that they allow for adjustments based on circumstances. Therefore relationships have a tradition that supports compromise. Conflicts are supposed to be sorted out between the parties directly, and the historical view was that drafting a legal document or contract invites the breakdown of any agreement.

Japanese colleges and universities are ranked with Tokyo University at the top. The very best Japanese universities tend to be public, in contrast to the United States, where the top universities are mostly private. Graduating from a top university ensures the graduate a choice of careers and jobs. At the National Police Agency, with its elite class of entrants, numbering around 20, the applicants are required to take the National Public Service Examination. Some of the top scorers often select the Ministry of Finance or other agencies that rank above the National Police Agency. Often those entering the "elite" program as assistant inspectors are graduates of Tokyo University. Many of these will move forward in lockstep along the promotional system with the majority enjoying brief periods as chiefs at one of the 47 prefectural police agencies. Most of the national government positions that carry responsibility are highly competitive, desirable, and primarily open to graduates of the upper-ranked universities. A significant number of high-ranking officers that I have met and interviewed over the past 30 years were graduates of Tokyo University. Of course, some step into top-notch positions in the private sector. However, while many professional career police stay in law enforcement for their entire career, some opt for private security and other non-governmental positions upon retiring.

One question I enjoyed asking police officers during field research in 1980 and in 2000 had to do with changes in police work. I simply asked, "What has changed most during your career?" Frequently officers commented on how citizens were aware of their rights and cited them in encounters with them. Of course, this was commented on as making their jobs more difficult. Not surprisingly, younger people were less deferential and compliant than their older counterparts. Human rights commissions exist in all the prefectures and, given the repressive history of police prior to World War II, it is perhaps predictable that citizens are not reluctant to cite their rights. One trend that continues to exist today is the weakening of traditional values, which have contributed to social control and have acted as a brake on criminal activity. Today there is greater reliance on law as a tool to control crime.

Some notes regarding the beginnings of Japanese police: the Tokugawa Shogunate, from 1603 to 1867, was the feudal period in which there were four classes. Samurai, who were the warriors and the tool of the feudal lords, or *daimyo*, were at the top. They were followed, in order, by peasants, artisans, and merchants. This was a strict system and upward mobility was very difficult—once you were born into a class you were resigned to staying in that class. Loyalty to the government and to your own family was critical, as formalized law barely existed. Hirano (1963) offered a note regarding this matter:

> It is not the awareness of punishment which serves to deter a Japanese so much as the awareness of the impact which the fact of his involvement in criminal proceedings would have on himself and, more important, on his family. (p. 291)

Eleanor Westney's 1982 work was very illuminating in her comparative study of several Japanese governmental agencies, including the postal service and the police. Around the time of the Meiji period, police started to appear. It was samurai attached to government agencies that acted as police. Magistrates oversaw their work in various communities and towns. Samurai alone were allowed to carry weapons and they wore two swords in their belts. One was three or four feet long while the other was two feet long. These two swords also served as a symbol of their rank. These samurai were expected to exercise power and also to act as a policeman in meting out justice. Modern-day Japanese police look to samurai as their models. Officially, samurai had the authority to draw their swords and kill commoners who deviated from the prescribed social role. Lower ranking samurai were sensitive, according to Westney (1982), about their status prerogatives and tended to draw their weapons at a minor provocation. One type of such behavior might be not bowing low enough when a feudal lord's procession was passing by. In the 1850s and 1860s, several incidents were reported involving Westerners who did not kneel when a feudal lord passed by, resulting in samurai cutting them down.

Japan was divided into 245 feudal domains, each controlled by a shogun, or overlord. Confucian notions that had come from China provided a framework for relationships in which the society had both vertical and hierarchical features. During the Tokugawa period the hierarchical dimension was very pronounced. This involved an elaborate system of social obligations that were indirect but nonetheless powerful forms of suppression.

It was a formidable task for the Meiji government to modernize Japan—a nation that had lived isolated for centuries. Some of these changes were linked to the treaties that had been imposed on the nation by Western governments. One objection was that Westerners had not allowed their citizens to be subjected to local law for criminal offenses and had demanded that they administer their own forms of justice. To remedy the situation, the Japanese adopted legal codes based first on the French model and later on the German one.

To understand the concept of human rights in Japan it is helpful to appreciate the role of the emperor in the early Meiji era:

> [He] possessed both political power and spiritual authority, [and] embodied the prerequisites of both the German emperor and the Pope. The people were not only the emperor's subjects politically but his followers spiritually. In addition to enacting laws, the emperor issued imperial rescripts on education, national esprit and morality. The people were required to observe the law in their overt behavior and were also obliged to order their consciences in accord with imperial rescripts. A portrait of the emperor was enshrined in every school, and the principal often read rescripts aloud. Moreover, all subjects were required to stand in awed attention when facing the emperor's portrait or when listening to rescripts. Insofar as the arbiter of spiritual values and political authority were one, ethics and power, public and private [*oyake* and *watakushi*], were completely fused together. (Kuno, 1978, p. 61)

Another view of the role of the individual in Japan at that time is the government's "The Way of the Subject":

> What we call our private life amounts, in the final analysis, to the practice of the Way of the Subject, and takes on public significance as

we carry out our duty to assist in imperial rule. Thus even while engaged in private activities, we must never forget our duty to devote ourselves to the emperor and serve the state. In our country everything one does—whether he is in government or in private business, whether he is a parent raising children or a son studying in school—is in fulfillment of his particular duty as an imperial subject. (Kuno, 1978, p. 62)

The requirements and obligations to the government were clear. Obedience to the state was necessary and the Meiji government wielded enormous power and was intolerant toward any opposition to its policies. Attempts to assert individual rights during this time period were crushed with the assistance of police.

It appears clear to this author that authoritarianism survives in some form today under the democratic structure that was imposed on Japan at the end of World War II. In this context, there has been a long history of obedience to the state although protest activity started to become much stronger by the 1960s. Today the democratic process is active and the responses from citizens and governmental officials in the wake of the 2011 earthquake and tsunami are testimony to this. Nonetheless, far right-wing groups would be delighted to see a restoration of a strong emperor, not just the figurehead version that was created by MacArthur at the end of World War II. Ike's 1972 comment on "paternalism" and Koschmann's 1978 statement speak to the issues linked to authority:

Never conquered by or directly confronted with external forms of political rule, they remained unaware of the potentially relative, fallible nature of all authority. Authority was a given, taken for granted as an unalienable part of the natural order (Kuno, 1978, p. 61)

The basic character of Japan's modern-day police force was evident in the early Meiji period. One example is the "routine family visits" to all households and commercial establishments that police still engage in today. They do this from tradition and not by law. Officers leave their *koban* and *chuzaisho* (*koban* are police mini-stations or police boxes in cities, while *chuzaisho* are rural police boxes that are residential) to make the visits at least once annually, maintaining careful records on their visits. *Chuzaisho* are typically staffed by a married male officer with living quarters in the rear of the building for a spouse and any children. In the 1980s, the wives were not paid for their work, but by 2000, they were compensated. Also, it should be noted that by 2000, women in general were engaged in most police work, but earlier had been relegated to duties such as juvenile work and traffic details.

During the early Meiji period, the country was faced with unrest and the government struggled to maintain order. Citizens were fearful and anxious about uprisings and bloodshed. Kanetake-Oura's comment is revealing:

> There was not lacking a rough element which, dissatisfied with the new Government, watched for an opportunity to rise against it. Moreover, many ruffians at large constituted a danger to the people. The main object of the police at that time was to arrest these malcontents and bravadoes. (1910, p. 283)

Not surprisingly, a strong police role emerged. The police force that was created was highly centralized and powerful, and their functions would be alien to Western police forces. Public health, sanitation, construction, and firefighting were all tied to the police. They were not considered public servants, but rather, their roles included surveillance and political control. One police chief was quoted as saying, "There would be no household in Japan into which the eyes of the police would not see and the ears would not hear" (Sugai, 1957, p. 4). Former samurai, numbering around 3,000, undertook this task and they were not properly trained or prepared for these duties. Historically, they were used to operating on the basis of their social status and now they were forced to operate without an organizational structure—a very different role indeed. Here is a comment from Sugai concerning the matter:

> This method of choosing men was singularly effective in guaranteeing their staunchness and relative immunity from corruption because of a system of morality peculiar to the former warrior class. On the other hand, this practice had certain drawbacks in that it tended to develop in the police an attitude of disrespect and superciliousness toward the people. (1957, p. 5)

One approach that the Meiji government seized upon to control the police of Tokyo was to select two-thirds of the personnel from the one province of Kyushu. The notion that police officers can be more effective working in areas away from their place of birth continues today. The concept is to avoid having to enforce the law in the region where family and friends reside.

The Tokyo Police Department was modeled on a combination of the Paris Prefecture of Police and the Yokohama Police Department. Eventually the Tokyo Police Department emerged as the model for all other Japanese police agencies (Westney, 1982). However, partly due to the large numbers of foreigners in Yokohama, it was actually the first police department in Japan. It was Westerners, who were familiar with police services, that demanded its creation. Before 1868, foreigners were responsible for their own policing and because Englishmen were predominant, the Yokohama police reflected the English structure of organization, drill, patrolling, and weaponry. Although the Tokyo police at the outset retained the English flavor of the Yokohama police force, with the transfer of the police agency to the Ministry of Justice, the police department was revised. Officials were sent to study police departments far afield—in France, Belgium, Germany, Russia, Austria, and Italy. The bias was toward the French, however, and it became the primary influence on the Tokyo Police Department. What appealed to the Japanese was the wide-ranging administrative functions and the extensive political involvement. Therefore, the Tokyo agency controlled other services such as firefighting, prisons, and health. It became a powerful and autonomous organization that, similar to its model, played a key role in the life of the national capital with close ties to the central government (Westney, 1982).

Police at this time started gathering information such as name, occupation, age, and social status of all residents. While today some residents do not respond to these police visits, the vast majority of people still open their doors. Once again, these visits have this long traditional history but are not required by law. More and more citizens cite their rights, but people comply often in the more conservative countryside. In the early period, the frequency of household visits was linked to one's status—those with a high reputation were visited just once a year. Those individuals who were unemployed or who had criminal histories were visited the most—three times a year. In the period prior to World War II, when political repression was rife, police behavior was also intimidating and repressive (Tipton, 1990). The police at that time focused on trends in the people's thinking and politics in addition to tracking their other activities.

In 1874, policing moved from the Ministry of Justice to the Ministry of Home Affairs. It was called the Police Bureau and continued to operate under the aegis of the Home Ministry until it was closed in 1947. Prefectural governors were given jurisdiction over their respective forces:

> Salaries, travel allowances, etc. of police officers above inspector's rank were paid from the national treasury; other expenses, such as maintaining policemen in lower ranks and providing and keeping up office buildings, were mainly met by local taxes but partially subsidized by the national government—the ratio of subsidies being four-tenths of all expenses for the Metropolitan Police Board and one-sixth for other prefectures. (Sugai, 1957, p. 4)

The cooperation in the Meiji period between the national and prefectural governments for managing police services is roughly similar to the organizational breakdown that presently exists between the National Police Agency and prefectural police agencies. For example, the National Police Agency currently pays the salaries of all officers at the rank of senior superintendent or above.

As noted above, the system of *koban* and *chuzaisho* also had its inception during the Meiji period, and there were more than 400 police boxes in the city of Tokyo by 1877. Staffing structure today has been maintained with a high ratio of supervisors to patrol officers. Typically, today one officer supervises three patrol officers at a *koban*. One officer walks a beat, one is stationed outside, and one stays inside doing administrative work. The pattern was quite similar around in 1877. These mini-police station buildings of today are for the most quite similar to the early structures. *Koban* are placed in various locations where people gather such as parks, transportation centers, shopping areas, major intersections, and locations where crime might be expected. The term *hashutsujo* was the term officially created for *koban* in 1888, but the term *koban* persists today.

The role of police during the Meiji era was described by Kanetake-Oura in 1910:

> The Emperor issues, or causes to be issued, the ordinances necessary for the carrying out of laws, or for the maintenance of the public peace and order, and for the promotion of the welfare of the subjects.… These regulations defined for the first time in Japan the sphere and aim of police authority, and indicated the functions of police administration.… The object of the administrative police is to anticipate evils threatening the people and so to preserve the latter's safety.… The local governor (except in the prefecture of Tokyo) superintends the police affairs of the locality, appoints police sergeants to their respective duties, and dispatches them, whenever necessary, to different places, to overlook policemen in the discharge of their duties.… The business of the police is divided into the following four parts: (1) Protecting the people from wrongdoers. (2) Acting as sanitary inspectors. (3) Checking lewdness and profligacy. (4) Detecting and proving against persons who contemplate acts contrary to the established laws of the land.… The police shall aim at preserving public welfare, and in no case shall one pry into petty incidents of family affairs, nor use his position to gain profit for himself. (p. 282)

Neighborhood associations were active during the Meiji period, and they were cohesive groups in which citizens assisted one another in a variety of projects including planting rice and building houses. They reflected the powerful role of groups in Japan. The Japanese term for this system is *tonari-gumi*. Within that framework, they were identified as *burakukai* in rural areas and *chonaikai* in urban settings.

The concept is important in considering crime control because they were the forerunners of crime prevention associations that have been very influential in modern Japan. When I first arrived in Tokyo to commence my Fulbright Fellowship in 1980, I was interested to note that one of the major organizational units within the National Police Agency was Crime Prevention. It existed along-side Patrol, Security, and Juvenile Delinquency, among others. Historically, leaders of neighborhood associations were reputed to be very loyal to the emperor, and Western officials during the occupation suspected them of being part of the authoritarian pre-war regime. The leaders used coercive and dictatorial tactics in its dealings with members and it was common for members to report secretly on citizens who drifted away from government policy.

In the pre-World War II period, the heads of the associations had close working relationships with the police in their neighborhoods. These *burakukai* and *chonaikai* had their own meeting halls and they provided community activity centers. Effectively, these associations were semi-official arms of the police and they were employed to keep order.

At the end of World War II, these organizations and their relationship with police changed. In place of the disbanded neighborhood associations, local crime-prevention groups have formed with a narrower framework. To some extent, the ties with the police remain close, but the associations' leadership is now elected, and some friction with the authorities has been known to occur, especially around election time, when it is not uncommon to have *chonaikai* members arrested for campaign violations.

In contemporary Japan, these *burakukai* and *chonaikai* continued but their strength has been sapped due to the unwillingness of single people living in apartments and condominiums to join. They also may have suffered due to the transience of modern-day life. The organizations themselves excluded these occupants because they were perceived as short-term residents. In reality, many of these residents did move every two years on average.

The network of relationships involving family and neighbors included participation in weddings and funerals. A variety of obligations and rituals were part of the fabric of everyday life. The network of relationships involved the complex notion of *giri*, literally "duty," which is a fundamental feature of social interaction in Japan. Most scholars agree that it has gradually weakened as the twenty-first century unfolds.

Strong suppression of radicals by the government was characteristic in the pre-World War II period and has been described by Mitchell (1976), Okudaira (1973), and Tipton (1990), among others. Their observations and analyses of the atmosphere surrounding the creation and implementation of the Peace Preservation Law, along with the sweeping enforcement of it by police and prosecutors, offers an ugly and frightening portrait. The turbulence of the era, combined with the rising influence of left-wing radicals, resulted in the passing of this law and some related laws in the year of 1925. The Police Bureau was very active and Okudaira's comments captured the mood of the time:

> The dangerous thoughts, which the Peace Preservation Law raised as the subject of control, implied, in the beginning, Communism and anarchism, and later the implication of the term "dangerous" became more and more stretched, and finally every anti-government thought— the identifications were made by the administration of each period— was regarded to be under the application of the law. The victims of the Peace Preservation Law were not only those who attempted to reform the then-existing Buddhism, the believers in Shintoism or in the numerous newly risen religions but also those belonging to "Jehovah's Witnesses," "Seventh-day Adventists," and the "No-church Independent Sect." On the other hand, the controlling authorities attached great importance to cultural movements along with labor and political movements. Consequently, students' researches in the social sciences or the liberal arts were the most important subjects of restraint. (1973, p. 49)

An earlier law that was also repressive in nature was the Public Police Law of 1900. This law was aimed at antigovernment political groups, but it also restricted organized labor. These political groups were required to register their programs with the police, and they needed permission to meet. Their meetings could be dissolved by the police and their organizations disbanded, and membership in secret organizations was prohibited. Violators of the Public Police Law could be punished by fines and up to one year in prison.

It was left primarily to the Home Ministry's Police Bureau to provide the repressive apparatus to subdue radicals and to control protest movements. Unlike the situation in Western countries, where political organization and publications were regulated through the courts, in Japan police used administrative techniques to maintain public order. Faced with increasing left-wing radicalism, in 1902 the government created a Higher Police Unit and a second unit, the Special Higher Police. The repressive machinery of the Japanese justice system of the prewar period appears to have emerged for a variety of reasons in addition to those already mentioned.

Mitchell's views on the subject were explained as follows:

> The reasons for thought control in Japan were complex and not confined to flaws in the Meiji Constitution, a tradition of authoritarianism, and the weakness of liberalism. Other factors less subject to direct

manipulation by Japan's leaders must be considered: the rapidity with which the whole world's economic system collapsed and the more un-compromising attitudes of China and the United States. These prob-lems, together with the rise of communism, signified the weakening of the old economic and political order. (1976, p. 192)

Prosecutors wielded enormous power during this period of the 1920s. Pros-ecutors dressed like judges and they identified with the judiciary. They assisted in drafting court documents and handling cases. One of the weapons in their arsenal was the designation of "charges withheld." Using this tool, a person was classified as neither prosecuted nor absolved of charges. The party was cast into a probationary limbo under the control of the prosecutor. Any fur-ther violations on the part of that person were sure to result in vigorous pros-ecution (Mitchell, 1976). Another element of the repressive atmosphere of this era is described by Okudaira (1962) in reference to the censorship that was en-forced through government policy. The policy shifted from pre-publication censorship to post-publication censorship in which heavy penalties were im-posed on writers and editors. The Home Ministry's Police Bureau was at the heart of the censorship process. Books that were deemed detrimental to the public peace were seized and destroyed.

It should be noted that while the authoritarian nature of the crackdown on perceived dissidents created anxiety and fear in the ranks of the general pub-lic during the pre-World War II period, the actual size of the police force was very modest. Ratios of police to citizens were comparable to Europe and the United States. In the late 1920s, Tokyo had 12,700 police for a population of 4.5 million, while New York has a force of around 12,000 police serving 5.6 million citizens (Tipton, 1990).

The terror and detention inflicted on Japanese citizens in this era was reflected in the actual numbers. There were 269,000 detentions in 1929, but that jumped to 473,000 in 1931. By 1933, the number detained climbed to 1.2 million (Tip-ton, 1990). Often police repeatedly pressured suspects with detention and, in effect, held them in custody without bringing formal charges. Some were held for two years and police actions were not subject to legal review. A Japanese per-son had no opportunity to appeal. In the twenty-first century, Japanese pros-ecutors still detain suspects for far longer periods than their counterparts in the United States. The process described above was part of the evolution of the Japanese state moving toward full-blown fascism by the time of World War II. Those who questioned or challenged authority were subjected to the arrogance and abuse of public officials. Today, Japanese citizens over 80 often have bit-ter and resentful feelings toward the police. Interviews I conducted with private citizens revealed a mixture of anger and anxiety that citizens felt toward the authorities of that time.

# Post World War II Policing

During the period in which the American occupation took root, two kinds of reforms were established (Terrill, 2007). With a new constitution, the police operation became linked to the constitutional rights of citizens. Police services were decentralized and somewhat modeled after the American system. In place of the national system, 1,600 independent police agencies were created along with public safety commissions. The latter were developed to give greater control of policing to private citizens.

Chwialkowski (1998) noted that much of the Japanese post-World War II police system had its origins in the role played by the American occupational force and particularly General Robert Eichenberger. Transforming a police force that had vaguely defined duties and whose major role was to stifle dissent, interfere in public elections, and arbitrarily arrest and imprison "political disturbers" was a major undertaking. A focus was on making the police force less authoritarian, more responsive to public opinion, restrained by a constitution, and accountable to local communities (Bayley, 1991). Paramilitary organizations were eliminated and the various neighborhood associations that had spied on citizens were removed. The Americans attempted to remove police who had been anti-democratic and police personnel were not allowed to be members of labor organizations (Cohen & Passin, 1987).

The basic outline of the Japanese constitution bore some resemblance to the American one—the right to counsel, the guarantee of a speedy trial, the right to cross-examine witnesses, the protection from forced confessions (Chwialkowski, 1998). However, as noted later in the chapter on criminal investigation, there have been many reported instances of Japanese police coercing confessions from those they have detained. These have come to the surface particularly in the last ten years. Japanese police were to concentrate on standards, identification, communication, training, scientific crime detection, and statistics.

While many of the reforms have been retained over the years, the decentralized structure of police forces was dismantled for the more traditional nationalistic approach. With the Police Law of 1954, the national character of police services was resurrected. Public Safety Commissions have been retained and all municipal-aided rural police agencies were integrated under the aegis of the 47 prefectural police departments.

In conclusion, this portrait of early Japanese policing is critical to understanding Japan's current police system. A number of the earlier features of the police such as the "routine family visits" that originated from the Meiji era have remained virtually intact. Legal concepts rooted on Confucian doctrine that affect dispute resolution are still evident in the early part of the twenty-first century and the democratization of Japan has given greater respect for human rights.

# 3

# The Role of Japanese Police

Japan has a decentralized structure of prefectural police agencies with the National Police Agency at the top of the hierarchy. The National Police Agency creates the policies and structures for police nationwide and operates under the umbrella of the National Public Safety Commission. The Police Act, created in 1954, empowers the national government to give each prefecture the authority to carry out police duties to "protect life, liberty, and property" and maintain public safety and order within its prefectural jurisdiction (Police of Japan, 2011). The National Police Agency is headed by a Commissionor General, who is appointed or dismissed by the National Public Safety Commission with the approval of the Prime Minister. The functions of the National Police Agency are presented in Figure 3.1. The rank structure for Japanese police officers is offered in this descending rank order:

Police superintendent supervisor
Chief police superintendent
Senior police superintendent
Police superintendent
Police inspector
Assistant police inspector
Police sergeant
Senior policeman
Policeman

In the United States, Americans have been wary of vesting too much power in a centralized police agency and have opted for the present decentralized system of municipal, county, and state police forces. Of course there are also specialized federal agencies such as the F.B.I., Secret Service, and Drug Enforcement Agency. In Japan, there are benefits that accrue to a well-organized and unified national police force. One feature that derives from this national system is a high level of professionalism among police. A professional is one who emphasizes public service, high standards of performance, and has a broad knowledge of a field. If one uses a professional standard of law or medicine, even

### Figure 3.1 National Police Agency Functions

• Planning and research on police systems;
• National police budget;
• Review of national policies on police;
• Police operations in time of large-scale disasters and disturbances;
• Formulation and implementation of plans for emergency situations;
• Measures against trans-prefectural organized crime;
• Traffic regulation on national highways;
• International criminal investigation assistance;
• Operation of the Imperial Guard;
• International emergency relief activities;
• Police training;
• Police communications;
• Criminal identification;
• Criminal statistics;
• Police equipment;
• Standards of recruitment, duties and activities of police personnel;
• Coordination of police administration; and,
• Inspection.

*Source*: National Police Agency, 2011.

highly qualified police in both Japan and the United States cannot meet this standard. This is primarily because independence of judgment and action is critical to a true professional. In the case of police, their independence is lacking because they must meet the demands of the organization in which they play a role.

One advantage Japanese police managers enjoy over their American counterparts is that they can implement policies unfettered by the demands of labor unions. Westney, in her 1982 history of Japanese policing during the Meiji period, noted that professionalism was:

> a means of reducing turnover in the force and of improving police standards of performance without a marked increase in expenditures, and it facilitated the standardization of police practice throughout the country. However, it had other, unanticipated consequences: It increased the autonomy of the police force, it reduced its responsiveness to its social environment, and it reinforced the social distance between the policeman and the public. (p. 35)

It is fair to ask if social distance between police and the community is too high of a price to pay for professionalism. In the modern era, the Japanese police have a strong record of dedication and commitment to their work. As one member of the legal staff of the American Embassy in Tokyo commented during an interview I conducted, "They're not wondering if they can step out of police work and find a better-paying job like some American police officers."

As of 2010, the total strength of all Japanese police was approximately 291,500. The National Police Agency portion was around 7,700: 2,000 police officers, 900 imperial guards, and 4,800 civilians. Prefectural police totaled around 283,800. Of that total, 255,200 were police officers, with the remainder being 28,600 civilians. The number of women officers has gradually increased over the 30-year span I have studied Japanese policing, and they are up to approximately 14,900, with an additional 11,800 women serving as civilian support personnel (Police of Japan, 2011). Female police officers have assumed greater duties as well. In addition to performing standard patrol functions, they assist crime victims(including sex crimes victims), and they attend to cases of stalking, domestic violence, and child abuse. Historically, they had been relegated to traffic details and juvenile work.

Police are paid under a "special pay scale" according to the National Police Agency, due to the "risks" associated with police work. On average, the salary scale is 15 percent above that of other comparable government workers. Those high-ranking college graduates who pass the National Public Service exam and enter as assistant inspectors (around 20 per year) are assigned directly to the National Police Agency or in top positions at Prefectural Police Headquarters. This would be equivalent to an American starting a military career as a second lieutenant. Applicants are administered exhaustive written examinations and given multiple interviews. Nationwide, in 2009, about 127,900 individuals took the examination, with only 15,000 making the initial cut.

At the entry level for new recruits to prefectural police agencies, the examination and selection process is vastly different. Training for those who are selected lasts 21 months for high school graduates and five months for college graduates. The percentage of college graduates who are accepted by the Tokyo Metropolitan Police Department has climbed steadily over the years and is now above 70 percent.

Initially, high-school graduates first attend a ten-month pre-service training course (six months for college graduates). During this period, they acquire basic community policing knowledge and skills. After completing this phase, they receive three months of on-the-job training under a senior officer. This is followed by a return to the police training institute to obtain further legal knowledge and skills linked to the police career they are about to embark on. At this juncture they are sent to a police station, where they work under a senior officer. Included in police training the recruit receives is instruction in judo, kendo, martial arts, and firearms. Budgets for police services are divided between the national government and prefectural governments. Generally, the prefectural governments pay all expenses associated with operating the prefectural police agencies, excluding a direct appropriation that comes from the national treasury department. All the salaries of high-ranking officers (senior superintendent and above) come from the national government that supports the services provided by the National Police Agency (Police of Japan, 2011).

Training periods for American police vary from several weeks to six months or more, and the standards are vastly different depending on the state, county, or municipality.

The training for the future managers of the National Police Agency (NPA) are very different from the training of prefectural police described above. Here is a description offered by the NPA of its management training:

> Assistant police inspectors receive five weeks of training and then are assigned as a sub-section chief at a police station. Police officers promoted to police inspector enter the National Police Academy in Tokyo for a two-month training program. They master management and leadership skills, and develop the practical skills for duties as the section chief of a police station. Further, the National Police Academy provides supervisory training for superintendents designated the given assignments as either a chief of a police station or section chief of a prefectural police headquarters. This is the highest-level training course available for police officers. The Highest Training Institute for Investigation Leaders, at the National Police Academy, trains police inspectors and above in leadership, management, and advanced techniques and technologies concerning criminal investigation. As a training institution for transnational criminal investigation, the National Police Academy's International Research and Training Institute for Criminal Investigation provides both foreign language training for Japanese police officers and training to police officers from other countries. (National Police Agency, 1998, p. 15)

Victims services were introduced in Japan in 1981 under the Crime Victims Support Act. The National Public Safety Commission has been charged with implementing the act and providing funding, counseling, and support to victims. Private victim support groups have been active, and the Crime Victims Relief Foundation has provided various types of support including scholarships to bereaved children. They have also provided counseling, escorts to hospitals or courts, and have helped to broaden public awareness of victims.

# Tokyo Metropolitan Police Department

My initial research on Japanese policing commenced in 1980 and included field research in 1980–1981, 1983, and 1999. Study and analysis have gone on and continue until the publication of this book. Many interviews have been conducted in various locations including Tokyo, Chiba, Kobe, Sapporo, Yokohama, Kyoto, and Okayama, among others.

In Japan, the annual salary for new police officers who were university graduates was 2,872,800 yen (National Police Agency, 1999), which is equivalent to $36,349, assuming a yen to dollar ratio of 79 yen to $1 (as of July 22, 2011). Similar to other government and private sector employees, police receive bonuses as well. They receive a 5.25-month salary bonus, and at the 2011 yen to dollar rate, that is an additional 1,206,575 yen, or $15,273. Add in a housing allowance of 104,400 yen ($1,320), and total compensation is around $52,942 per the yen to dollar rates of 1999. Currently, the National Police Agency for 2011 reports that salaries for high-school graduates is 15 percent higher than other government administrative personnel due to the fact that the work is "inherently dangerous" (Police of Japan, 2011). For police personnel in the United States, the median salary of all police and sheriffs was $51,410 in 2008 (U.S. Department of Labor, 2009).

One piece of public relations literature published by the Tokyo Metropolitan Police Department (MPD) states: "Tokyo is the center of government, business, culture, and transportation of Japan, with a population of some 12 million in an area of 2,171 square kilometers (828 square miles)." The total personnel of the M.P.D. was 50,613, which included 2,901 civilians. There were approximately 1,330 police boxes, which included 237 residential *kobans* (Tokyo Metropolitan Police Department, 1998).

After a direct introduction to high-ranking staff of the Tokyo MPD by a member of the Tokyo Public Safety Commission, I commenced the original field study of working police in 1980, and the follow-up field studies took place in 1983 and again in 1999. Personal introductions are critical in Japan, and it is clear that the various field study experiences could not have taken place without support from various scholars and officials.

As I noted in an earlier publication, my first visit to the headquarters of the Tokyo MPD was very impressive:

> The headquarters loomed like a fortress near the Imperial Palace grounds. The atmosphere inside was very formal and a bit startling if one is unprepared for the military demeanor of the police personnel on duty. Officers guarded the entrance and inside the building uniformed

women await visitors behind a desk. Arriving officials were greeted with the equivalent of a snap to attention and were crisply saluted. Impeccably dressed officers issued identifying badges to visitors, who were required to wait for an escort before proceeding to a particular conference area or office in the eighteen-story building. (Parker, 2001)

At the outset, my purpose in studying Japanese police was to begin at the grass-roots level and observe the day-to-day work of police officers on the beat—the work of officers assigned to the various *koban* and *chuzaisho*. A variety of stations in Tokyo were visited commencing with the Tsukiji/Ginza station, which was a major entertainment and shopping center. Later I visited the Shitaya station in an older commercial and working-class section of the city. Seijo represented a quiet upper-class area away from the downtown area. There I visited the police station and *koban* associated with Akabane—a commercial and lower middle-class area. After that it was on to Motofuji—an area including the campus of Tokyo University. Interviews were first conducted with ranking personnel at the various police stations, including detectives, and these sessions were inevitably followed up by visits to various *koban* and *chuzaisho* that operated under the police stations. In considering the role of the *koban* system, it is useful to think about it as part of the Japanese penchant for order. In this national system of policing, working hours are quite different from the various schedules that occur in American cities, towns, and states. American officers typically work swing shifts. Officers may work a "graveyard" tour of duty, or 11 P.M. to 7 A.M., and several weeks later shift to 7 A.M. to 3 P.M. or 3 P.M. to 11 P.M. Assignments are often tied to years on the job and/or union contracts. The Japanese approach is very different. Police stationed at *koban* and assigned to patrol typically work the following schedule:

> 1st day: Full day (a 24-hour period, from morning to morning)
> 2nd day: Off day
> 3rd day: Normal day (morning to evening)

*Koban* typically have several small rooms. A room in the front has a desk. Rooms at the rear, and occasionally upstairs, include a *tatami* mat area for sleeping and an area to make simple meals. *Tatami* mats are approximately three feet by six feet and have a thick straw base of woven rushes. A safe is available to lock up weapons when an officer is sleeping or off duty. Police boxes come in various shapes and sizes but are often crowded and similar to much of Japanese housing. Regulations require that the front door remain open at all times and during the high heat of summer months it makes working in the police boxes very unpleasant. Air conditioning units are useless.

Summer temperatures are comparable to those in Washington, D.C. On the exterior of police boxes are billboards, and "most wanted" persons posters can be viewed along with other announcements that pertain to the local area in which the *koban* is located. Occasionally officers brighten up these drab gray (often concrete) buildings with bright flowers or bowls of fruit. Often local shops deliver noodle dishes or sushi to the officers, or they may bring a meal from home. When *koban* police officers go out for a meal, regulations require them to go out of uniform. This policy is tied to the emphasis on sensitivity to citizens—some older citizens have not forgotten the arrogance of officers prior to World War II. The Tokyo MPD has a rank of superintendent general—the only such rank in the entire county and reflects the "queen bee" status of the Tokyo MPD. Only the commissioner general of the National Police Agency ranks above the chief of the MPD and he is in charge of police for the entire nation.

In my first series of police visits, I started with the Tsukiji station and met with the older graying chief who was friendly and open to my inquiries. I experienced what became a pleasantly familiar ritual—green tea was served. Often several assistants and the station's interpreter would join the meeting with the ranking officer. The Tsukiji station encompasses the famous Ginza district, popular with thousands of tourists. The Ginza district is just 2.5 square kilometers, but has over 3,000 pubs, restaurants, and other "public morals businesses," as the police call them. Approximately 9,800 households with 23,000 residents exist in the area—the low number reflecting the commercial character of the area. However, around 200,000 individuals work in Ginza, and 500,000 people, including visitors and shoppers, flow in and out on any given day. Ten police boxes operate under the Tsukiji station and total personnel number around 400. A highlight for a tourist visiting Tsukiji would be the giant fish market, visited by 70,000 persons daily. The MPD patrols the periphery, but private security are employed in the fish market.

In my research over the years, one of my favorite questions has been, "What are the types of situations do you typically encounter on any given day?" In the early 1980s, when I asked the Tsukiji police chief this question, his response was that "citizens rarely use weapons. While they may punch or strike out, it's almost unheard of for guns to be used—even the use of knives is unusual."

# Emergency Calls

Reacting to an emergency, a person dials "110," equivalent to "911" in the United States. This can result in an officer being dispatched from a *koban* or *chuzaisho* on foot or in a patrol car. Domestic violence continues to be underreported in Japan. In interviewing officers on the subject, including several who became personal friends, they acknowledged that spouses were often too embarrassed to report such incidents. They claimed physical violence was at a low level. Loss of face, important in many Asian countries, undoubtedly plays a role. More often police received complaints about excessive noise or an unpaid loan from an acquaintance.

In the United States, of course, officers are not infrequently called to residences on matters of domestic violence, and historically these cases can be among the most lethal in police work. During 1996, on a national level in Japan, a "110" call was received every 5.1 seconds and a total of 6,198,980 calls were logged for the nation (National Police Agency of Japan, 1998). By 2009, the number increased to over 9 million calls nationwide. This translated to about one call every 3.5 seconds.

# Residential and Commercial Visits by Police

As noted earlier, a unique feature of Japanese policing is the visits of police from the *koban* or *chuzaisho* to residences and businesses in their area. This is done by tradition and not by law. Again, most Japanese comply but some do not respond to a knock on their door. For the Tokyo MPD, a patrol officer is responsible for approximately 450 households or businesses. Officers fill out cards on each of the visits and the information is filed back at the police box. A copy of a pamphlet issued to all police recruits is provided (see Figure 3.2) that gives the recruit advice on how to approach these visits with suggestions on etiquette, conversational ploys, and dos and don'ts.

On one visit, when I accompanied a police sergeant to interview the manager of a ten-story commercial building, the officer asked about crime or any problems. The interviewee stated there had been no crime in his building, which was several blocks from the center of the busy Ginza district. He noted that drunks occasionally slept at night under the roof of the building. Of course, some officers enjoy the visits more than others; often they are older, more experienced officers. Overall, police work in Japan is more low key than in the United States and patrol officers keep a lower profile than their American counterparts, and there is less "muscle flexing" than one observes in the United States. Drinking is widespread in Japan but it is unlikely to result in the bloodshed that is not uncommon in American cities. Often the most common request at police boxes in cities is for directions. This is because Japanese streets

**Figure 3.2  Suggestions for Police Recruits**

---

I.   Etiquette

    1.   Dress properly and neatly.

    2.   Knock on the door or ring doorbell before entering.

    3.   Do not peep in windows or touch articles such as decorations at the entrance.

    4.   When offered a chair or *zabuton* (cushion), sit down and greet the person properly.

    5.   If a woman receives you, keep the door open unless she asks you to close it.

II.  Communication

Offer appropriate greetings, indicating why you have come. If you are visiting the house for the first time, introduce yourself. For those who are not familiar with routine visits, explain and ask for their cooperation. Select appropriate words. Make your speech clear with a choice of language appropriate to the person you are addressing. You may use the local dialect if there is one in your area.

III. Note the Occasion

    1.   Avoid ceremonial occasions, when there are guests or when people are occupied with work.

    2.   When there is no one at home and contact is difficult, ask the neighbors when the family might be at home in order to carry out the routine visit.

IV. Note the Content of the Conversation

    1.   Speak of familiar, interesting matters and make the conversation easy to understand.

    2.   Do not say things that may hurt the feelings of the residents. Avoid rumors concerning neighbors and political topics.

---

in many cities have no names and are numbered in an odd way. Therefore a first time visitor may have to go to the nearest *koban* to seek help in locating an address. Gun control is strict in Japan and gun-related incidents are very low, as I noted earlier. I recall my interviews during my first research study in 1980, when I asked police officers about how often they drew or used their gun. I was shocked that after many interviews—perhaps 50—I finally found an officer who acknowledged drawing his weapon. In that instance he had been called to a bank robbery in progress, but had not been required to discharge his gun. In follow-up interviews with police officials in 1999, a similar outcome was reported—no change in the frequency with which officers drew their weapons. While sections of Tokyo may appear similar to big American cities like New York and Chicago, the level of crime is vastly different.

Henry Kamm's (1981) comments describing his experience in the Ikebukuro section of Tokyo are revealing. He noted that the area was a combination of pawn shops, Turkish baths (that serve as a cover for prostitution), bars, cheap eating places, and "love hotels," where rooms can be rented by the hour. Nonetheless, he observed that no crime was reported, no complaints were lodged, and no arrests were made. The only suspects questioned were men pushing bicycles that, despite arousing patrolmen's suspicion, proved to be owned and registered by the suspects. The only harsh treatment meted out was by an angry mother coming to reclaim her two small daughters who, instead of doing their homework, went in search of their father at a game parlor but lost sight of him.

A police officer's typical day is presented in Figure 3.3 (National Police Academy, 1998).

In the early 1980s, I sometimes went on patrol with *koban* police, both walking and in patrol cars. On one occasion, while interviewing an officer in the early morning hours at the Tsukiji Fish Market police box, I asked an older officer about his experience. He commented that the area was relatively crime free with only occasional pickpockets. In earlier years there had been more frequent problems with "toughs," and once in a while a knife fight, but shop owners had bonded together to get rid of these undesirables. The main objective of officers at this police box was to provide crime prevention information while doing routine visits to the shops in the huge market. Like other interviewees, he reported less responsiveness from citizens compared with earlier years. He stated, "Before and right after World War II, the police were both respected and feared, but today some people are tempted to abolish the *koban* system because of the decreased level of activity. I believe it should be maintained, but patience is required."

Another officer in the study, working in the Hongo area of Tokyo, summarized the changes he had witnessed by remarking, "They used to treat us like members of the family and invite us in for coffee or tea; today that would be unthinkable." The problem of weakening of ties between police and citizens has continued over the span of my study, from 1980 to 2012. For some Japanese police, they view it as an inevitable byproduct of modern industrialization. One outcome of the weakening ties has been a reduction in "clearance rates" on crimes, as reported earlier.

One theme from my interviews and connections with Japanese police over the years has been that in older residential neighborhoods, and with the shopkeepers in these areas, there is a stronger relationship with police. These are typically more conservative areas with older residents, and they have much to gain from closer ties with the police. Therefore, they provide the backbone of crime prevention activity. Crime rates are often lower in these neighborhoods.

## Figure 3.3 *Koban* Officer Log

8:30 Work starts at police station
- Receives instruction from police chief and community section chief.
- Gets uniform and equipment checkups.

9:00 Desk work
- Instructed by *koban* chief to pay special attention to sneak-thief as they have many reports reported recently.
- Receives a report from citizen that he left his bag behind in a public phone booth.

10:00 Patrol
- Gives crime prevention guidance focusing on residential areas frequently targeted by sneak-thieves.
- Receives a command from police radio and rushes to the house of the resident who made an emergency call to police for being troubled by a peddler not leaving a house.

11:00 Desk work
- Upon a report, conducts traffic control for a traffic accident in the neighborhood until handling over the duties to traffic officers from the police station (11:10–12:00).

12:00 Lunch

13:00 Desk work
- Receives a report finding a bag left in the telephone booth and takes contact to its owner after confirming what it contains.
- Gives geographical guidance.

14:00 Routine visit to home and work places
- Gets a hearsay information that a suspicious looking man haunts a nearby park at night.
- Visits ten households on the beat (two of them were absent) and tells them to watch out for sneak-thief.
- Visits a home which previously had a thief sneak in and asks if there is anything unusual after that.
- A resident seeks advice about his son frequently being tempted by a group of delinquents to go out after dark.
- Officer notes physical features of the son and tells he would visit his home again for the further discussion.

16:00 Desk work
- Persons who consulted before claiming and being claimed for making noise by playing Karaoke; visit *koban*.
- Officer mediates between the two and presents a solution (16:30–18:00).

19:00 Supper

20:00 Desk work

21:00 Joint patrol

- Cracks down on drunken driving, with other *koban* officers in the same precinct.

1:00 Night patrol

- Detects a few youngsters in a park and advises them to return home.

2:00 Nap

- Upon a fire report, rushes to the scene and rescues people (2:30–3:30).

7:30 Traffic control for school children

- Controls traffic for schoolchildren on their way to school—in cooperation with community residents.

8:30 Desk work

- Files a document.

9:00 Handing over Duty

Armed robberies in Tokyo have continued to be far lower than in New York City over the past 30 years, notwithstanding New York City's dramatic drop in violent crime.

In 1980–1981, there were 225 times more armed robberies in New York City. One interesting difference between American and Japanese police practices is that Japanese police rarely go to court. Information they gather on a criminal case gets turned over to a prosecutor. The court does not require the personal appearance of the officer. The prosecutor's written statement is usually sufficient. American police officers spend a significant amount of time in court, waiting for a case to be heard.

# Women in Police Work

Overall, women have gradually assumed more status in Japan but are still not treated as equal to men. As women have achieved better paying jobs and higher status positions, there has been an increase in divorce rates, apparently attributable in part to their greater financial independence. In April of 1998, there were 8,100 women police officers in Japan, but by 2009, the number had grown to 14,900 (Police of Japan, 2011). The NPA reports greater efforts in 2011 to support the role of women in police work, including the introduction of a babysitter service. Furthermore, the growth in the status and income of women is in parallel with their enhanced opportunities in business and government. The Gender Equality Law, passed in mid-1999, may have had a mod-

Table 3.1  Women in the Workforce, 1985 and 2005

|  | Percent of All Management Jobs Held by Women | |
|---|---|---|
|  | 1985 | 2005 |
| Philippines | 21.9% | 57.8% |
| United States | 35.6 | 42.5 |
| Germany | 25.8 | 37.3 |
| Australia | 17.6 | 37.3 |
| Britain | 32.9 | 34.5 |
| Norway | 22.0 | 30.5 |
| Singapore | 12.0 | 25.9 |
| Malaysia | 8.7 | 23.2 |
| Japan | 6.6 | 10.1 |
| South Korea | 3.7 | 7.8 |

est impact, but the *Japan Times* (August 28, 1999) noted that the legislation lacked "specific compliance measures." One later development that has been a huge plus for women is the growth of the Internet. By 2000, Japan became the largest user of the Internet in the world. Stephanie Strom (*New York Times*, 2000), reporting on this development in Japan, quoted Jiro Kokuryo of Keio University, who specializes in e-commerce: "It is changing people's point of view and empowering them to challenge traditional ways of doing things." Women have banded together on the Internet. By 1998, some 25.6 percent of the 14 million Japanese using the Internet were women according to the Ministry of Posts and Telecommunications, up from 17.8 percent a year earlier. One woman, Naoko Utsonomiya, was quoted as saying that it will help "crack the bamboo ceiling." The historical practice of face-to-face male business negotiations and the groups of males that drink sake together at night has made it difficult for women to advance in the business world. As one Japanese friend of mine, and a former language instructor at Yale once said to me, "everything gets done over drink in Japan." Cyberspace is offering new opportunities for women, and they can work from home just like men. This is important with limited child-care facilities and strong pressures on mothers to stay at home. Historically, the vast majority of women have left their jobs at the time of marriage or after having children—the result of traditional conformity pressures imposed by male-headed businesses and government enterprises.

Table 3.1 presents a picture of women managers in the Japanese work force in 1985 and 2005 (Fackler, 2006).

Even though increases in women in management jobs in Japan can be noted, the increase is from just 6.6 percent to just 10.1 percent. The United States and Western nations have far more progressive policies, with the United States demonstrating an increase from 35.6 percent to 42.5 percent over the same 20-year span.

## Police Special Projects and Programs

One interesting experience that I was offered during my visits to police stations and *koban* was an invitation to a "Single Men's Kendo and Judo Tournament." Kendo has a long tradition in Japan generally, and the police have incorporated it into their programs for many years. I described it as follows in my last book on the Japanese police (Parker, 2001):

> Kendo is a form of fencing with a bamboo sword. Officers, outfitted in medieval-looking robes and wearing face shields, utter war cries as combat is joined. The contestants received a rousing send-off by the chief at an early morning ceremonial gathering in the upstairs gym of the Shitaya police station. This included the beating of a huge drum, a sake toast, and a pep talk by the chief. The contestants then traveled twenty minutes to the site of the tournament, where they met teams from eight other police stations. After a brief warm-up period, there was another short ceremony for all the participants. One of the reasons one rarely encounters an overweight Japanese police office is that, as mentioned earlier, all officers are required to take either judo or kendo, and promotions at the lower levels require proficiency in these sports. Physical exercise is continued by most police long after the required years of training are over. Moreover, foot and bicycle patrols are still far more common than motorized patrols, and this contributes to the trim appearance of most personnel. (p. 60)

One of the organizations within the Japanese police system is the riot police. They have been called upon more often during earlier periods, such as the student riots of the 1960s that to some extent mirrored the similar student uprisings in the United States and Europe. In the 1980s, there was the stand-off at Narita Airport, outside of Tokyo, in which farmers rallied against the expansion of runways. They engaged in physical combat at times. Overall, they have rarely been called upon over the past 15 years or so. Each prefecture has its own riot police unit available for a quick response to emergency. They include specialized squads—a counter-terrorism group, an ordinance and explosive disposal squad, and a water rescue squad. Eight prefectures have special assault teams that can be deployed in hostage-taking situations.

A Digital Forensics Division was established in 1999 to support cybercrime investigators and provide digital forensic services. Other high-tech developments by the National Police Agency since 2000 include a mobile radio communications system and new communications command systems to assist in the dispatching of police units to crime scenes and emergencies. These units, in all prefectures, handle 110 calls. These automated systems allow for car locator and mapping systems to assist in identifying and dispatching police to particular locations (Police of Japan, 2011).

Various dissident groups are monitored by the police including extreme right-wing and ultra-leftist organizations. One organization that caused a number of deaths in 1995 was Aum Shinrikyo, whose members released sarin gas on Tokyo subways during rush hour. The leader, Shoko Asahara, was arrested and is serving a life sentence after a lengthy trial. The organization has now split, with one group of followers adhering to the teachings of the arrested leader, while another group distanced itself from the founder. As of 2011, three followers of Asahara were on the NPA's most wanted list (Police of Japan, 2011). Around 2010, far-right nationalist groups attacked Chinese fishing boats after a Chinese vessel collided with a Japanese Coast Guard patrol boat. The event was not accidental. During 2010, 1,757 rightists were arrested by Japanese police.

Tensions between North Korea and Japan have continued for many years, sometimes heating up. Cases that are still open involve a number of Japanese nationals (around 17) who were believed to have been abducted by North Korean government agents and transferred to North Korea. Several cases go back to 1977.

Earlier I mentioned the critical importance of personal relationships in accomplishing my research in Japan. I felt fortunate to develop friendships with several police officers, lawyers, and justice officials. I was invited to their homes for dinners and parties, and I sometimes played tennis with them, joined them in going to nightclubs, jazz shows, coffee shops, etc. This was not only enjoyable but it offered an opportunity to check on various issues that came up during my official visits and interviews with other personnel; and it allowed me to clarify or refute points that had arisen during these more formal sessions. One patrol sergeant was particularly helpful and an excellent English speaker. He was a college graduate and very bright and personable. Also, to my surprise, he was familiar with a number of American criminal justice scholars and had read a number of their books. Here is one informative comment that he offered:

> Policemen who are ambitious do a lot of questioning of citizens. For example, when patrolling the streets, it is fairly easy to do. If someone has a light out on his bicycle, he can be stopped and rather easily persuaded (if he is initially evasive) to give basic information about himself—what his name is, where he is from, where he is going. He will cooperate, although reluctantly at times. I might do this six or seven times a night. (Parker, 2001)

The above description reveals how police **penetrate** into Japanese society as David Bayley (1991) has noted. If American police were to undertake their duties in a similar way, they would typically encounter strong resistance and citizens would argue their "rights." Occasionally foreigners report problems with the police—often on what Americans would consider minor issues. One incident stands out that was reported in the first phase of my research:

> A professional woman employee of a U.S. government office in Tokyo offered the following episode as an example. This Japanese American spoke fluent Japanese and had lived in Tokyo for a number of years. She stated that she and an acquaintance, a male American scholar, were stopped by two men in business suits while heading for lunch in the Akasaka area of Tokyo. The officers inquired where the couple were going, to which she responded by asking who they were. The men immediately furnished their police identification cards. She then asked why they had been stopped, but they did not reply. The officers repeated their questions and the woman reluctantly replied that they were headed for lunch. One officer smirked and again repeated his question, to which she angrily retorted, "To lunch!" The police then asked about the nature of their relationship and in the process discovered that her companion was not carrying his alien registration card, which all foreigners are legally required to have with them at all times. The officers then asked the couple to accompany them to the nearest police box, despite the woman's protest that the man's alien registration card was easily accessible—a three-minute walk to his office. At the police box, the man was asked the purpose of his being in Japan, and he informed the officers that he was seeking employment. They responded that there was no way that they could be assured of the veracity of his statement. The American visitor was then asked to provide further identification and to sign a form letter of apology. In

addition, he had to promise to report back with the alien registration card. This incident illustrated the ease with which Japanese police can make inquiries at their own discretion (a privilege that would be the envy of American police) and the indignant and angry feelings of foreigners subjected to such tactics. (Parker, 2001, p. 63)

Some *koban* had bulletin boards near the building with various notices, including "Most Wanted" posters, often with photos. Sometimes the Tokyo Metropolitan Police Department headquarters would circulate information or provide posters. One "permanent" poster spotted in several *koban* read, "To have good contact with people and show understanding, to get the confidence of people." Another stated, "Don't take it out of the holster, don't put your finger on the trigger, don't point it at people." Another one said, "Try hard to stay in good condition mentally and physically," and another, "Try your best to be responsible and maintain a sense of duty." A more detailed one listed "five goals":

1. Try to meet each person honestly and try to gain the respect and understanding of the local community.
2. Try to melt into or fit into the community by taking the initiative and grasping the area of your jurisdiction.
3. Try actively and constructively to question people on the street in order to prevent crime and make arrests.
4. Be alert and be nimble in terms of organizing your activities in order to solve each case as quickly as possible.
5. Work properly, correctly, and with dignity. Be fully alert in preventing any crime or accident. (Parker, 2001, p. 65)

Sanya, one of the fewer lower-class districts in Tokyo, had many transients and was one of the most crime-ridden areas in the city. A small district of run-down, single men's rooming houses and hotels, it often provided a safe haven for offenders attempting to elude the police. Overall, though, this neighborhood's criminal activity paled in comparison with high-crime rate areas of American cities. By and large most Japanese urban areas were clean and pleasant by American standards. In Sanya, there might be a mugging or purse snatching, but rarely a serious assault or homicide.

## Policing Hokkaido and Okayama

Field research was undertaken in both Hokkaido and Okayama prefectures—to assist in expanding the understanding of police activities outside of Tokyo. Hokkaido is second to Honshu in size among Japan's five major islands

**Figure 3.4  Organizational Chart of Hokkaido Prefectural Policing**

GOVERNOR

HOKKAIDO PUBLIC
SAFETY COMMISSION

AREA
PUBLIC
SAFETY
COMMISSION (4)

HOKKAIDO PREFECTURAL
POLICE HEADQUARTERS
CHIEF OF HOKKAIDO
PREFECTURAL POLICE

AREA
HEADQUARTERS (4)
CHIEF OF AREA                                                    POLICE SCHOOL
HEADQUARTERS
                            POLICE STATION
                                          MUNICIPAL POLICE DEP.
                KOPBAN/POLICE BOX
                RESIDENTIAL POLICE BOX

*Source:* Hokkaido Prefectural Police Website.

and accounts for 85,513 square kilometers. It is primarily rural with major employment in areas such as farming, fishing, and forestry. It has some industry—particularly paper mills and beer breweries. It is first in the nation in the production of agricultural products such as wheat, soy beans, potatoes, sugar beets, onions, and milk. Sapparo is the major city and the site of the 1972 Winter Olympics, with a population was around 1,900,000 in 2000, and it is the fifth largest city in Japan. A very cold area during winter time, temperatures average minus 5 degrees centigrade in January and February. The prefecture enjoys a heavy snowfall, and along with mountainous terrain, it is appealing to skiers. Hokkaido's police had not been studied by Western scholars in any depth. As of 1997, the Hokkaido Prefecture employed 9,224 police officers. Figure 3.4 presents the organizational chart of the Hokkaido Prefecture Police. There are many more *chuzaisho* in Hokkaido (506) as opposed to *koban* (291), given the rural character of the prefecture.

One Hokkaido police administrator noted that there needs to be a balance between being friendly to citizens but also maintaining some distance in order for an officer to properly do his job. Being too friendly may bring charges of favoritism. Also administrators believe that being too close could make an officer vulnerable to corruption, and this helps explain why officers are rotated in their assignments every few years. Officers operating in the countryside do have the luxury of spending more time with citizens during their household visits. In the most rural areas, officers often do not have the fellowship of other officers and must seek out neighbors and family for companionship. When first arriving in a new assignment at a police box, the officer must try to get to know people in his area. This is usually undertaken as part of the household survey. The task is more challenging if he is officious. Police recruits in any country tend to undertake their duties "by the book" or the "proper" way as taught at the training academy. For example, if an officer rigorously enforces traffic regulations, he or she may not be approached by citizens in terms of information on criminal matters. As noted earlier, women are now compensated for the work they do in supporting their husband's job at the residential police box. Although women are far more integrated in police work in recent years, men still staff *chuzaisho*. Women are now compensated at around 1 million yen annually (77 yen = $1 as of August, 2011).

"Lost-and-found" is an interesting phenomena in Japan. In Tokyo, many items, from cell phones to cash to even cigarette cartons, have a strong likelihood of finding their way into police lost-and-found centers (Onishi, 2004). In Tokyo, in a four-story warehouse, hundreds of thousands of lost objects are meticulously catalogued according to date and location of discovery and the information is put in a computerized database. These lost-and-found centers are based on a 1,300-year-old system that preceded Japan as a unified nation. In 2002, individuals brought to the Tokyo center 23 million dollars in cash, 72 percent of which was returned to the owners once the party was able to confirm to the police that it was their money. About 19 percent went to the finders after no one claimed the money after six months. Many finders do not make claims and the money reverts to the Tokyo government. One woman, Hitomi Sasaki, found $250 in a tray under a plant outside the restaurant where she worked, and since no one came to claim it after six months, she received it. She commented, "I used to live in Chicago so I can tell you how wonderful this is" (Onishi, 2004). Children are taught early on to hand in anything they find to the police. Therefore many of the hundreds of people who come to the Tokyo center everyday take the system for granted.

On a recent morning, shelves were heaving under bags containing lost items that spoke of the rhythms of commuting life: keys, glasses, wallets, cell phones, bags. A small bicycle helmet with "Suzuki" on it and a toy horse testified perhaps to a child's fickleness. Skis and golf bags attested perhaps less to misplacement than to an abandoned hobby; unclaimed wedding bands perhaps spoke of the end of something larger. Wheelchairs and crutches were harder to explain, though Nobuo Hasuda, 54, and Hitoshi Shitara, 47, veteran officials of the lost-and-found system, had well-rehearsed lines. "I wonder what happened to the owners," Mr. Shitara said. Mr. Hasuda said with a smile, "If they didn't need them anymore because they got better, it's a good thing." One floor was a sea of umbrellas, the most commonly lost item—330,000 in 2002, or 3,200 for every good rainfall—and, at a rate of 0.3 percent, the least reclaimed. The low rate is an indication of how rapidly Japan has grown rich in the span of a few generations. "In the past," Mr. Shitara said, "one person barely had one umbrella, or a family had to share one. So your father scolded you if you lost an umbrella." (Onishi, 2004, p. A4)

In the eighteenth century, finders were given certain rights and were rewarded with a partial value of the found property. Finders who did not hand in objects were severely punished. According to one account in 1733, two officials who kept some clothing were led to the back of town and executed.

Returning to the subject of the Hokkaido Prefectural Police, one officer I interviewed at the Konbu *chuzaisho* observed that the attitudes of rural citizens were different than their urban counterparts. He commented that when he worked at the busiest police station in Sapporo (the largest city on the island prefecture), people gave only necessary minimum information but in this rural outpost (hundreds of miles from Sapporo) people sought him out for conversation and volunteered information. An elderly man came regularly for conversation and the officer occasionally invited him for breakfast. Because of the heavy snowfall in this mountainous area, the officer sometimes helped people shovel out their cars. This Konbu *chuzaisho* was responsible for 114.3 square kilometers, but there were only 450 houses and commercial buildings in the area. A mini-patrol car was provided, but much of the officer's time was spent on the routine family visits and an occasional investigation of a traffic accident. When I asked about domestic disturbances or husband-wife fights he said none had been reported in the previous year. One *chuzai-san* that I always recall, because it was such an enjoyable visit, I described in the first edition of my book in 1984:

> This man was one of the most delightful police officers I met during my stays in Japan. He was a *chuzaisho* officer working in an outlying area covered by the Tokyo Metropolitan Police Department. I spent several days at his police box observing his daily routine and his interactions with citizens. I was surprised to find that there are residential police boxes under the M.P.D.'s jurisdiction until I learned how large and diversified Tokyo metropolitan area is. This man—Officer Saito let us call him—was thirty-seven years old, married, and had three

daughters. He was a sergeant. He had always sought a residential police box assignment. Born and raised in an agricultural community
far to the south of Tokyo, he had considered taking over his parents'
farm but had decided against it. "These days," he said, "the oldest son
is not automatically expected to take over the farm. Rather, the son who
likes the work will take it over." He traced his early interest in police
work to the "little kindnesses" he had observed the local officer offering to neighbors in his community. He had hoped to avoid working
in a large city, but it proved to be his only access to police work. After
completing high school, he had been assigned to Nakano for police training. Later, he took evening courses at his own expense at Nippon University, a Tokyo-based institution with over a hundred thousand
students. Eventually, he received his degree. He had been a policeman
for seventeen years and had worked in a variety of other police assignments, including traffic control, and his last assignment before
receiving this posting had been in a jail working with presentence detainees. As mentioned earlier, police administrators agree that married, slightly older officers like Saito are the best choice for *chuzaisho*
assignments, but, according to one official in Chiba Prefecture, they
are increasingly difficult to find. Saito was friendly and outgoing and
appeared to enjoy thoroughly the most trivial, mundane encounters
with citizens. He went out of his way to make such meetings agreeable.
His police box was gaily decorated with flowers, and a colorful bird chat-
tered in a cage near the window. This *chuzaisho* is located in a park across
the street from a cemetery, and there are some cherry trees nearby. It
was the first *chuzaisho* I visited, and the setting was so idyllic that I
found myself wondering at the time whether or not it had been "spruced
up" for my benefit. Later, after visiting other flower-bedecked *chuzaisho*, my skepticism vanished. Saito said he found his job very enjoyable because it allowed him to get to know people and that, in his
opinion, was the most important part of a *chuzai-san*'s job. This
seemed evident when he conducted the residential survey, visiting
neighborhood homes, shopkeepers, and the residence of a Buddhist
priest. His wife was cooperative and helped by answering the phone
and occasionally assisting with a drunk. He noted, "When drunks are
talking to women, they are less aggressive." In discussing police work,
he remarked that most officers are very committed, that morale is
high, and that while some people, like his brother, feel that the police
take their duties too seriously, he disagreed. He added that the disci-
pline of police work creates a sense of pride in many officers. (p. 101)

Yes, there are police officers like Saito in the United States, and they can often be found in small towns and villages. They have more time and are less pressured and can develop relationships with citizens like in Japan.

# The Okayama Prefectural Police

Okayama is a prefecture in the Western part of the county and around 500 miles from Tokyo. I was able to do research in this area in 2000 because of my 20-year friendship with a recently retired chief of the Okayama Prefectural Police. He had received rotating assignments, like all National Police Agency ranking officers, and was back in Tokyo at the time of this field study. His assignment at that time was in the "public security" section in Tokyo. This assignment involved intelligence gathering on radical groups in Japan. This phase of the research centered on Okayama City, the capitol of the prefecture and a beautiful and appealing area to tourists. The Chugoku Mountains provided the backdrop along with Japan's Inland Sea. The population of the prefecture was around 1,950,000, and the police force included 3,028 officers and 530 civilians. There were 23 police stations and a total of 305 police boxes under the prefectural headquarters. A ranking officer commented that around 90 percent of citizens responded but 10 percent denied access. The use of guns in 1999 was such a rare event in the prefecture that one supervisor stated that there were just two or three incidents in the previous year in which an officer had been required to draw his gun. Those were events in which, he stated, a "foreigner might be armed." Fifty or 60 arrests of Chinese had taken place in 1998, primarily for illegal entry, larcenies, and overstaying tourist visas. None had committed homicide. Some South Koreans arriving legally, engaged in pick-pocketing, slashing bags, and other petty crimes. Overall, a small group of foreigners were residing in Okayama. In 1998, there were just 104 felonies reported, including murders, rapes, robberies, arsons, and kidnapping. Suicides officially numbered 401 in 1997 and 484 in 1998. Of course, suicides in many countries are underreported.

I made an inquiry regarding organized crime—a topic to be covered in greater detail later. The officer at the Okayama-Higashi Police Station commented that *boryokudan* (organized crime) members often were involved in the sale of stimulants (mostly amphetamines), prostitution, the sale of pornographic materials, and loan sharking. Approximately 130 individuals were members of organized crime in this prefecture. Most were armed with knives and clubs as opposed to guns. However, nationwide, although there was a low incidence of firearms throughout the country, a significant portion of handguns seized were owned by *boryokudan*. The amendment to the Firearms and Swords Control Law of 1995 made it a more serious offense to possess guns and this has aided law enforcement. Nonetheless, Japanese police and organized crime have co-existed in interesting ways in which *boryokudan* (historically called *yakuza*) have been allowed to operate within certain unwritten but generally understood parameters. Some occasions in which organized crime members violated the unwritten policies are described later in this book. Suffice it to say that both the police and *boryokudan* have conservative members and view their legacy as going back to the ancient samurai warriors. When I asked the chief of the Okayama-Higashi station as to why there wasn't a greater crackdown on these openly operating organized crime figures in his prefecture, he claimed certain difficulties. He stated, "The biggest reason is they have invested in legitimate businesses and that it had been difficult to follow the money trail; money laundering laws don't have the same teeth in the United States." One of his colleagues who had worked with U.S. law enforcement agents noted, "In the United States the burden is often on the organized crime figure to prove that he got his money legitimately, but here the burden is on the prosecutor. However, in some cases we have been effective in using the tax law to tax their illegal funds or make an arrest" (Parker, 2001, p. 111). Still, there had been 80 arrests of organized crime figures in Okayama during 1998 and 1999. No homicides among gang members or involving Japanese citizens had been reported in the prefecture during the previous two years.

In this station, eyewitness matters were handled by published sketches in newspapers and *koban* bulletin board postings of artist's sketches, along with television presentations of photos and sketches. As in the United States, photos are often presented in arrays, but Japanese have often used one-on-one encounters of suspects (called "show-ups" in the United States). These have been found to be illegal, according to a ruling of the United States Supreme Court, because of the prejudicial impact of asking a witness, "Is this the person?" The subject of retirement was briefly discussed with the chief of the Okayama-Nishi Police Station. Mr. Matsumoto, a gregarious person, said he had been a police officer for 37 years. He was scheduled to retire at age 60. Often due to this somewhat early retirement system, retired officers take jobs in other areas such as private security—also a common occurrence among American officers. But these retirements bring meager pensions for the Japanese, which contribute to their desire to seek post-retirement jobs. His pension was scheduled to be around 3 million yen (equivalent to $41,000 at 73 yen per dollar). Street crime units have been popular for many years among city police departments in the United States. Chief Matsumoto commented that only in special investigations such as a kidnapping did the station resort to the use of large numbers of undercover or plain clothes detectives. In such an event, perhaps 100 detectives would be organized. The aggressive use of undercover officers, as in New York City, was viewed as unwarranted in Japan.

Another common, albeit controversial, police practice in the United States is "hot pursuit." In Okayama City there was no official policy on this matter, but there would be hot pursuit on waterways where the marine police operate. However, with "hot pursuit" it was unnecessary as other methods could be used to identify the violators.

One memorable incident took place in Okayama when I was out on a bike ride. It reflects the politeness and the consideration given to *gaijin*, "visitors":

> Having stopped for a brief lunch on a twenty-mile bike tour of the surrounding countryside, I pulled out a map at my table to try to locate my position. I asked for the assistance of a young Japanese man in his twenties at the adjacent table. He introduced himself as a junior high school geography teacher. He not only offered assistance, but dashed to his car to get a more detailed map of his own so he could draw a clear map of my route. I thanked him, and we both headed out onto the road. After I had been biking for a mile or so he drove up beside me and stopped. He apologized for having made a mistake on one of the turns he had drawn on the map and wanted to set me straight. This Japanese penchant for being helpful to foreigners is very widespread, and while I used to think it was a wonderful, friendly gesture (that I experienced many times over the years), I came to understand that it also springs from the sense of obligation that Japanese feel for visitors. This sense of obligation translates, of course, not only to a willingness to assist a foreigner but to various interpersonal relations among Japanese. It also contributes to the greater cohesiveness of Japanese society compared to American society. (Parker, 2001, p. 121)

A visit to the railway police office in Okayama shed light on the role of railway police units. Railway police provide a deterrent role as well as an investigative function. They patrol trains and stations and they handle low-level crime such as petty theft. Occasionally they get involved in the investigation of accidents, in the protective custody of lost children, and sometimes they provide counseling like their counterparts at *koban*. All prefectures have a railway unit, and crime prevention is a key function as evidenced by many posters. Some offer advice on protecting valuables, while others offer cautions to young people. A hotline number is offered, but the offices I interviewed rarely encountered serious crime. One poster stated, "Stop Molesters. It Takes Courage. Report a Molester to the Railway Police Bureau, Tel. 086-222-7405. Complete Confidentiality

For Victims." Japan has been notorious for men molesting women on crowded trains and subways. The Japanese film (2005) *I Just Didn't Do It* highlighted the problem in a true story of a falsely accused college-aged man riding a subway in Tokyo during the morning rush hour period. Finally one of the objectives of the railway police was to search for "wanted offenders" as part of a nation-wide effort. Their mug shots were often displayed on bulletin boards.

# 4

# The Investigation of Crime, Prosecution, and the Courts in Japan

While crime rates have dropped considerably in the United States over the past few decades, they still exist on a much higher level than in Japan, as I described in an earlier chapter. In Japan, while the criminal justice system has much to recommend it in terms of efficiency and quality, it is still the nature of the society that acts as a powerful social control on criminal activity. Crime does not pay in Japan and while clearance rates have gone down over the past 30 years, the chances of being caught are infinitely greater than in the United States. Unlike in the United States, there is no plea bargaining in Japan. Interestingly, while poverty, racism, drugs, and family breakdown are identified as major factors in crime causation in Japan, a lot of attention is focused on the highly competitive educational system, which also results in a rash of suicides in the spring when students receive their college entrance examination scores. Experts have linked juvenile offenders in schools to parents who have overly indulged their offspring, but also to the "pressure cooker" atmosphere. It can start at an early age when parents seek to give their children an edge by getting them accepted at top kindergarten schools. School dropouts, depression, and assaults (occasionally on teachers) are part of the picture. Some youngsters who have dropped out seek group support in motorcycle gangs, referred to as *bosozoku*. Occasionally they try to hook up with low-level *yakuza* or *boryokudan* in response to the crisis of being a drop-out in a society that places a premium on achievement. In my previous book on Japan, I reported on a case of a mother who had killed a two-year-old girl who had taken her daughter's slot in a prized nursery school:

> A two-year-old girl, who had just passed an entrance exam, was killed by the mother of a child who failed the exam. The enraged and jealous mother admitted that she had strangled Haruna and stuffed her body into a bag. She then boarded a train to dispose of it near her

own parents' home on the outskirts of Tokyo. Of course, numerous editorials decried the homicide and railed against the system that places intense academic pressures on children at this absurdly young age of two. Still, discussions of this type, which have been common in Japan for decades, have not yet contributed to any significant reforms. The shocking nature of the case plunged the Japanese into a related discussion of family life in general and the pivotal aspect of a mother's role (they are often called "education mamas" because of their central role in supervising the education of their offspring) in all of this. Some of the discussion explored the emptiness of some mothers' lives that appeared to have propelled them into "desperately projecting so many of their aspirations upon their young children." (Parker, 2001, p. 123)

A variety of incidents and responses to juvenile problems in schools have been highlighted in press reports. A major industry is interwoven into the problems of juvenile crime in Japan. It is the existence of *juku*—the cram schools, which students and parents believe are necessary to provide many extra hours of study in order to be academically successful. Most Japanese agree that in order to get a good job one has to graduate from a prominent university. In the United States, students can drop out and get a second or third chance to graduate from a college or university. While graduating from a high-ranking Ivy League college such as Harvard or Yale can be important, it does not carry the same clout as graduating from Tokyo University or Kyoto University. If one doesn't perform well in the early years in Japan the door will be closed. Japan scholars claim that their system has historical roots from the Meiji era of the 1860s, when the nation was trying to catch up with the West. It is true that Japan emphasizes egalitarianism, but the cut-throat academic approach has taken its toll. Howard French (2002) described some problems regarding schools that shocked the Japanese. Historically, Japanese classrooms were serene and students respected teachers and conformed to the demands of teachers. In the early 1980s, I visited a junior high-school near my apartment on a number of occasions. There was no evidence of the turmoil or disruption that has engulfed some Japanese classrooms over the past decade. I never even viewed any instances of rudeness toward teachers. However, here is a description of in a school district in Yokohama concerning developments in later years:

By fourth grade, they are using obscene language, often directed at the teacher or written on the blackboard. And by sixth grade, a growing generation of preteenage rebels has begun walking in and out of classrooms at will, mocking the authority of adults and even attacking teachers who try to restrain them. "When I was posted to this

school in April last year, the sixth graders were so disorderly that teachers couldn't start classes," said Masakuni Kaneshima, 57, the principal of an elementary school in Kunitachi, a Tokyo suburb. "About a
third of the students, that is, about a dozen from each class, wouldn't
even enter the classroom. Together with the head teacher, my job became bringing these children to their classroom." A plague of similar
troubles have many Japanese asking whatever happened to their country's school system, not long ago the envy of much of the world for its
reputation for producing not just wave after wave of high-achieving
children, but of conspicuously well-behaved children, as well. (French,
2002, p. A6)

One report released by Japan's National Institute for Educational Policy Research stated that 32.4 percent of 6,614 elementary school teachers surveyed believed that at least one classroom had experienced "collapse." "Classroom
collapse" was excessive disorder, with students insulting teachers, leaving the
classroom, wrestling with one another, talking out of turn, etc. Higher grades
also reported similar problems, with nearly half of all high schools reporting
violence, high drop-out rates, and student prostitution (French, 2002). Many
of these reports have resulted in anguished debates among parents and educators
as to the causes of these developments. Predictably, it has created a blame game
with parents voicing concern that teachers have abdicated their responsibilities.
But educators have responded by citing the parents' inability to properly raise
their children. One education expert, a Mr. Ogi, said that students were victims of high expectations with overly demanding parents—often in single-
child households. Ogi remarked, "Even if only a few kids in the class rebel, the
others enjoy watching and they love bullying the teacher. At home, they have
to play the role of the perfect child or they don't get the affection from their
mothers, but when their mother is not present they tend to act out." Here is
another description offered by French of classroom chaos:

At the Idogaya Elementary School in Yokohama, a four-story building with a large, open sandlot that looks from the outside like the very
proto-type of the Japanese elementary school, officials said that bits
and pieces of all those factors had played a role in a classroom breakdown problem the school said it had brought under control last year.
In a reflection of the shame that attaches to social problems in Japan,
among dozens of schools that were approached, Idogaya was the only
one that would both acknowledge it had experienced class-room collapse and allow itself to be identified. A tour of several classrooms,
however, showed no traces of the problem. In a sixth-grade music

class, students practiced Beethoven's "Marmotte" on their recorders, following the teacher's cues almost to perfection. Likewise, in a fourth-grade calligraphy class, there was nary a hint of giggling as students practiced writing characters. Despite the scenes of wrinkle-free order, the principal, Chuji Yamada, said he had been sent to the school because of his reputation as a problem solver. There had been disorder in a second-grade class, he said, in which "three or four kids would run out of the classroom and ignore the teacher's instructions." (p. A6)

There are strong psychological pressures in Japan's cohesive society to conform and obey the law. Individuals who come to the attention of justice officials typically feel a sense of shame, along with their family members. This atmosphere helps to deter criminal behavior. Family members feel responsible for delinquent or criminal acts committed by their offspring. In a study I undertook in 1983 on the role of parole and community-based programs for offenders in Japan, I discovered that in some instances families disowned the incarcerated family member upon release. The person was then left to fend for himself (Parker, 1986).

Also contributing to lower crime rates is the greater number of intact families in Japan. In Japan in 2008 there were 251,000 divorces and the rate was 1.99 per 100,000, but it had climbed slightly from 1.78 in 1997. Since 2008, the rate has stabilized and decreased slightly. In the United States, the rate was 4.4 in 1995 and was at 4.95 by 2004. By 2009, the Center for Disease Control and Prevention estimated that the rate was 3.4. As noted in the earlier discussion of the role of women in Japan, many are now more independent financially and feel less pressure to marry at an early age. On average at present, Japanese women are 27 years old when they marry, compared to 24.2 in 1971. Some even feel free not to marry. Overall, there is less stigma to obtaining a divorce in Japan than 20 or 30 years ago. In the United States, there has been very little stigma associated with divorce generally, although in some ethnic groups and in some religious circles, divorce is frowned upon. In summary, by including the many co-habitating couples and single parents in the United States, there are significant differences between the two countries regarding in-tact families. Japanese children often have two parents to nurture them far more often than do children in America. Data provided by the National Center for Health Statistics reported that the proportion of unmarried teenagers giving birth continued to increase in 1998 to 78.8 percent of those teenagers (Lacy, 1999).

Guns continue to play an infamous role in American society and gun incidents in Japan are rare, as noted earlier. There are daily reports of gun homicides in the United States and occasionally there are major gun-violence events such as the Columbine High School deaths in Colorado. The widespread availability of guns clearly contributes to the onslaught, and one person with an automatic weapon can kill many. It is estimated that there are over 200million guns across the United States, both registered and unregistered.

Criminal investigations in both nations often begin with a citizen report of a crime. Japanese report crimes closer to the level of the actual incidence. This statement is supported by "victimization" surveys in both nations. In Japan, a survey of citizens found the number of unreported crimes to be at 1.005 times the actual number. In a parallel study in the United States, the numbers revealed the unreported rate of crimes to be double the rate of reported crime to police departments.

Several writers have commented on the role of police detectives as informants (Ames, 1981; Adelstein, 2009). While initial investigations are handled by *Koban* police, more serious investigations are handled by detectives. Jake Adelstein offers numerous examples in his book about his role as an American working as a Japanese newspaper reporter on the police beat for a prestigious daily, the *Yomiuri Shimbun*. Some of his reporting dealt with organized crime figures—the *yakuza* or *boryokudan*. As he noted, organized criminals have strayed from the days in which they left the general population alone. Adelstein reports that "people who are supposed to be policing *yakuza* are easily deceived by them or perhaps even knowingly working in collusion with them."

Peter Hill's (2003) illuminating work on Japanese organized crime offered an interesting historical note on their origin:

> The groups commonly referred to as *yakuza* lay claim to a long lineage. While much of this is of dubious historical validity, the *yakuza* mythology is important in conditioning the perceptions, held by both the gang members themselves and the wider society, of the place the *yakuza/boryokudan* hold in Japanese society. Historically the term '*yakuza*' itself is imprecise in that it is commonly used to refer to two distinct groups, the *bakuto* (gamblers) and the *tekiya* (itinerant peddlers). The derivation of the word itself, from the '*ya*' (eight), '*ku*'(nine) and '*sa*' (three), making up the worst possible hand in a traditional Japanese card game, shows clearly its original reference to gamblers. (p. 36)

One dimension of the historical relationship between *yakuza* and mainstream society is Hill's description of how *yakuza* developed relationships with right-wing politicians, thereby helping to insulate these organized crime figures (Hill, 2003):

The links between the postwar *yakuza* and, usually right-wing, politicians are well known. This is not so much due to fearless investigative journalism or mass-arrests of corrupt politicians as to the extraordinary degree to which these links were openly displayed for much of this period. In some cases during the period of immediate postwar chaos, the links were in fact so close as to make it impossible to differentiate between the authorities and gangsters. During the immediate postwar period in Nagahama city in Shiga prefecture, the boss of the Hakuryu-sha *yakuza* group not only sat on the city council, but also served as head of the city's police commission (Iwai 1963: 692). The Hakuryu-sha therefore ultimately controlled both formal and informal markets for protection. This was largely made possible due to attempts by the occupying authorities to impose a decentralized system of policing in Japan. (p. 54)

One prominent gangster refused an invitation to join the Socialist Party (*KantoOzu-gumi*), but was persuaded to run for the Diet (Japanese Parliament) by the leadership of the Liberal Democratic Party.

It was perhaps a bizarre development, by American standards, but the Japanese government purchased *yakuza* protection in 1960 amidst the widespread discontent and rioting opposing the Japan-American Security Treaty. At that time, the government feared for the safety of the projected visit of President Eisenhower to Japan.

Relationships between police and organized crime have been described by a variety of scholars and the consensus seems to acknowledge that no serious attempt to break the group has ever been undertaken. This is in contrast to the formal statements of the National Police Agency and Ministry of Justice. In returning to the post-World War II period of turmoil, one of the preconditions for *yakuza* control over the flourishing black market was the absence of efficient alternative providers of protection. However, this also reflected the weakness of police during the period and the role of MacArthur's staff in the post-war reshaping of various policies (Hill, 2003).

Ironically, many Public Safety Commissions were packed with gangsters. Also, corruption played a role in the post-World War II decentralized police forces. The small autonomous police agencies were unable to adequately share information and coordinate law enforcement activities. This is a problem that the United States, with its decentralized system, still confronts today. This situation in Japan was central to the government's creation of a national integrated system of policing and criminal justice.

Finally, a number of Western scholars, in discussing the *yakuza*-police relationship, acknowledge or suggest that the police welcomed the existence of organized crime as providing a "hammer of the left" and, in addition, a force that played a role in discouraging disorganized crime (Hill, 2003). Incidentally, in some American cities, there have been similar discussions as to how Mafia neighborhoods are safer areas to live in for average people.

# Cybercrime

As in many countries, cybercrime and financial-related crime has increased in Japan. Cases cleared in 2009 reached a record high of 6,690, an increase of 369 from the previous year. The police report there have been many cases of Internet fraud. Some involve child prostitution, pornography violations, and the breaking of copyright laws. Unauthorized computer access crimes that were cleared by the police increased by 45.6 percent from the previous year. To deal with cybercrime, including crimes against children, the National Policy Agency created the "Internet Hotline Center" in June 2006. The NPA has also increased, by necessity, its international contacts with various countries, including the G8 nations.

In the 1990s, due in part to the economic "bubble" and the recession that followed, banks and financial institutions were stuck with huge amounts of non-performing loans.

# Sex Trafficking

Sex trafficking has been a major problem in Japan, as Adelstein (2009) reported in his book *Tokyo Vice*. Onishi (2005) observed that for many years Japan denied having a problem. When Adelstein brought documented evidence of the serious abuse of foreign women, the police argued that even if the evidence supported the allegations, it was pointless to pursue the cases because the women entered illegally and would be deported before the guilty parties could be tried and convicted. Revisions in a Japanese law in 2005 have strengthened the government's ability to obtain convictions in these cases. Foreign women who are exploited by criminal elements end up everywhere, from Tokyo's red-light districts to country-side areas unfamiliar to foreigners. They are on street corners, serve as sex performers, and work as hostesses in clubs that expect them to date customers. Onishi (2005) reported on the case of a Columbian woman who spent four years as a prostitute, mostly to repay the $45,000 she owed criminals who bought and sold her. Finally, she dashed to the Columbian Embassy for help. She stated, "We shouldn't be treated as criminals to be deported out of Japan, but as victims." In 2005, the government severely restricted the number of "entertainer" visas—which have been used as covers for persons who were not legitimate entertainers by any stretch of the meaning. Some women coming in were fooled, but many knew they would be working in the sex industry. Few knew that they would incur huge debts to the traffickers who typically took their passports and restricted their movements. The Japanese government was notorious during World War II for the use of Korean "comfort" women, who were sex slaves to the Japanese military. Overall, the victims are said to number in the thousands, with the three largest sources being Thailand, Columbia, and the Philippines. Columbia's embassy claimed that 3,500 Columbian women worked as prostitutes in Japan. In an interesting twist on the notion of *gaijin*, women being at a lower level than their Japanese counterparts, Yoko Yoshida, a lawyer for a network against sex trafficking, reported that Japanese women do not stop their husbands from hiring prostitutes. The women report that if the husbands fell in love with these foreign women it would be a problem, but as long as that did not occur there was little sense that the foreign women would be a risk to their marriage, as they were "not human beings" like themselves.

# Violence

Much as in the United States, the Japanese press carry reports (although far fewer) of dramatic and violent criminal incidents. Psychologists at the National Research Institute of Police Science shared their views with me during an earlier phase of my field research. In discussions with Japanese police psychologists over the years, they stress that aggressive behavior is frowned upon and that interpersonal communication is nuanced and subtle. The parties generally seek harmony. Verbal exchanges are more polite and less confrontational. Japanese see the value in candor, but they also see the price as rudeness and hurt feelings. Of course, Americans become confused in their meetings with Japanese as the subtlety of Japanese communication baffles them. Here is a distillation of some comments from the police psychologists:

- The low level of violence is significantly related to the socialization process. At a very early age, parents teach their children that aggression will not be tolerated.

- Teachers exert strong controls on the expression of violence and/or aggression. Two- or three-day suspensions from classes are not unusual if a child acts up even in a minor way.
- The homogeneous nature of Japanese society, with less than 1 percent of the population being non-Japanese, contributes to a greater degree of empathy for one another.
- There are relatively few broken families in Japan and the divorce rate is low (as noted in the earlier discussion).
- The environment is less stressful in Japan according to these social scientists, several of whom had studied at the University of Chicago or at Harvard. While life is fast-paced, particularly in the major cities, there are environmental supports that help to cushion the consequences of modern urban life. Notwithstanding some weakening in the lifetime employment scheme, most Japanese employees still have more job security than their U.S. counterparts. The emphasis on group life, in which fellow workers, students, or neighbors offer emotional and social support to one another is important.
- Family life and child rearing are a high priority for Japanese couples, notwithstanding the increasing number of women working outside the home.
- Japanese society offers many forms of recreation and leisure activity. It is common for groups of workers to go off together to a resort for a few days of fun and recreation, enjoying the camaraderie that they prize. Workers frequently drink sake together or play popular games like mah-jongg or *pachinko* after work. (Another outlet is provided by the attention and caresses of Japanese hostesses in nightclubs and cabarets.) (Parker, 2001, p. 133)

In more recent times, it appears that there are at least some additional "stranger" types of crimes in Japan in which the offender strikes without apparent motive. They were rarely reported in the early 1980s at the time of my first study. These types of offenses have been far more common in the United States, and we are less shocked by them because they are no longer unusual. In one instance, a disturbed man tossed a firebomb into a Tokyo bus, killing several people. In another example a middle-aged man stabbed two women and two children to death on a Tokyo street and then took the women hostage. However, it is important to keep in mind that the overall level of crime, as reported earlier, is much lower than in most countries, including the United States.

# Role of the Public Prosecutor

Prosecutors wield enormous power in Japan and in more recent years their reputation has been tarnished a bit. In a presentation sponsored by the Japan Society in New York in 1980, a Japanese prosecutor described the role for his American audience:

> Each prosecutor is authorized to decide on the appropriate scope of investigation, to decide whether to prosecute at all and, if so, on what charges and, finally, to request the imposition of sentence as he feels appropriate. Decisions are to be based only on the interplay of the individual prosecutor's conscience with the "substantive truth" as he discovers it. Thus, he is not merely an assistant to the agency head but is vested with independent powers. In this sense, a prosecutor's decision-making process is similar to that of a judge. (Japan Society, 1980, p. 5)

A public prosecutor may suspend prosecution at his or her own discretion even if the evidence is sufficient to convict, if he or she believes it to be in the best interest of the offender and society.

Terrill (2007) states that the rationale for the suspension of prosecution is that it can contribute to the rehabilitation of an offender. In 1995, approximately 38 percent of non-traffic offenses were suspended from prosecution. The suspension of prosecution for homicide was 4.3 percent, for robbery it was 6.5 percent, and for larceny over 41 percent. Also, consideration is given to compensation and the victim's feelings in any suspension of prosecution.

The Supreme Public Prosecutors Office heads up Japan's prosecutorial service (Terrill, 2007). It is part of the executive portion of the government. The minister of justice also has some control over prosecutors. Prosecutors retire at age 63, with the exception of the prosecutor-general (age 65).

One article by a British journalist, who wrote a highly critical piece that appeared in the *Asahi Evening News* (Kirk, 1981), has always resonated with me as I had reflected on the power of Japanese investigators (both police and prosecutors) and the extremely high conviction rates recorded in Japanese courtrooms. In his highly condemnatory piece of writing, Kirk pointed out that Japanese believe that a confession is the "king of evidence." In various media reports in recent years, there is ample evidence that there are significant numbers of false confessions. In light of this, police and prosecutors are reviewing their investigative and interview tactics. The conviction rate has continued to stay at around 98 or 99 percent, depending upon the source that is cited. The Japanese justice authorities have always denied that they have coerced confessions, but recent evidence speaks to the contrary. Prosecutors and police for years have acknowledged that despite the constitution, which states the presumption of innocence, individuals are believed to be guilty if they are brought to trial. The chance for acquittal has been extremely unlikely. If a witness changes his testimony, the state can still use the written record even if the defendant does not appear in court for any reason. For example, if the witness fled or died or was ill, the state could still move ahead if it had an earlier written record about the case. This is unlike the United States and Great Britain, where witnesses must appear in court to answer questions. One huge advantage for police and prosecutors is that a suspect can be held for up to 23 days while the prosecutor decides if he or she has enough evidence to present an indictment. Prosecutors in modern day Japan have a broad range of situations and vehicles to exercise their prosecutorial roles. The prosecutor typically acts as a supervisor during an investigation that has been initiated by the police. A brief statement on the role of prosecutors was offered in a statement by Horiuchi:

> They investigate criminal wrongdoing by interrogating suspects, interviewing witnesses, and examining written and physical evidence gathered by the police; they decide whether or not to formally charge suspects with a crime; they present the state's case at trial; and they supervise the execution of sentences imposed by the courts. (1995, p. 70)

A major focus of public prosecutors is to separate out those parties who might be acquitted if prosecuted from those who will be prosecuted and found guilty. As noted above, this is in addition to those who might be convicted, but are not prosecuted for various reasons by governmental choice. Also, this is in the context of a system that has neither a grand jury nor an examining magistrate, and therefore relies on police and prosecutors for evidence and prosecutorial decisions (Horiuchi, 1995). Warrants are obtained at the arrest stage by a judge. Two exceptions include a circumstance in which a party is committing or has just committed an offense, and when a person may be arrested for an offense punishable by up to three years imprisonment because of "great urgency"—for example if the person poses a risk of fleeing. Once a person is in custody the prosecutor must inform the person immediately of the offense and of his right to defense counsel. The prosecutor requests a detention order from the judge and then initially the person can be detained for ten days. Usually the judge grants the request. Later the prosecutor may request an additional ten days of detention. The maximum period of detention before bringing an indictment is 23 days. Bail is not available during the detention period, but after prosecution a judge can offer bail. Prior to the bail decision the judge typically weighs opinions from both the defense and the prosecution. At that point, the judge fixes the condition of bail including the amount.

A wiretap law was passed by the Japanese government in 1999 that allowed justice officials to wiretap telephone conversations, faxes, and email messages.

One consideration in looking at the low crime rates in Japan is that many offenses considered crimes in the United States and other Western nations are not identified as crimes in Japan. Examples that have been offered include vagrancy, homosexuality, and public drunkenness. Therefore, law enforcement resources have not been tied up on these victimless crimes. At the conviction stage, Japanese prosecutors also weigh the rehabilitation prospects of the offender. Here is Nagashima's (1963) comment on this matter:

> Before the second Code of Criminal Procedure, there was no provision giving procurators a discretionary power of nonprosecution. Nevertheless, it gradually became general usage for the procurator to decline prosecution of less serious crimes. Because the investigation and disposition of the matter were carried out by the procurator in closed chambers, the identity of the offender against whom prosecution was declined was rarely disclosed to the public; consequently, the offender could continue in the community as a good citizen rather than with the stigma of a criminal. This system contributed so much to the rehabilitation and reentry of the offender into society that it was explicitly approved and extended in the second code. Even an offender who had committed a rather serious crime might be relieved from prosecution if he was a first offender, if the injuries caused by the offense were compensated for, and if there was reasonable ground to believe that he would not commit another offense. (p. 299)

It is important to keep in mind that even in cases where prosecutors decline to prosecute, the accused may still be "marked men" in the eyes of police and prosecutors. These decisions have been strongly influenced by factors such as confessions, "sincere repentance" by the suspect and forgiveness by the victim. Confessions, however, have come under a dark cloud in recent years along with the activities of some prosecutors.

Masayuki's powerful film, *I Just Didn't Do It* portrayed the enormously critical role that confessions and attempts at coerced confessions play in the Japanese system. Based on a real story of a college-aged male who was accused of fondling a young female during rush hour on a Japanese subway, the flawed processes of Japanese police practices were highlighted. While the young man refused to confess to a misdemeanor crime, he ended up by having to do two years of prison time. Early on, the law enforcement authorities tried alternately to pressure him and harass him to confess or seduce him by saying that if he admitted the crime he could walk away with a minor misdemeanor. Even his defense team found themselves encouraging him to admit to the crime or otherwise face the 99 percent conviction rate and the extended period of detention even before going to trial in a very drawn-out legal process. Eventually, his defense team became strongly convinced of his innocence, but to no avail. He was convicted after a more liberal and sympathetic judge was replaced by a harsher one. Other problems of false and coerced confessions have come to light, but they have been suspected for years. In a notorious case in which suspects were accused of vote-buying, all were subjected to repeated interrogations and in several instances, months of pre-trial detention. In one instance, the police ordered a woman to shout her confession out a window, and in another example a man was forced to stamp on the names of his loved ones. All together, 13 men and women from their early fifties to mid-seventies were indicted. Six succumbed to the pressure and confessed. One man died during the trial, apparently from stress, while another tried to commit suicide. The judge ruled that the defendants had "made confessions in despair while going through marathon questioning."

In another case, in Saga Prefecture, a high court upheld the acquittal of a man who claimed he had been coerced into killing three women in the late 1980s (Onishi, 2005). Other than the confession which had been drawn out of him after 17 days of interrogation that went on for more than ten hours a day, there was no additional evidence to support the state's case. In Toyama Prefecture, the police admitted that a taxi driver, who had served almost three years in prison for rape in 2002, was innocent after they found the real culprit. The taxi driver claimed he had been browbeaten into affixing his fingerprint to a confession drawn up by police after three days of interrogation. Suspects are told that if they confess it is the first step toward rehabilitation. In the vote buying case, Onishi (2005) described some of the experiences of the accused:

The police started by accusing Sachio Kawabata—whose wife, Junko, is the assemblyman's cousin—of giving cases of beer to a construction company in return for votes. Mr. Kawabata said he had given the beer because the company had sent guests to an inn that he owned. Mr. Kawabata soon found himself enduring nearly 15 hours of interrogation a day. Locked in a tiny room with an inspector who shouted and threatened, he refused to confess. So on the third day, Mr. Kawabata recalled, the inspector scribbled the names of his family members on three pieces of paper. He added messages—"Grandpa, please hurry up and become an honest grandpa," and "I don't remember raising you to be this kind of person." Drawing no confession after an hour, the inspector grabbed Mr. Kawabata by the ankles and made him trample on the pieces of paper. "I was shocked," recalled Mr. Kawabata, 61, who was hospitalized for two weeks from the stress of the interrogation. "Man, I thought, how far will the police go?" Mr. Kawabata, who was never indicted, recently won a $5,000 judgment for mental anguish. Trampling the pieces of paper, it turned out, had its roots in a local feudal practice of ferreting out suspected Christians by forcing them to stomp on a cross. The police then moved on to more potent alcohol. According to the trials verdict and interviews with 17 people interrogated by the authorities, the police concocted a description of events according to which the assemblyman spent $17,000 to buy votes with shochu, a popular distilled spirit, and gifts of cash. One of the first to confess was Ichiko Fujimoto, 53, a former employee of the assemblyman. After a couple of days of interrogation she broke down and admitted not only to distributing shochu and cash to her neighbors, but also to giving four parties at her home to gather support for the assemblyman. "It's because they kept saying, 'Confess, just confess,'" Ms. Fujimoto said in an interview at her home. "They wouldn't listen to anything I said." Everything in her confession was made up, a court concluded. But it was enough for the police to start extracting confessions from others for supposedly receiving shochu and money at the parties. One neighbor, Toshihiro Futokoro, 58, began despairing on the third day of interrogation, even though he had yet to be formally arrested and was allowed to go home after each day's questioning. "They kept saying that everybody's confessing, that there was nothing that I could do, no matter how hard I tried," Mr. Futokoro said, adding, "I thought that nothing I said would ever convince them." At the end of the third day, Mr. Futokoro tried to kill himself by jumping into a river but was pulled out by a man out fishing. He then confessed. Another man, Kunio Yamashita, 76, succumbed after a week of interrogation. The police told him that he was the lone holdout and that he could go home if he confessed. "I hadn't done anything, but I confessed, and I told them I'd admit to whatever they said," said Mr. Yamashita, who eventually spent three months in jail. (p. A1)

In another example of the flawed system of criminal investigation and interviewing, Dickie (2009) illustrated the case of a man who had suffered for over two decades at the hands of the state. He spent 17 years in prison convicted of murder. Police had claimed he was responsible for the 1990 murder of a four-year-old girl. Courts had repeatedly affirmed DNA evidence linking him to the crime and stated that he had already confessed. Later tests found that Mr. Sugaya's DNA did not match samples linked to the crime. The new tests, once again, pointed to the dangers of jailhouse confessions even when they are later recanted. Sugaya claimed, "they were pulling my hair and kicking me, saying 'you did it, you did it.'" Death penalty cases, while rare in Japan—there were just 15 executions in 2008 and in some years there are much fewer—have been under review over the last few years along with many other serious convictions. Some scholars hope that jury trials, introduced again in 2009, will allow private citizens (sitting with judges in a different framework from that found in the United States) to play a stronger role in these cases. Satoru Shinomiya, of Kokugakuin University Law School, believes the public will put less store in confessions signed in custody and more on other factors than judges do (Dickie, 2009). Other critics of the interrogation process are asking for video-taped records of the police interrogation. Toshikazu Sugaya has now become famous and an outspoken critic of false imprisonment (Fackler, 2009). He has written three books, one entitled *Falsely Convicted*. He claimed that during his many years behind bars, other inmates stated they had also been falsely convicted due to coerced confessions. A second defense lawyer who later took up Sugaya's case noted that there had been a misplaced faith in a rudimentary DNA test. Police rationalized that mistakes were made because they were under intense pressure to solve the murder of the three girls. Some retrials of cases have been held including one in a 1967 robbery-murder in which two men were incarcerated based solely on confessions they later recanted. In summary, Sugaya's greatest disappointment was not seeing his parents again during his confinement. His father died two weeks after his arrest and in a revealing example of the attitudes of many family members toward a convicted murderer, his mother refused to visit him. She told police that she hoped he would be executed and "sent home in a box" (Fackler, 2009).

The conservative and best selling Japanese newspaper *Yomiuri Shimbun* declared in the fall of 2010 that there was a "serious deterioration" in the quality of public prosecution that had led to a "terrifying abuse of power" (Dickie, 2010). A series of defeats by prosecutors served as the background for the harsh judgment rendered by the newspaper's editorial board. There have been suggestions that political considerations had tainted some cases. Until September 2010, Tsunehiko Maeda was a proud member of an elite corps in one of Japan's most prestigious agencies, but Maeda sat in jail in October, one month later. Maeda was accused of falsifying data. The case collapsed against a highly respected welfare figure, but was just one among a series of prosecutorial failures. Another instance involved a case of murder that was prosecuted based only on a confession that was coerced. Maeda was charged with tampering with evidence in the case of the welfare minister, and fellow prosecutors were left to fend off accusations that they have overstepped their authority. Demands have increased for oversight and a system has been introduced whereby prosecutors' decisions can be reviewed by panels of citizens selected by lottery.

In another example of what appeared to be a political decision, prosecutors decided to release a Chinese fishing boat captain who was at the heart of a diplomatic firestorm (Dickie, 2010). Another case that appeared to have strong political ramifications involved a prominent and famous political figure — Ichiro Ozawa. One of the most powerful figures in the ruling Democratic power was spared prosecution over alleged abuse of political funding rules. The review panel claimed the case should never have been dropped when guilt was a possibility. This case again pointed to prosecutor's decisions to pursue only cases that will reach the 98 and 99 percent level of success against defendants.

## Juries Return

One major recent development in Japanese criminal justice — some say the most significant in recent decades — has been the introduction of juries again. They were briefly introduced by General MacArthur and his staff at the end of World War II but were abandoned after a brief period. Reformers hope that juries will create a better balance in a system heavily weighted toward the prosecutorial side. Prior to the commencement of actual trials in 2009, the government introduced the system to a highly skeptical public by running a series of mock trials (Onishi, 2007). Concerns regarding the success of these hybrid juries has been linked to deeply rooted cultural obstacles. For example, a reluctance to express opinions openly and in public — particularly in the presence of high-ranking authority figures such as judges. Also, there is discomfort associated with arguing against and questioning authority. Over 500 mock trials were held across Japan, but 80 percent of citizens polled dreaded the change and did not want to serve on juries. In the mock trials, citizens preferred directing questions to judges and rarely engaged their fellow mock jurors. Judges had to draw out citizens' views and responses were typically couched in ambiguously polite language. In the new system of hybrid juries, judges and jurors each have one vote. Also, unlike in the United States, jurors can ask questions in the courtroom. Six jurors and three judges are part of the new framework. A not guilty ruling by at least five jurors can affect a guilty ruling by the three judges. On the other hand, even if all six jurors vote guilty, the ruling will not stand unless one of the judges also votes guilty. In general, the new jury system has been set up and designed to encourage greater citizen participation in the administration of justice and for citizens to rely less on governmental authority. It is an innovation that, despite Japanese citizen anxieties, seems to be enjoying some success. Two actual cases follow.

In August of 2009, Japan's first jury trial ended in the murder conviction of a 72-year-old man by the name of Katsuyoshi Fujii. He was charged with fatally stabbing a 66-year-old female neighbor with a knife (Tabuchi & McDonald, 2009). Although reluctant at first, all six lay jurors asked questions during the four-day trial. Often trials can drag on for months or occasionally years. The lack of transparency in trials has often frustrated citizens. This was an intensely covered event by the Japanese media. Jurors are selected from election rolls and must be at least 20 years old.

In a case two years later, Tatsuya Ichihashi was put on trial and the prosecutor demanded a life term for the rape and murder of Lindsay Ann Hawker, an English teacher from the U.K. (Kamiya, 2011). In this case, Ichihashi was accused of strangling the 22-year-old Briton. The case started when police found Hawker's nude corpse in a sand-filled bathtub on the convicted man's balcony in Chiba Prefecture. Ichihashihad spent 32 months on the run before being captured. On July 21, 2011, the accused was convicted and given a life term. Prosecutors stated that he was spared the death sentence as there was only one homicide (Kaninya & Hongo, 2011). One issue that caused concern among court observers was the repeated errors by the interpreter in the translations linked to the trial of the Japanese accused and his British victim.

# Courts In Japan

In the early legal system of Japan, around the fourth century, a legal procedure at the time was called *kukatachi*, an ordeal by fire or boiling water. It was a primitive judicial procedure, in which after swearing their allegations were true, both parties were made to grope for a heated clay object in a stove or huge container of boiling water. Judgment was rendered in favor of the person whose hand was not scalded (Supreme Court of Japan, 2009).

Much later, after World War II, the legal system was reshaped, which reflected, in part, the role of General Douglas MacArthur and the American Occupation authorities. Characterization of the overall legal system also reflect the continental European system of justice. In short, the system is a hybrid of the European continental model and the Anglo-American model. Some structural changes at the beginning of the twenty-first century have been implemented that were designed to create a speedier procedural system in the courts and in trials, along with a stronger legal defense system. The latter has been very weak for many years.

**Figure 4.1 Homicide Case—Charge Sheet—Tokyo District Court**

Charging Sheet

Date: June 26, 2009

To:
         Tokyo District Court
From:    Tokyo District Public Prosecutors' Office

         Prosecution is hereby instituted in the following case:
                Hiromichi Suzuki
                Public Prosecutor
                Tokyo District Public Prosecutors' Office

THE ACCUSED:

(under detention pending trial)
         Name:                    Taro Yamada
         Date of birth:           August 5, 1967
         Occupation:              Restaurant Employee
         Registered domicile:     4–1, Hayabusa-cho, Chiyoda-ku, Tokyo
         Residence:               Jingu Heights Room 504, 7–6,
                                  Jingumae, Shibuya-ku, Tokyo

CHARGED OFFENSE: Homicide

CHARGED FACTS:

The accused, having determined to take the life of Akiko Mori (then 26 years old),
with whom he had once cohabited, in a rage against her on account of her indiffer-
ence to him, called on her at Fuji Tavern, located at 7-1-1, Shimbashi, Minato-ku,
Tokyo, on the night of June 3, 2009, and at approximately 11:30 P.M. on the same
day, at the same place, stabbed her in the left side of her chest with a knife in his possession, thereby causing her death soon afterwards at the same place from excessive
bleeding, and thereby murdered her.

APPLICABLE PENAL STATUTE:
         Article 199 of the Penal Code

*Source*: Supreme Court of Japan, 2009.

A hypothetical case handled by the Tokyo District Court (Figure 4.1) in
2009 describes the charge sheet in which the former lover of a woman restau-
rant employee murdered her (Supreme Court of Japan, 2009). After gathering

## Figure 4.2 Outline of Steps in a Court Case

| | |
|---|---|
| Questioning the Accused for Identification | |
| Reading of the Charging Sheet Aloud by the Public Prosecutor | |
| Notifying the Accused of Rights | Opening Proceedings |
| Giving the Accused and the Defense Counsel an Opportunity to Make Any Statement Concerning the Case | |
| Opening Statements by the Public Prosecutor and the Defense Counsel | |
| Disclosure of the Results of the Pretrial | |
| Arrangement Procedure | |
| Examination of Evidence Requested by the Prosecutor | Examination of Evidence |
| Examination of Evidence Requested by the Defense | |
| Questioning the Accused | |
| Closing Argument by the Public Prosecutor | |
| Closing Argument by the Defense Counsel | Closing Arguments |
| Final Statement by the Accused | |
| Pronouncement of Judgment and Sentence | |

*Source*: Supreme Court of Japan, 2009.

evidence, the suspect, Taro Yamada, was arrested after a warrant was issued by the court. Murder and manslaughter are not distinguished in Japan as long as the act was committed knowingly and with intent. He was told of his right to counsel and the constitution, much like in the United States, provides that no person shall be compelled to testify against himself or herself (the right to remain silent). As in the United States, all defendants are entitled to the right of counsel regardless of their income.

One recent development, and not unimportant in strengthening the defense of clients, has been that the scope of eligible cases was expanded. A sketch of a typical case at the trial level is offered in Figure 4.2. Appeals are allowed in the Japanese system and prosecutors as well as defense counsel are allowed to appeal court rulings. A party may file a final appeal, called a *Jokuku* appeal, to the Supreme Court.

**Figure 4.3  Structure of Courts**

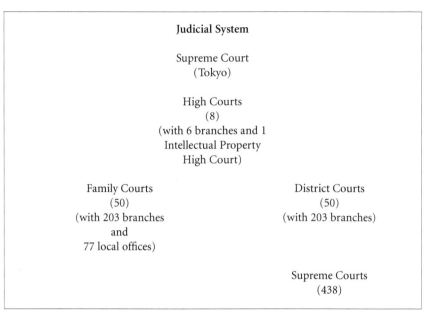

*Source:* Supreme Court of Japan, 2009.

Figure 4.3 offers an outline of the court structure in Japan as of 2008. There are four tiers of courts. The 438 summary courts are staffed by 806 judges. Summary court judges are not career judges (Wikipedia, 2011). These appointee judges mostly handle small claims civil cases and minor criminal offenses. In the case of criminal offenders, these judges are not able (with few exceptions) to imprison these defendants. At the second tier are the district courts, and there are 50 with 203 branches. Except for minor cases, trials require a three-judge panel and many trials now are tried by jurors made up of judges and lay persons.

There are eight high courts and they typically have three-judge panels. They exist to handle appeals from the judgments rendered by district courts. At the top of the system is the Supreme Court, which has 15 judges sitting on the bench. They either sit together on the Grand Bench (nine or more justices) or on a "Petty Bench" (three or more judges). As in the United States, some appeals are ruled as groundless and no oral arguments are heard. Every case or appeal is first heard by one of the three Petty Bench judges (Supreme Court of Japan, 2010). In family court proceedings, court probation officers conduct investigations into the facts of cases and search the background of family members and juveniles who are brought into the courts. These family courts focus on domestic relations cases and matters involving juveniles. They also deal with issues concerning guardianship of adults, permission to adopt a minor, designation of parental authority, division of estates, marital disputes, and divorce matters. Juveniles who are under 20 years of age are handled by these family courts (Supreme Court of Japan, 2010). Cases brought to family courts are handled by a single judge or a three-judge panel.

The death penalty exists in Japan, but is not widely employed. Of the Group of Eight industrialized nations, only the United States and Japan execute defendants. As of August 2010, Japan had 107 inmates on death row. From 2000 to 2009, Japan sentenced only 112 people to death and executed only 46 (Tabuchi, 2010). Japan has long been criticized by the United Nations Human Rights Committee for maintaining the death penalty. The United States executes more, but China, as will be noted in a later chapter, executes more than all other countries put together. As increasing numbers of false confessions have surfaced, Japan is under greater pressure to abolish the death penalty. Inmates on death row are not told when they will be executed until the last minute. Lawyers and family members are informed afterwards. Inmates can remain on death row for as long as 40 years (Tabuchi, 2010). Interestingly enough, a majority of Japanese support the death penalty. All death cases are carried out by hanging. There are seven execution sites in Japan. Human rights advocates are critical of the prison conditions—inmates' death row cells are about 50 square feet, or 4.65 square meters in size.

# 5

# Corrections, Probation, Parole, and Juvenile Offenders in Japan

The Japanese correctional system operates under the Ministry of Justice. The Bureau of Corrections is the administrative agency for the prisons, detention houses, juvenile prisons, and the women's guidance home. The Rehabilitation Bureau handles probation, parole, and the community release program (halfway houses). Organizationally, it sits in parallel to the Bureau of Corrections under the Ministry of Justice. In the mid-1980s, I undertook a comparative study of probation, parole, and the community-based programs, and compared these services with those in the United States (Parker, 1986). The Prison Law of 1908, along with the Penal Code, provided the foundation for the modern day prison system of Japan (Correction Bureau, 2008). French and German concepts played a role and to some extent the policies of the American post-World War II administration helped shape these functions (Terrill, 2007).

As of January 2008 there were 187 total correctional institutions—60 prisons, eight juvenile prisons, seven detention houses, eight prison branches, and 104 branch detention houses. The Ministry of Justice has a policy of conducting spot inspections at all facilities at least once a year. Nonetheless, there have been some problems over the past decade that have put pressure on the Correction Bureau to institute reforms. These have been triggered by deaths and injuries inside prisons. In the case of the Nagoya Prison, in 2002 and 2003, deaths in that institution shed light on problems generally on the correctional administration and management of inmates. As a result, the Ministry of Justice established a Reform Council to generate recommendations. In May 2005 and June 2006, the Japanese Diet passed legislation supporting some reforms. Both sentenced and un-sentenced offenders were impacted by the legislative changes and these developments continue to unfold as of 2012. One impact of the legislative reforms was to increase the staff by approximately 1,200. In 2007, total staff of all in-

### Figure 5.1 Daily Prison Population in Japan

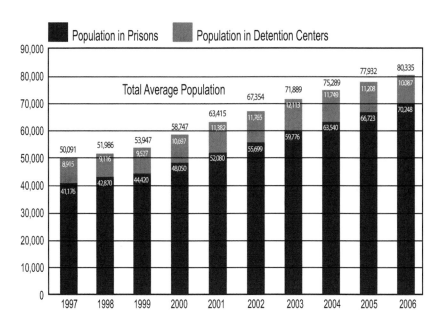

*Source:* Correction Bureau.

stitutions numbered 18,226 (Correction Bureau Ministry, of Justice, 2008). In 1990, the prison population stood at slightly less than 47,000, with approximately 7,000 individuals in detention centers and the balance of 40,000 in prisons. Recidivism rates have been around 46 percent. By 2001 the prison population had risen to 63,415, or 48 offenders per 100,000 in the overall population, but at the end of 2009 the population had risen again to 75,250, or 59 offenders per 100,000 population (see Figure 5.1). Overall, the total number of prisoners in Japan was 80,523 in 2010 and 2,304,115 in the United States (*The Economist*, 2011). In the United States, the prison population for both state and federal prisons had risen enormously for many years (see Figure 5.2). Only in 2009 did the United States witness a modest decline. This decrease represented a surprising confluence of conservative and liberal policies and attitudes for reducing prison populations. Many of the previously existing conservative policies had proved ineffective in the eyes of liberals, who had advocated more probation and community-based treatment particularly for non-violent offenders. In addition, both political sides recognized that many drug-related offenses were best dealt with through mandatory treatment. Data in pilot programs

Figure 5.2  Incarceration Rates—United States

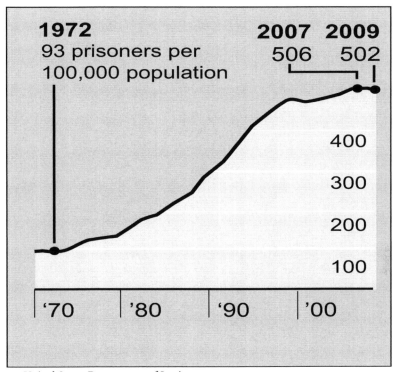

*Source:* United States Department of Justice.

demonstrated the value of treatment over prison. However, a major concern for conservative elements was the huge cost of incarcerating individuals. The United States, with 5 percent of the world's population, accounted for 25 percent of the world's inmates (Savage, 2011). Reducing prison time for low-level drug offenders, eliminating or reducing "technical" violators of parole (and thus avoiding returning a parolee to prison), and strengthening re-entry programs have already saved huge amounts of money. Also, the U.S. Supreme Court played a role by ordering the state of California to reduce severe over-crowding in prisons in 2010. Unlike Japan's rate of 59 offenders per 100,000 people in 2009, the United States rate was reported to be 502 per 100,000 in the overall population for the same year. It had declined slightly from 506 per 100,000 in 2007. *The Economist* (2011) reported that recidivism rates for the United States were at 43 percent. For 2009, this was defined as the percent returned to state prisons within three years. Federal prison data was not included in this report. In addition, one in every 100 American adults was in prison or jail. Furthermore, the cost to taxpayers has been around $60 billion per year, which is a rate of around $45,000 per year per person. Harvard University is cheaper! (*The Economist*, 2011.) Not surprisingly, most released offenders in the United States are returned to their old neighborhoods, where drug and alcohol abuse are common. Few are high school graduates and, with a criminal history, a job, of course, is difficult to obtain.

In returning to the subject of Japanese prisons, the Correction Bureau (2008) sketched what it claimed was a typical day for a sentenced inmate:

> Sentenced inmates get up at 6:45 A.M. in the morning. Following face-wash and the toilet, a morning roll call is taken. The main purpose of the roll call is to confirm that there have been no escapes. However, this also serves as a daily checkup of inmates' mental and physical health.
>
> After the roll call comes breakfast, following which sentenced inmates go from their rooms to the prison workshops. Usually, small groups organized by the group room units of the dormitory walk in line to the workshops, and on their way to the workshops, they will change their clothes to work clothes. At this time, a body search is conducted to confirm that there has been no unlawful trafficking of property and to check the condition of their health. After entering the workshops, sentenced inmates take part in brief physical exercise and are notified of some basic rules of their work in order to ensure smooth proceedings for the day. Prison work begins at 8:00 A.M.
>
> Before the working hours finish at around 4:40 P.M., there is time for lunch, short breaks for more than 20 minutes, and exercise for more than 30 minutes. During working hours, the sentenced inmates have visitors (such as from family members), are provided with guidance for reform, and take baths on bath days. After the working hours finish, the sentenced inmates return to their rooms, and answer the roll call in the same way as in the morning.
>
> Following the roll call and supper, the sentenced inmates are given free time from 6:00 P.M. During this period, they may use this time to sleep, relax, watch TV, or listen to the radio. Also, some sentenced inmates spend this period reading letters or writing letters to their family members, which may enhance their yearning for their future life after release. Penal institutions provide such assistance as lending books for effective use of the free time.
>
> At 9:00 P.M., the day is over and the sentenced inmates go to bed.

# Complaints and Criticisms of Japanese Prisons

This benign picture of Japanese prison life is in sharp contrast with both anecdotal reports of former inmates and Amnesty International's analysis of Japan's prisons. For example, Susan Chira (1988), writing for the *New York Times*, reported on the case of Chisako Tezuka and her experience in a Japanese jail:

> Chisako Tezuka was arrested last year on suspicion of fraudulently obtaining a loan. She says she was taken to the police station, stripped naked, subjected twice to a genital search, and forced to urinate while male police officers watched.
>
> She was questioned for twenty days in sessions in which she was handcuffed and roped around the waist, she said. She was never indicted, and the police discovered she had paid back the loan two months before.
>
> The police acknowledge that the questioning and genital search took place, although they dispute some of the details of Ms. Tezuka's account and deny that what happened constituted mistreatment.
>
> "Japanese people do not know what is going on," Ms. Tezuka said. "The Japanese press has covered very little about this, even though it is a very serious issue for Japan." Yasuhiro Maeda, a public relations officer for the Metropolitan Police, said that Ms. Tezuka's account was inaccurate and that abuses in detention cells were exceptions, not the rule. He said that Ms. Tezuka was searched because there was a danger she might commit suicide and because her behavior had led the police to believe she might be hiding something in her sexual organs.
>
> "We paid attention to her feelings and did not make her take off all clothes—we allowed her to wear clothes on her upper body while checking her lower body," he said.

Although anecdotal, the following report from an ex-United States Marine created a stir in both the Japanese and American press (Allen, 2004). Rochico Harp was sentenced to seven years of hard labor for his role in an abduction and rape of an Okinawa school girl in 1995. He claimed he was required to assemble cell phones or make auto parts after he was convicted and incarcerated. The Japanese prison, near Yokosuka, is where most convicted U.S. servicemen serve their time. He said, "You had no choice, if you refused to work in what inmates called a chill box, they forced you to sit rigidly all day at a desk until it was time to eat and sleep. If they thought you were rowdy, they put you in a straitjacket in a padded room." Harp's lawyer, Michael Griffith of New York, claimed that it was a gross violation of international law to force prisoners to work for commercial purposes. Japanese officials disagreed and argued that the products were not exported to foreign countries and therefore were immune from international law.

In another case, testimony was presented to a Congressional Subcommittee on Asia and the Pacific in 2004, and included the testimony of an American incarcerated in Fuchu Prison outside of Tokyo. The prisoner, Christopher Lavinger, was sentenced to 16 months on drug charges. He testified that he was struck with an electric baton twice when he shifted from a rigid position on a chair during the time he was required to sit motionless for 12 hours a day. Furthermore, he claimed he was subjected to this treatment after he refused to produce goods for Sega and several Japanese department stores, working for the Japanese equivalent of three cents per hour (Allen, 2004). One legal opinion offered on this and related cases in Japan states that "forced labor violates the General Conference of the International Labor Organization's convention, ratified by Japan on November 21, 1932." Concerning the Japanese death penalty practice of giving short notice to inmates on death row before hanging, Amnesty International has charged that inmates have been driven insane. They claimed that death-row inmates are exposed to "cruel, in-humane, and degrading treatment" (McCurry, 2009). Amnesty International issued a 72-page report on the practice, and it included interviews with inmate's relatives and lawyers. Families claimed they were only told of the death of the family member after the execution had been carried out. In another example, a questionable confession — extracted after 20 days of interrogation — the spotlight was on Japanese investigatory procedures in the case of Iwao Hakamada, a former professional boxer. The 73-year-old had been on death row for 41 years, until 2009. He was convicted of the murder of four members of a family but, in the evidence presented to a three-judge panel at the time, one believed he was innocent. In 2006, in a psychiatric exam, a psychiatrist claimed that Hakamada was suffering from "institutional psychosis." The Amnesty International report portrayed a distressing picture of inmates on death row — they were given two or three opportunities for exercise weekly and just five-minute meetings with lawyers or relatives. Silence and isolation was routine for these inmates (McCurry, 2009).

Amnesty International reports (2009) substantiated some of the abovementioned allegations of abuse:

All detention facilities in the country operate extremely strict disciplinary regimes with inmates forced to comply with arbitrary rules rigorously enforced by staff. Prisoners are often not allowed to talk with each other or even make eye contact. Punishment for flouting these rules includes being made to sit in the same position for hours at a time, sometimes over several months, and not being allowed to wash or exercise. Punishment also apply to all those who complain. According to Amnesty International, some penal institutions still hold prisoners in a "protection cell" (*hogobo*) as means of punishment. *Hogobo* cells are special cells constructed for housing prisoners who are deemed to show certain aggravated signs of instability or vulnerability. Inmates are held in metal or leather handcuffs, which are kept on even while they eat. They are made to excrete through a hole cut in their pants (*mataware pants*).

In a later statement in the same Amnesty International Report (2009), Nagoya Prison officials were arrested:

Prosecutors reportedly arrested five Nagoya Prison officials on 8 November this year for using restraining devices: leather hand-cuffs and manacles to restrain a 30-year-old prisoner on 25 September. As a result, the prisoner suffered internal bleeding, and required hospital treatment. Recent reports suggest the same type of restraining devices and physical violence by Nagoya Prison officials were used against the 49-year-old prisoner who died in May.

## Japan's Aging Group of Inmates

In a significant development that in part reflects the weak Japanese economy and the elderly, lonely and often left to their own devices, more aged Japanese are in prison. The number aged 60 and over doubled to more than 10,000 from 2000 to 2010 (Yamaguchi, 2010). While the crime rate is low, the spike is another sign of economic stress on older adults. Most have been convicted of minor crimes such as shoplifting, reflecting the lack of family support in a society that is less cohesive. About 50 percent are repeat offenders and some set themselves up to get caught in order to seek the relative security of a prison. Despite spartan conditions, the elder inmate receives three meals a day and a twice-weekly bath. Some even committed more serious offenses to lengthen their prison stays. One 70-year-old male stated, "I'm worried that there would be no work for someone like me upon release" (Yamaguchi, 2010). Also, and similar to younger offenders, this man expressed concern that his younger brother might shun him upon release. A contributing factor to the increase in the elderly prison population is that elderly inmates have little chance of parole without family or community ties. The social welfare system of Japan is very limited, with many people falling between the cracks—a topic to be addressed in a later chapter. In 2010, 1.3 million families were on welfare, of which 44 percent were elderly.

In the United States inmates age 55 and older in state and federal correctional institutions grew 76 percent between 1999 and 2008. However, those age 60 or older numbered 35,900 or just 2.3 percent of the total, a much smaller proportion than in Japan. The growth in American senior offenders has at least one cause— laws mandating harsher sentences.

At one Japanese prison in Onomichi, the inmates worked six hours per day. One ranking guard at Onomichi Prison stated, "we have to provide the kind of attention like an ordinary nursing home." Shoplifting has grown for all age groups across Japan, but in the case of financially struggling single seniors, they typically stole food, cosmetics, or other small items worth less than 5,000 yen (Yamaguchi, 2010). Prison administrators are trying to reduce recidivism rates for this population by increasing vocational training and welfare programs to assist in their reentry into society, but it remains to be seen if this policy will be effective.

In a study done by the Tokyo Metropolitan Police Department, 24 percent of those 65 and over cited loneliness as the reason they stole from stores (Kyodo News, 2009). One elderly man who was apprehended was found with 21 yen in his pocket (77 yen = $1 U.S.). Unlike younger offenders, who experience highly disciplined and sometimes harsh prison treatment, these older inmates also receive special diets along with expanded medical treatment. However, due to the general attitude of Japanese people toward those who commit crimes, families sever ties and these older inmates rarely receive visitors (Onishi, 2007). Finally, it should be noted, prisons for the elderly are usually free of violence.

# Probation, Parole, and Aftercare

The Rehabilitation Bureau oversees the programs associated with probation, parole, and aftercare in Japan. Similar to programs in Europe and the United States, their goal is to keep offenders out of prison or to assist them when they are released. Counseling and assistance to offenders in Japan are provided by a large core of volunteers. Probation officers, who double as parole officers, typically supervise the volunteers who handle most of the day-today contact with the offenders. A large number of those given suspended sentences are released to the supervision of the volunteers (Parker, 1986). Probation officers often directly supervise the high-risk clients. Volunteers come from a wide variety of backgrounds, but are often older or retired (more than 70 percent are retired), and some critics argue that this is a weakness. Japan has fewer than 1,000 full time probation officers, but volunteers number around 48,000. On average, each volunteer supervises two offenders, with their primary responsibility being the assistance of offenders in their reintegration with their families and/or society (Hoover Institution, 1996). The Ministry of Justice appoints volunteers for a term of two years, but many are reappointed several times. While no special training or background is required, the applicant must be respected in the community and financially stable. They come from a variety of occupations—fishermen, farmers, religious leaders, housewives, and retirees. Ninety percent are at least 50 years old.

An adult prisoner may be conditionally released on parole by a decision of a Regional Parole Board, but must have served at least one-third of the sentence. In 2009, of the 30,178 inmates released, 14,854 (49.2 percent) were released on parole. Screening for release is conducted by a parole board (UNAFEI, 2010). General conditions for probation and parole are somewhat similar to the United States—maintaining a good attitude, providing relevant information to professional and volunteer probation officers, residing at the designated residence, and responding to requests for interviews by professional and volunteer officers.

The United States probation and parole system has serious problems—enormous caseloads that prevent effective interviewing and counseling. On average, the nation's 35,000 probation and parole officers must supervise 100 convicts each. As the Hoover Institution noted, "With so many charges, the typical officer is lucky if he can find his parolees or probationers, let alone monitor their movements." The inability to provide good support and supervision results in a high percentage of these offenders violating their conditions of parole and thus returning to prison.

# Juvenile Offenders in Japan

In an earlier chapter discussion was offered concerning the problem of young school-aged students creating problems and crises in classrooms. Overall, the picture of juvenile crime reveals that there have been a variety of spikes in juvenile offending from 1949 to 2009. Since the beginning of the twenty-first century, crime for this population has declined, despite press headlines to the contrary. Larceny is the largest category of crime, numbering 54,784 from the total of 90,282 in 2009. Violent offenses were 7,653 and intellectual offenses numbered just 1,144. The largest number of juvenile offenders were from the ranks of senior high school students (34,857), followed by junior high school students at (30,015).

Juveniles are defined as under the age of 20 in Japan. The highly competitive nature of the Japanese educational system has contributed to drop-outs and youngsters joining *bosozoku* or motorcycle gangs. Members of *bosozoku* are seeking support through the group, and not unlike juvenile gangs in the United States, they provide a type of family or sense of community that is otherwise lacking in their lives. These motorcycle gangs often engage in dangerous or reckless driving, such as weaving in traffic, not wearing helmets, and running red lights (Wikipedia, 2011). The leading driver is the *sentosha*, or gang leader, who is responsible for these behaviors. Police sometimes use a vehicle to trail the groups of riders. Not infrequently, the motorcycle gangs roar through suburbs, creating a loud disturbance, waving a Japanese imperial flag, and occasionally starting fights with wooden swords, metal pipes, baseball bats, and Molotov cocktails. Typically they are made up of people under 20 years of age. In the 1980s and 1990s, they would often gather up to 100 riders and would en masse move down an expressway (Wikipedia, 2011). Like many groups, the individuals are far more assertive when participating in group outings. As individuals they sometimes appear weak and lack strong egos. The numbers of people in these groups appeared to peak at around 42,510 in 1982, and by 2011 their numbers had dropped to around 9,064 (Kyodo News, 2011). Although these individuals have been regarded as ideal candidates for *yakuza* or organized crime, a crackdown by police in recent years has weakened these groups considerably (Chapman, 2008).

While larger biker gangs of up to 100 have been on the wane, smaller groups of around 50 or 20 still exist and they follow certain disciples and in recent years use the Internet to connect. Afraid of being caught, they don't wear gang colors. One police officer stated, "I think young people today have a stronger desire not to be bound by a strict group hierarchy" (Chubu Connection, 2010). In general, the police report that offenders often are younger than in earlier years. As noted earlier, there is more divorce in Japan and fewer intact families have resulted in a weakening of the fabric of family life. Greater transience in Japanese family life, consistent with the rapid growth of urbanization, has also taken its toll. This weakening of the nurturing and disciplining of children appears to have played a role, and while these characteristics help explain the current level of juvenile delinquency, it must be kept in the broader perspective of the picture presented. Namely, that overall there have been declines in juvenile delinquency from the rates of 2001 with major juvenile penal code offenders at just around nine per 10,000 persons in 2009.

Two areas of concern to criminal justice authorities involve child prostitution and child pornography. The government, in an attempt to crack down on offenders in these areas, passed parliamentary (Diet) acts to address these issues. The Act on Punishment of Activities Relating to Child Prostitution and Child Pornography and the Protection of Children became effective in 1999, with a further revision of these laws in 2004 (Police of Japan, 2011). In 2009, 1,515 individuals involving 2,030 offenses were arrested under this legislation. For child prostitution, 865 persons were arrested, associated with 1,095 cases. Included in this number were 336 offenders who were using online dating services, and 65 persons linked to telephone dating services. Child pornography arrests numbered 650 persons. In June 2009, the National Police Agency developed a new strategy called the "Strategic Program to Combat Child Pornography," which focused on issues linked to the investigation and the prevention of distribution of pornographic materials (Police of Japan, 2011).

During 2009, the number of child abuse cases reached 335, an increase of 28 or 9.1 percent from the previous year. The police offer Juvenile Support Centers and give advice and guidance to parents in cooperation with Child Counseling Centers.

# Juvenile Offenders in America

Turning to some of the data about juvenile offending in the United States, the picture is far different. Juveniles are usually identified by the federal government by and most states as age 18 and under, making comparisons with the Japanese data (juveniles are classified as 20 and under) somewhat difficult. In 2008, United States law enforcement agencies made an estimated 2.11 million arrests of individuals younger than 18 (Office of Juvenile Justice and Delinquency Prevention, 2009). Overall, there were three percent fewer juvenile arrests in 2008 than in 2007 and juvenile violent crimes went down by two percent, continuing a decline over recent years. The data is drawn from the F.B.I.'s *Uniform Crime Reports*.

Juveniles did account for 16 percent of all violent crime arrests and 26 percent of all property crime arrests in 2009. The number of juveniles involved in murder in 2008 was 908 or nine percent of the total homicides. Of course, juveniles were sometimes the targets of violence—perhaps due in part to gang conflict. Eleven percent of all murder victims were younger than age 18. Astonishingly, more than 38 percent of all juvenile murder victims were under age five, but it varied across demographic groups. In 2008, about one in ten murder victims (1,740) was a juvenile. Afro-American offenders, while accounting for just 16 percent of the population, accounted for 52 percent of juvenile violent crimes and 33 percent of property crime arrests (Office of Juvenile Justice and Delinquency, 2009).

One interesting dimension of the juvenile crime picture is that research shows they are more easily apprehended than their adult counterparts. In looking at the broad category of the "Violent Crime Index" (murder, robbery, forcible rape, and aggravated assault) the data showed declines from 1994 through 2004, but increases in the following two years to 2006. However, from 2006 to 2008, the United States witnessed declines in these "Violent Crime Indexes."

Most arrested juveniles were referred to courts in the United States. Briefly, the juvenile justice system and courts were first established in Chicago in 1899. During the last 30 years they have undergone significant changes, as they have adapted to changing societal trends.

# 6

# Social Problems in Japan: Alcoholism, Drug Abuse, Mental Illness, Suicide, Homelessness, and Joblessness

## Alcoholism in Japan

Issues linked to alcohol abuse and alcoholism were always a bit of a mystery to me during my various visits to Japan, including my first year-long experience in 1980–1981. Yes, I learned very early on, before my first arrival in Japan, that "everything gets done over drinks in Japan." A Japanese language instructor at Yale University, who later became a friend, made this comment in the context of watching a classic Japanese film about family life. In the film, by the renown filmmaker Ozu, a group of elderly Japanese men urge one of their widower colleagues to arrange the marriage of his daughter. Alcohol consumption by the participants in the film is frequently observed. It is common for Japanese to indulge in sake and other alcoholic beverages with co-workers after work. Japanese typically drink alcohol and entertain business clients after hours—sometimes in private clubs. Executives feel pressures to drink, and sometimes complain that they have to "dry out" on weekends. Often they are indulging in alcohol for five consecutive evenings, and it is not unusual to see men staggering around on subway platforms at around midnight as they struggle to get home. Usually police do not intervene, but a friend may be needed for support. Furthermore, alcohol is also easily available to juveniles as vending machines dispense alcoholic beverages until the late evening hours.

Japan ranks sixth in the world for the largest consumption of beer, after China, the United States, Germany, Brazil, and Russia. Most social occasions require it and people drink to fit in (Japan Inc., 2007). There has been some science that states that Asians biologically process alcohol differently from other races (these are references to enzyme differences). As a result, it has been assumed, rightly or wrongly, that Asians are more immune to alcoholism. Nonetheless, various research studies have identified a rise in this disease in Japan. For example, statistics in 2007 from Japan's the National Hospital Kurihama Alcoholism Center claimed that 2.4 million Japanese are problem drinkers. Prince Tomohito Mikasa, the 61-year-old cousin of Emperor Akihito, admitted he suffered an alcohol breakdown. A former director of the National Institute of Alcoholism in Japan stated that there was no question that alcoholism was on the rise, but that the scale of the problem had gone undetected for a long time (Japan Inc., 2007). This is despite the fact that alcohol consumption in most industrialized countries has declined since 1960, but that it has quadrupled in Japan. The country is not in a strong position to support treatment as less than 1,200 hospital beds exist nationwide to treat the illness. Private clinics are becoming more common, but it is extremely difficult to get admitted to a clinic even for severe cases. Furthermore, there is a lack of support in Japan for alcoholics and their families. Most Alcoholics Anonymous meetings have been created for and supported by foreigners. Part of the reason is that it is a taboo subject in Japan, according to a writer for *The Japan Times* (Johnston, 2009). The author cited the example of an unidentified tenured professor. Well known in his field, and a consultant to major business leaders, his addiction nearly cost him his job. But he was fearful that revealing his problem would get him fired, so he did attend the Kansai chapter of Alcoholics Anonymous. He commented, "Heavy drinkers are admired for their strength and forgiven for their rude behavior, which is ignored the next day."

Laws against drunk driving have been toughened since the 1990s so many drivers are careful and can take the highly efficient public transportation system home. A survey by Susumu Higuchi of the National Hospital Kurihama Alcoholism Center revealed the extent of the abuse (Johnston, 2009): "In fiscal 2003, people aged 15 and above consumed about 7.7 liters of alcohol annually. Almost 8.6 million people consumed more than 60 grams of alcohol daily, which is considered excessive."

# Drug Abuse

Drug abuse has a very different character in Japan compared to the United States, not just in the choice of drugs but in the overall scale of abuse. Stimulant abuse, including paint thinner, is high on the list of drugs abused by adolescents. It started to peak around 1984, reaching 24,372 cases, but abuse declined to less than 20,000 cases by 1989. The trend has shown a flattening out with slight ups and downs through 2007 (Ministry of Justice, 2008). Among organized crime (*boryokudan*), the percent convicted under the Stimulants Control Act rose to 53 percent of the total by 2007. In addition, there has been a rise in convictions associated with the use of opium and cannabis over the years 1978–2007. When Japan entered the 1990s the abuse of new drugs such as cocaine and psychotropics became rampant, particularly in the entertainment and media sectors of society (Education in Japan Community Blog, 2002). Reports from the Japanese Ministry of Health, Labor, and Welfare have indicated that most drugs of abuse have been smuggled into the country from North Korea, Macau, and China in container ships. Paint thinner is abused from domestic sources. Illegal foreigners, particularly Iranians, have accounted for the largest number of foreigners engaged in the illegal importation of drugs.

Japan has instituted treatment programs in correctional facilities for drug offenders, and as of 2007, there were 74 institutions that provided rehabilitation programs. As mentioned above, the character of illegal drug use is quite different in the United States. Three major heroin epidemics have occurred in the last few decades in the United States. Periodically, cocaine use has also been a cause for concern in America, particularly with crack cocaine linked to violent crime in the last two decades of the twentieth century. Overall, there has been far less drug abuse in Japan compared with the United States.

# Mental Illness and
# Its Treatment in Japan

There have been some significant criticisms leveled against Japan and its treatment of the mentally ill—some of it tied to its culture. Widely stigmatized, mentally ill individuals have been reluctant to seek treatment. Bringing shame to one's family plays a role: "Mental illness remains a problem that is often silently shoved into corners of ignorance and oblivion" (Lehavot, 2001). One characteristic of the plight of the mentally ill is reflected in the lack of acceptance that it is a disease with chemical and biological causes. Rather, the more accepted notion is that it is a shameful condition of personal weakness. At the beginning of the twentieth century, around 1900, the law in Japan required that the mentally ill be isolated and confined to their residences (Rosen, 2001). Therefore this dark view of the Japanese population toward mental illness has, of course, profound implications for the diagnosis and treatment of illnesses such as schizophrenia and manic-depression (bipolar) disease. Individuals become embarrassed and afraid to seek help. Bringing shame to one's family is more critical than bringing shame on oneself. Sometimes if a person seeks counseling they withhold this information from their families. Even as children, the Japanese have been taught to repress expression of their emotions and beliefs in public, and sometimes even in private (Lehavot, 2001). Japanese place a high value on reciprocity, in addition to the hierarchy and harmony discussed earlier. True feelings are often in contrast with their publicly expressed views. As a result, restraining one's feelings is the standard. This indirectly works against the expression and openness required in the acceptance of mental illness.

Another tradition that impedes the successful treatment of the mentally ill is the tradition of relegating the care of the elderly—sometimes victims of mental illness—to women. The burden often falls on women in the home rather than on institutions that can manage mental illness more effectively.

The problem of being mentally ill in Japan was highlighted by *The Economist* (2001):

> Eiko Nagano was still at school when doctors first diagnosed her depression. Friends and teachers bullied her, she dropped out of school, and spent years drifting in and out of mental hospitals. At 48, Mrs. Nagano has learnt to keep her condition hidden. If people knew, she says, she would lose her apartment, and her children would be bullied as she was. Despite this, Mrs. Nagano considers herself blessed: she has her freedom. Mostly, Japan still treats its mentally ill by locking them up, in brutal hospitals in the mountains. There have been attempts at reform. In 1987, the government passed a law that was supposed to encourage less institutionalisation and more community-based care, following earlier reforms in the West. Yet nothing seems to change. Japan has three times as many mental-hospital beds per person as Britain, and seven times as many as the United States. In America, patients stay in mental hospitals, on average, for eight days; in Japan, for more than 400. Most disturbing are the conditions inside these hospitals. Most of them are privately owned, built with soft government loans in the 1960s and 1970s. Under Japanese law, however, mental hospitals are entitled, per patient, to only one-third the number of doctors and two-thirds the number of nurses that regular

hospitals are guaranteed. The mental hospitals' trade association claims that, because of poor funding, its members barely break even. That is a lie, says Toshio Fujisawa, former director of a large Tokyo mental hospital: "They make profits by sacrificing their employees and their patients."

Governmental policies to treat emotionally disturbed people in the community have lagged, despite advances in drugs that can dampen if not prevent disabling symptoms. By the mid-1990s the government began to develop community-based services (Matsuda, 2009). This approach, resembling the U. S. plan to deinstitutionalize the mentally ill in the 1960s, established a policy to shift care from institutions to community-based programs. It estimated that 69,000 people could be discharged from hospitals if community services were available. As of 2012, the policy had only gradually moved forward due to lack of adequate funding. Legislative committees searched for ways to change the fee structure of public health insurance for the purpose of supporting the shift from institutionalization to community-based treatment.

# Managing Mentally Ill Offenders

The Medical Treatment and Supervision Act of 2005 aimed to provide intensive psychiatric treatment to emotionally disturbed offenders with a focus on assisting them in their reintegration into society (Nakatani, 2011). Statistics demonstrated that the number of incarcerated psychiatrically ill offenders had steadily increased from 2000. Many are substance abusers, and while some have been transferred from general prisons to medical ones, a substantial number remain in general institutions that lack psychiatric treatment options. Among the 365,577 individuals charged with non-traffic penal code offenses in 2007, 1,270 (up 20.5 percent from the previous year) were found to be "mentally disabled" (Ministry of Justice, 2008).

In general. three types of psychiatric admissions exist in Japan. The first is voluntarily, where a patient signs a consent form. The second is a compulsory admission, in which two psychiatrists examine the person and agree that the person must be hospitalized to prevent the person from hurting himself or others. Finally, the third type of admission is also compulsory, and is typically the result of a police arrest and the person is brought to a municipal psychiatric hospital for evaluation and placed in a secure unit.

# Suicide

In the fall of 1999, I was returning to the campus of International Christian University on a fast train operated by the Chuo Line and the train abruptly stopped at a station halfway to my destination. The doors stayed open for over an hour. I had never experienced any such disruption on Japanese trains or subways. Periodically there were public announcements, but I could not comprehend them. I asked fellow Japanese commuters, and one responded with the brief comment "probably an accident" and offered a shrug of his shoulders. After finally arriving at my destination, Mitaka, and taking a bus ride to meet my Japanese colleague at the campus of International Christian University, I apologized for my late arrival. My fellow Japanese professor explained that my delay was probably due to a suicide, someone throwing himself or herself in front of the train. I was unaware at the time that the Chuo Line had become infamous for suicides and had been nicknamed the "Chuo-cide Line." Astonishingly to a *gaijin*, the company (JR East) charged the families of the suicide victim a fee depending on how long the train was delayed. Deaths on this line correlated with the rising number of suicides in Japan overall.

A later development, initiated by this line, resulted in the creation of large mirrors near various sites along the rail line where people had frequently jumped to their deaths. The JR East line had not collected data to determine if the mirrors had any impact (Pilling, 2007). In 2006, 32,155 people had taken their lives according to the National Police Agency, or approximately 90 a day. Among the Group of Eight countries—Japan, Russia, France, Germany, Canada, Italy, Great Britain, and the United States—Japan ranked second only to Russia in the highest number of suicides. Russia's rate was 39.4 per 100,000 persons compared to Japan's rate of 24.1 per 100,000. The U.S. rate for 2006 was around 8 per 100,000 (Pilling, 2007). Later data in 2009 revealed that the number of Japanese suicides had reached 34,427. This number placed the rate at about 95 suicides a day (Fackler, 2009). This ratio meant that Japanese suicides were almost three times as great as those in America. Finally, for 2010, the National Police Agency identified 31,690 suicides, a modest decline of three percent from 2009 (Yamaguchi, 2011). Yamaguchi reported that "failing to get jobs" was a key reason for suicides. Sadly, about one-third were in their twenties and fresh graduates.

Some Japanese have seized on some bizarre techniques of committing suicide. The strategies have even been detailed and illustrated on the Internet. For example, one 14-year-old girl followed the advice from a website that gave precise instructions for ending one's life (*The Economist*, 2008). The site provided instructions for creating hydrogen-based gas by mixing toilet-bowl cleanser with bath salts. That technique claimed around 60 lives in April of 2008 — many being in their teens or twenties.

A top tourist site turned into a frequented location for suicide has been the towering cliffs of Tojimbo near the Sea of Japan. Yukio Shige has walked along the rocky slopes searching for "lone human figures, usually sitting hunched at the edge of the precipice"(Fackler, 2009). By the end of 2009, Mr. Shige and a group of volunteers had collectively saved 222 people. Astonishingly to a Westerner, he has received criticism from Japan's conformist society that looks dimly on individuals who draw attention to themselves by engaging in social activism — even of this humanitarian kind. The local tourist association has complained about his efforts as they believe his activities are bad for business. In Sakai, a small city in Fukui Prefecture where the Tojimbo cliffs are located, outdoor lighting has been installed along with two pay phones along with 10 yen coins to enable a person to dial the national suicide hot line. Yukio Shige claimed his approach was quite simple—when he finds a potential suicide near the cliffs he walks up and gently starts a conversation. Typically a male, he claims they are usually open to conversation about their pain. A former police officer, Shige had been appalled by the number of bodies he had to yank out of the sea in his earlier days (Fackler, 2009).

Attempts by scholars to explain the high rate of suicide in Japan sometimes leads to the historic role of the samurai code of glorification of suicide as an honorable exit. However, from the 1960s through the mid-1990s the Japanese rate, while high, was not escalating. A key point seemed to be in 1988 when companies started laying off thousands of employees—that year the number of suicides increased by 35 percent. Many of the suicides in recent years do correlate with the bursting of the economic bubble and the following 20-year period of recession.

In addition, the Japanese media has focused on school bullying as a cause, but these have represented a smaller number of cases. However, the country has for years seen a spike in Japanese adolescents who have committed suicide around the time they received their exam scores, which make or break their opportunity to attend a good university. The National Police Agency surveyed reasons for suicide in part from notes left by the victims. They included "domestic problems" (1,043), "job-related problems" (709), "other" (645), and "relationship problems" (295). A different perspective, offered by Jeff Kingston of Temple's University in Japan, focused on the continuing growth of the elderly as a percent of the population. As they age, they encounter more severe health problems (Pilling, 2007). In addition, the services needed to help with depression and crisis have been lacking. Just a few hotlines and crisis centers exist, and as previously noted, mental health and counseling services are weak and only starting to become established. Culturally, Japanese society gives few second chances to bounce back from the perceived shame of failing, including the shame of something like bankruptcy. Japan's main religious faiths—Buddhism and Shintoism—are neutral on suicide (*The Economist*, 2008).

## Joblessness and Homelessness

The poverty rate hit a record high of 16.0 percent in 2009, according to Japan's Welfare Ministry (Kyodo, 2011). The rate, which represents the percentage of people slipping below the median national disposable income, was the highest since the ministry started compiling data in 1985. Also, the child poverty rate rose to a record high 15.7 percent in 2009. Fackler (2010) offered an example: Satomi Sato, a 51-year-old widow, was having it rough raising a teenage daughter on the equivalent of $17,000 per year doing two jobs. Still, she was surprised that her income had dipped under the official poverty level. After years of economic stagnation, and widening income disparities, this once proud nation is belatedly realizing that it has significant poverty. The Labor Ministry disclosed in late 2010 that approximately 20 million people lived in poverty in 2007, and the announcement stunned many in the nation, with many Japanese continuing to believe the myth that it's mostly a middle class society. Shockingly, the government acknowledged that it had kept the matter secret since 1998, denying that a problem existed. The economic pain had been further masked by Japanese attempting to put up a middle class appearance—they feared losing face to their neighbors and becoming stigmatized. Experts have claimed that up to 80 percent of those living in poverty are part of the working poor holding low-wage temporary jobs. Years of deregulation and competition from low-wage Chinese jobs have added to the misery. Adding insult to injury, the poor are largely uncovered by Japan's minimal safety net. A vicious cycle appears to be unfolding in which the one in seven children who are poor cannot pay for the after-hours cram schools that are so critical to academic success. In this high-pressure academic system this can mean being permanently assigned to low-wage work. Japan is one of the nations in which the die is cast early in life, and unlike in the United States, one gets few second chances.

There are many transient workers—sometimes called day laborers in the United States—that operate under the radar in Japan. Recruiters head to the poor areas of big cities in Japan, such as Osaka, and recruit thousands of older workers, who spill out from homeless shelters, flop houses, and parks for day jobs—often doing construction work (Onishi, 2008). One recruiter, Takuya Nakamae, claimed that too many men in this Osaka neighborhood were over the unofficial cutoff age of 55. Nonetheless, he acknowledged that the older men had known how to work hard as they had played a pivotal role in the economic boom of earlier decades. In the larger picture, there have been many dreary tales of divorce, illness, and decline among Japan's "disposable workers" (Onishi, 2008).

Painfully, Japan lacks a solid safety net for the less fortunate that have lost jobs. An example was offered in the city of Oita (Fackler, 2009). Forty-seven-year old Koji Hirano, along with some fellow workers, were called into a cafeteria operated by the Canon Digital Camera Company and told they were being laid off. Shocked and frightened, the men were told to vacate their employer-owned apartments. Mr. Hirano, with no savings from his modest take-home monthly pay of $700, faced homelessness. As short-term employees, they had none of the rights of "salarymen" or even the factory workers of many small companies. Adding to the distress, they could expect little in the way of unemployment or welfare benefits. The Japanese Labor Ministry noted that about 131,000 layoffs occurred between October of 2008 and February of 2009. Only around 6,000 were drawn from the majority of Japanese workers, who traditionally hold full-time jobs. A large number, around 125,000, were identified as "nonregular workers" on short-term contracts and at lower pay with few benefits (Fackler, 2009). Starting in the second decade of the twenty-first century, around 34 percent of Japan's 55 million workers are "non-regular" employees, while historically there used to be far more "permanent" employment jobs available. Individuals like Koji Hirano face a stark future given the weak social safety net. With practically no savings, he had applied for welfare a half dozen times in two months, only to be denied by officials who told him he was not searching hard enough for full-time employment. There are many similar tales of Japanese who have been left with nothing. Some have starved to death.

An appallingly sad tale is of a "starving man's diary" that circulated on the web, and which brought the matter home to millions of Japanese. In this case, a thin notebook was uncovered along with a partly mummified corpse in the Summer of 2007 (Onishi, 2007). The diary recounted his last days, and included the comment, "This human being is still alive," and "I want to eat rice, I want to eat a rice ball." These were the words of a 52-year-old urban welfare recipient, not a lost hiker in the mountains. His benefits had been cut off, and he was one of three men who had died over a three-year-period in the western city of Kitakyushu. In all three cases it appeared starvation was the culprit. The diary embarrassed local officials, but they initially claimed it was a "model" case. Critics argued that these cases demonstrated how far authorities had gone to achieve their "flat welfare rate." Historically, the county has always been tough on welfare cases with applicants expected to seek help from relatives and expected to use up their savings. Welfare is considered less of an entitlement than a *shameful* handout. A welfare expert in Tokyo noted "those in need are not citizens—only those who pay taxes are citizens" (Onishi, 2007). With no religious support of a welfare tradition, and few soup kitchens (a handful are run by Christian missionaries from South Korea), individuals are left to fend for themselves. The national government provides 75 percent of welfare costs and shapes the policy nationwide—similar to most governmental policies, including the police.

Many homeless are treated with contempt and worse in Japan. A report emerged in 2003 in which three youths pounced on Masahiko Sugai in Kawasaki, beating him with sticks and fists (Onishi, 2003). It appeared to be typical of a new kind of crime—attacks by young boys on older men who have lost their jobs and became homeless and are "useless"—to use the harsh rhetoric of Japan's post-bubble economy. Less than a month later, ten boys (age 10 to 16) assaulted three homeless men. They told police they were "killing time" and "disposing of society's trash." The deputy chief of the police station stated that they claimed they didn't realize they had done something bad (Onishi, 2003). Deputy Chief Kenyo Hondo explained that it was part of a shameful trend to "target the weak." Over 1,000 homeless people were living in Deputy Chief Honda's city—a city that had experienced economic decline.

Many had set up wooden shacks neatly spaced in Fujuni Park, but others had resorted to cardboard boxes near the train station. Many of the homeless that were interviewed claimed that they had sought work, but claimed that if you were over 50 years of age it was very difficult to find jobs.

One pioneer in a campaign to address the jobless problem in Japan has been Makoto Yuasa (Murphy, 2009). Perhaps for a decade his efforts were swept aside and ignored by many in Japan. Undoubtedly, part of Japan's jobless problem involves being blind to the situation and holding on to the myth that the country is all middle class. Yuasa's rise to fame has symbolized the sea change in the country's awareness that it had a serious poverty and jobless problem. As already observed, Japanese looked at the problem as one of laziness and as an embarrassment to the proud nation. The scale of the problem and extensive media coverage has gradually resulted in a modest shift of attitudes on the part of Japanese citizens. Going into the second decade of the twenty-first century some Japanese have become sympathetic to the plight of the homeless and poor. Mr. Yuasa arranged a stunning publicity stunt in which 500 recently laid off workers were put up in tents in Hibiya Park in Tokyo, directly across the street from the Ministry of Health, Labor, and Welfare (Murphy, 2009).

The demonstration drew thousands of volunteers eager to help the homeless. Of course he has had critics who charge him with profiting from the people he claimed he was helping. Still, he was able to get enough support to open a drop-in center to assist the homeless and offer health check-ups. Volunteers accompanied the needy to government offices to apply for housing and the modest unemployment benefits that are offered.

This concludes the chapter on a discussion of the social problems that are impacting the lives of Japanese citizens—alcoholism, drug abuse, mental illness, suicide, homelessness, and joblessness. To varying degrees, I have pointed out how these quality of life issues impact crime and the criminal justice system.

# 7

# Chinese Historical, Political, and Legal Background

## Introduction

As China robustly charges into the twenty-first century, many issues are at stake that will impact the current and future criminal justice system. China experts and scholars continue to debate if the present authoritarian communist government will genuinely adopt the rule of law or only pay lip service to the approach. Some scholars say that the nation is no longer "communist" in any sense, but rather the country operates under a collective dictatorship. They claim there is little evidence of the Marxist-Leninist communist political philosophy that was embraced by the early communist Chinese leaders in the early 1950s. Clearly "market forces" or a type of capitalism prevails in the economic arena. Chinese leaders eschew the term "capitalism," but it actually operates that way.

The future is up for grabs and scholars such as Cheng Li offer several future scenarios as this vast nation moves forward toward 2020 (Li, 2007). In a nutshell they are as follows:

> *The emergence of a democratic China*—A wealthier and better-educated middle class, a stronger currency, and a more robust civil society, among other phenomena, lead to greater cultural and political pluralism.
>
> *Prolonged chaos*—Economic disparities among urban and rural populations, rampant corruption among the elite, health crises, and environmental degradation trigger intense socio-political and economic crises that undermine the stability of the Communist regime.
>
> *A resilient, authoritarian China*—Problems among the world's democratic countries make democracy less appealing to the Chinese peo-

ple, while stable development strategies by the party-state are necessary for growth and economic stability, further entrenching the ruling power of the CCP. (p. 18)

Any number of economic, political, and leadership factors could emerge that would sway the outcome. There are a variety of excellent arguments that one could generate that support each of these three scenarios or a combination of them. Of course, the most optimistic scenario offered by Professor Li is the initial one. In this scenario, "the emergence of a democratic China" might be linked to the growth in the rule of law and legal institutions that have rapidly evolved over the past few decades. After the upheaval of the Cultural Revolution (1966–1976), the Chinese government has promulgated, in addition to a constitution, an immense number of laws and regulations. It has educated a huge number of legal functionaries (lawyers, judges, prosecutors, and police personnel) and created hundreds of law schools. Notwithstanding the fact that while the system has all the "trappings" and appearance of a bona fide legal system, it remains to be seen if the government will actually implement the rule of law (Cohen, 2007).

While in the present period of the early twenty-first century, the Chinese leadership has been operating in a collectivist technocratic fashion, it is possible that a single strong leader will emerge that could contribute to the third scenario—"a resilient authoritarian China." Possibly, a continuance of the collectivist present structure, as exemplified in the Politboro, will continue to hold the reins of power. Since the country is so massive, both geographically and in population, it may prove too difficult to govern given the present Communist Party structure. A vast number of voices already clamor to be heard, whether it's on the Internet, in blogs, on cell phones, etc. The infamous state security system is already struggling to censor many of these dissident voices, and may have greater difficulty in the ensuing years. Therefore, scenario number two, "prolonged chaos," may prevail.

Chinese written history goes back to around 4,000 years ago and its tumultuous history of wars and chaos has been widely explored by many sinologists. Today, it has a land mass of around 9,560,900 square kilometers, and the population is around 1.3 billion individuals. There are 139.7 persons per square kilometer (*The Economist*, 2011).

# China's Diverse Population

Unlike homogeneous Japan, China has a diverse and heterogeneous population more like that found in the United States. While the Han population predominates, other ethnic groups such as the Tibetans, Mongolians, and

Uighurs exist in sizeable numbers. Furthermore, these populations tend to exist in enclaves in remote geographical locations. The Uighurs, for example, have a Muslim tradition and have lived in the far western region near Russia for over 1,000 years. As early as the mid-1950s Chairman Mao Zedong had called for young people to "open up the west" (Jacobs, 2009). After about a month-long trek across the vast Gobi desert, thousands arrived to discover that the factory jobs, hot baths, and telephones in every house did not exist. Now, many decades later, members of the Han majority have reshaped this remote Muslim region near Russia. Shihezi is a city of 650,000 and a showcase of the Xinjiang Production and Construction Corps. Ethnic unrest has not ceased despite the fact that the province's 2.6 million people are now primarily Han (95 percent). Just 5 percent are native Uighurs. The latter view the Han as colonists, who have tried to displace the Uighurs from their original home. Overall, however, for the entire region, the Han have grown to 7.5 million (40 percent), whereas the native Uighurs have fallen to 8.3 million or 45 percent.

There are many grievances that the Uighurs hold against the settled Han. The area has enormous mineral wealth and has increased the prosperity of the Han, but policies have marginalized the Uighurs economically and they have not enjoyed the same economic growth. Uighurs have complained about the repression of their Islamic faith and official polices have restricted their language. Government jobs go to the Han. During periods of various hostile encounters and conflicts, many lives have been lost and many arrests have followed. Police stop many cars and buses, but only Uighurs are searched and required to present identification cards.

In June of 2010, thousands of Uighurs took to the streets in Urumqi to protest the treatment of fellow workers (Teague, 2010). Local authorities were caught off-guard, and when security personnel arrived to quell the crowd an incident (apparently unidentified) took place that triggered violence. Each side claimed the other was the culprit, but the Chinese government chose to describe it as an outside force of terrorism. Other deadly incidents involving large numbers of demonstrators have occurred over recent decades in which the local government authorities have had to organize large numbers of armed police to maintain control of the area. Similar to their treatment of the Uighurs, the government has attempted to relocate members of the Han to other areas such as Tibet and Inner Mongolia. Local native populations have fought back and resented the erosion of their traditional ways of life, and deadly conflicts have occasionally resulted in armed and deadly encounters.

In Hohnot, Mongolia, ethnic Mongolians took their anger to the streets when two Han Chinese drivers killed two Mongolians in separate incidents in the capital city of Inner Mongolia (Jacobs, 2011). The protests drew more than

100 in the city center and resulted in a series of arrests. Earlier demonstrations took place in other parts of the region. Alarmed Chinese officials announced they would file murder charges against a forklift driver accused of striking and killing Yan Wenlong, who was among 20 people protesting a coal mine near the city of Xilinhot. Along with another activist, killed by a truck driver five days earlier, the incidents galvanized the local Mongolian population. Previously the Chinese authorities had met protests with a heavy-handed police response, but backed off after these widespread protests. Mongolians make up less than 20 percent of the region's 24 million people but, like other minority populations, are angered at the dilution of their language and culture (Jacobs, 2011). Large deployments of police ("public security" personnel) and soldiers indicated that the government was trying to nip this mayhem in the bud and avoid the deadly encounters experienced earlier from Uighurs and Tibetans. The Inner Mongolian Autonomous Region, as it is known officially, occupies 12 percent of the total Chinese landmass, but has become a critical source of coal, natural gas, and rare earth elements that are essential to supporting the Chinese economy. One source of conflict is the environmental degradation that results from coal mines and fragile pasture land along with the livestock harmed. During the Chinese government's attempts at quelling these large disturbances they resort to shutting down cell phones and Internet service—sometimes with only modest success. Not infrequently, some clever Chinese have found ways to outwit the government's censors and release information that government agents have attempted to block to the wider public.

Bordering Russia and the Inner Mongolian Autonomous Region is the independent country of Mongolia. Two decades after the collapse of the Soviet Union, Mongolia now enjoys full independence, but it feels locked-in economically by the two giants—China and Russia (Banyan, 2011). This nation has great mineral wealth including copper, gold, and coal, which China would happily enjoy commanding. The local population is disdainful of its giant neighbors, but relies on both for trade and economic growth. Under the ethnic Manchu Qing dynasty, which collapsed in 1911, China ruled Mongolia cruelly (Banyan, 2011). About twice as many Mongols live in China (5.8 million) as in Mongolia (2.8 million). To date, Mongolians have managed to live peacefully with their giant neighbors.

In Tibet, a hotbed of dissent and unrest since the Chinese claimed it in the 1950s, there are occasional waves of self-immolations by monks in the Tibetan region of Sichuan Province. In 2011, the Chinese government increased the public security budget, and Human Rights Watch stated that this had been in response to "heavy-handed" tactics by local security forces (Wong, 2011). Human Rights Watch went on to claim that public security (police) spending in the Tibetan region was three times the average for non-Tibetan parts of Sichuan. In 2007, a new "anti-terrorist unit" of the Ministry of Public Security participated in a "strike hard" campaign in the Tibetan region. Chinese government officials have claimed that these widespread notorious campaigns, that have been periodically unleashed to tackle crime, have been abandoned since around 2010.

In a riot in 2008, China sentenced 55 Tibetans for their role in a March 14 uprising in the major city of Lhasa (Wong, 2008). These Tibetans were convicted of arson, robbery, and disrupting public order, among other crimes. Envoys of the Tibetan spiritual leader, the Dalai Lama, had met to discuss policies in Beijing with government leaders. The Dalai Lama had called for Tibet to have autonomy but not outright independence. Chinese government officials reject his claim and counter that he and his followers seek outright independence. He had fled Tibet for India in 1959. Over the ensuing decades many reports have reached supporters of Tibet that involve detentions and executions of many people (including monks and nuns) by the Beijing government.

While eastern parts of China have witnessed an economic industrial boom over the past 30 years, many other sections of the country have retained a much lower level of prosperity and there is economic hardship and outright poverty. Most of these areas are where agriculture is the main source of income. As the transition from state-owned enterprises to more free-wheeling entrepreneurial endeavors have taken place, and mostly in the special "economic zones" of the coastal areas, many citizens of the underdeveloped central and western regions have suffered by comparison. As a result, millions of Chinese citizens have participated in a vast migration. Most young people flee from the agriculture backwaters of the country and take their chances for a job in the huge cities where enormous factories with sweat shop labor conditions and minimal wages exist. Some reports claim 114 million migrant workers have left rural areas to seek work in the cities. Many arrived with just their shirts on their back or a single suitcase. Of course, given the free enterprise spirit of the nation, some farmers and small businesses are thriving in these sparsely populated rural areas. However, by mid-2012 there was evidence that many workers were returning home. An example is Jintang County. Poor and deep inland, around 180,000 left (out of a population of 900,000) for the factories of Guangdong Province on the coast. Officials say that in 2011 the number of local laborers migrating within the Chongqing region exceeded the number leaving for other provinces. Similar patterns appear in other areas such as Henan (*The Economist*, 2012).

Even though the government has shed many of the state-owned enterprises from the earlier communist period, they still represent perhaps 40 percent of the total urban employment (Terrill, 2007). Lifetime employment schemes such as "Iron Rice Bowl" of the earlier communist era have also vanished since market forces have been unleashed. Business heads have acknowledged that under the state-controlled enterprises they employed thousands of workers, even if they were not needed.

Many thousands of workers that have been discharged from previously guaranteed state jobs have mobilized and created unrest in many parts of the country. Typical, for example, is Jiamusi, a remote industrial outpost near Siberia. Tens of thousands of disgruntled workers staged a massive protest (Rosenthal, 2003). Discharged workers were left with nothing to live off and 80 percent of those laid off were in their forties—receiving at most the equivalent of $20 per month. Those retired had no way to pay for medical expenses. Strikes, collective petitions, and acts of violence continue today to threaten security and "social stability." Many of the policies and activities of the Chinese leadership of President Hu Jintao have focused on maintaining social stability in an effort to retain the levers of power, and social stability has become a major goal of communist leaders. They continue to offer modest compromises to avoid large-scale conflict with citizens.

Chinese police literature offers many prescriptions for "managing" rather than "crushing" these large scale protests, but public security forces do not often listen and a considerable number of attacks on citizens have been reported. As a consequence, over the past decade even local officials have attempted to compromise and meet some of the protestors demands. The workers of Jiamusi turned to angry protest after realizing that less aggressive measures were not accomplishing anything. A credo of laid off workers emerged, stating that "a small disturbance leads to a small solution, a large disturbance leads to a big solution. No disturbance leads to no solution" (Rosenthal, 2003). The gap between rich and poor has continued to grow over the past thirty years and this has had a powerful impact on the Chinese masses. Earlier, they may have been uninformed, but now the Internet spreads the word. In a recent example of a dispute involving a metropolitan area of Guangzhou, 25 people were arrested in a conflict that erupted between street vendors and security guards. In this encounter, bottles and bricks were exchanged, but it was just one incident among over 127,000 mass protest incidents recorded by authorities in 2010 (Wines, 2011). Often government-approved land seizures, which have displaced large numbers of residents, have resulted in riots and public protests. In another incident, in Lichuan, approximately 2,000 protesters stormed a government headquarters to protest the death of a legislator, Ran Jianxin. Mr. Ran, a member of the local People's Congress had been investigating accusations of corruption in a city-backed land deal (Wines, 2011). Ran had been interrogated by police when he died under mysterious circumstances. His family claimed that false charges had been filed in an attempt to silence him and get him to abort his investigation. A relative stated that his body bore signs of an "unnatural death" and photos online of his bloodied corpse seemed to confirm the relative's allegation. A large gathering of the People's Armed Police with armored vehicles were required to move into the area to quell the uprising.

From the examples offered of Tibetans, Mongolians, and Uighurs, the problems of minorities in China have been explored. While China has attempted to control these regions, tensions and unrest continue to thwart their efforts.

# Historical Legal Sketch

China has a history of more than 5,000 years, and its traditions have played a role in the creation of the modern legal system. China's situation differs markedly from that of Japan because Japan drew on Western models, such as Germany and France, in its creation of a modern legal system, starting at the time of the Meiji era (1860s). Also, Japan did not suffer the cataclysmic eruptions of its large neighbor to the west (Chen, 2004). China struggled to modernize due to enormous changes and disruptions that took place from the end of the Qing dynasty in the early twentieth century to the Sino-Japanese war of the 1930s, to the civil war in the late 1940s which pitted Chiang Kai-shek and the Kuomintang against Mao Zedong and his communist armies. The communists won the civil war, of course, and the Kuomintang retreated to Taiwan and set up the dictatorship that only in the early twenty-first century became a democratic nation. Mao's government adopted the model of Marxism-Leninism that had prevailed in the Soviet Union, although with distinct Chinese features.

The Qing code embodied the norms of Confucianism. The founder was Confucius (551–479 B.C.) and his concepts and followers had contrasting views regarding the roles of law and morality. China's modern-day criminal justice system provides evidence of the legacy of Confucianism. Confucianists made the case against extensive reliance on law, but rather advocated the merits of government by education (Chen, 2004). Citizens should learn what was right and wrong and internalize these values with the *li*, or moral codes of conduct. That would allow them to behave properly, and good behavior would be linked to their conscience and not imposed on people as a result of their fear of punishment from a coercive legal system. The rulers were to behave virtuously to set proper examples for their citizens. In this approach, the government and rulers would win over their underlings. In a nation dominated by *fa* (law), individuals would be dominated by their self-interest and resort to litigious remedies, and they would try to manipulate the law to suit their own ends. In a nation dominated by *fa* individuals generally would develop the skills of a shyster lawyer and shame would be subordinated (Chen, 2004). With the *li*, Confucianists believed that disputes and conflicts could be sorted out in a more amiable fashion. Disputes would be negotiated through mediation and compromise, and individuals would not pursue their full self-interest. Social harmony would prevail and litigation would be avoided. It will be recalled that one of the reasons set forth for the low crime rates in Japan had to do with the Japanese emphasis on interpersonal harmony. This was a concept borrowed from China along with many other ideas and traditions.

Another argument against the reliance on *fa* or law was that each event, for example a crime, had its own unique features. Therefore a law, by its "boiler-plate" nature, could not fit a particular set of circumstances. Of course, this philosophical model was never fully implemented by Chinese emperors and modern-day leaders, but it managed to survive in various forms over thousands of years. Other political and social ideals emerged over the centuries, such as Taoism and Buddhism, and these were powerful forces that helped to form Chinese culture and society. In general, Confucianism provided a framework for the morals and norms of the emerging nation. It offered a hierarchical structure in which each individual played a role based on his or her position in the complex of social and interpersonal relationships. Again, recall that Japanese society, which emerged at a later date, stresses hierarchy as a framework for social networks of relationships. Confucian norms clarify the relationships among various family members—father and son, brother and brother, husband and wife (Chen, 2004). Respect for authority was very important, and the nation overall was viewed as an extended family with absolute loyalty and obedience to the emperor. The emperor was obligated to treat his subjects as if they were his children. He was expected to take care of them and teach them along with providing an upstanding moral example. Most emperors, however, over the long course of Chinese history, never came close to the ideal and some were outright cruel and tyrannical. Finally, the emperor was to hold his office by the Mandate of Heaven (Chen, 2004). Given the emperor's elevated status, Confucianism was more than a philosophy of life—it was a supernatural phenomena. The emperor had a sacred responsibility that was owed to heaven.

Along with the impressive and detailed code implemented by China's early rulers, the state was always predominant. China was much less concerned with the defense of an individual's interests and rights, and was more concerned with protection of social and political order (Leng & Chiu, 1985). Along with a well-developed judicial system and a system of appeals to higher authorities, including the emperor himself, much of the administration of justice was left to those at a lower level. A county magistrate had to perform the duties of judge, prosecutor, and police chief. The primary objective of Chinese justice was to assert the power of the state and to punish those who violated the rules of order and good conduct (Leng & Chiu, 1985). An individual was at an extreme disadvantage when confronted by the power of the state. Among the disadvantages were the presumption of guilt, the non-existence of defense counsel, the use of torture to extract confessions, and the enforcement of group responsibility and group punishment. Again one sees a similarity with Japan—groups play an important role in society. Emphasis on the interests of the group, the family, the community took priority over the individual's rights. Concerning punishment, cruel methods were often relied upon, although some of the worst were eventually terminated. The "five punishments" were tattooing, amputation of the nose, amputation of one foot or both feet, castration, and death (Chen, 2004).

Definitions of crimes and offenses were often vague and this practice is still evident in some modern-day courtroom cases. There was no fundamental separation of the prosecutor and the judge. Even today the roles of public security, prosecutor, and judiciary lack independence and the Communist Party often intrudes in the overall administration of justice. Additionally, citizens were reluctant to draw on the formal legal apparatus as corruption reared its ugly head.

There were, therefore, solid reasons for Chinese to stay away from the courts and judicial system and only consider litigation as a last resort. Many extra judicial agencies and remedies were relied on historically, and they continue to be drawn on up to the current time. They included neighborhood committees during the Mao era—that is individual's appointed by party leaders. Now, with the huge growth in the professionalization of the legal system, including courts and defense lawyers, the role of these block committees has waned, but informal means of mediation and conciliation still find appeal among Chinese citizens as they seek to resolve conflicts.

Historically, for example, civil disputes such as those involving land or family matters were often resolved through mediation offered by respected leaders or elders of clans, villages, and guilds in accordance with customary rules and concept of morality. These arrangements stressed offering concessions and focused on the parties' need to achieve social harmony and avoid litigation and self-interest (Chen, 2004).

# The Legal System under Mao

After the emergence of the communist People's Republic of China (PRC) in 1949, the nation looked to the Soviet system to a limited degree. What was critical in the building of the PRC legal system were variations of the *li* and *fa* characteristics from earlier centuries. Two models of law, *jural* and *societal*, formed the foundation of the system created at the time of Mao Zedong. The *jural* model is the formalized legal model that comes closer to a Western conception of a legal system. It provides a detailed codified system of law that is enforced by administrative agencies and a judicial structure. The *societal* model is reminiscent of the *fa*. It is an informal conception that stresses socially approved norms, values, and involves political socialization (Leng & Chiu, 1985). The latter is enforced by extrajudicial agencies and social organizations. During Mao's time, it was evident that he and the Communist Party founders preferred the *societal* model. It fit with his preference for the "mass line" and notion of a continuous revolution, and it politicized the overall legal system. The communists recognized the value in formalized law but viewed it as mechanistic and limiting the value of the political process. Extrajudicial devices were emphasized in settling disputes. Sometimes the standard judicial system was relied upon but often summary proceedings of revolutionary tribunals were drawn upon. If one sought a divorce the process might be mediated by a unit at one's factory before thought was given to relying on the courts. Many of the judges who heard the court cases were not professionally educated. They were often joined on the bench by "peoples assessors" or selected Communist Party members who sat next to the judge. This was another example of how the judicial process was interwoven with communist political thought.

Modern judicial systems in the West featured the rule of law, equality under the law, humanism, constitutionalism, democracy, majority rule, elections, judicial independence, due process, the jury, procedural fairness, and defense lawyers—all foreign to the Chinese legal system (Chen, 2004).

For a period of time, during the late 1950s, the *jural* model became stronger as the communist government began to experiment with a constitution. The PRC created laws linked to the People's Courts and the People's prosecutorial arm (People's Procuratorates). The Supreme People's Court was given the sole authority to administer justice. However, class elements were a critical factor in how a person was treated by the courts. Individuals identified as "reactionaries" or "class enemies" had no rights under the constitution—there was no equality before the law (Leng & Chiu, 1985). Presumption of innocence was out the window along with other Western ideas of jurisprudence, and were labeled "theories of bourgeois jurisprudence." In actual practice, the criminal process became completely controlled by Communist Party committees who administered the public security system.

As noted above, one's status, class, and origin became critical in how one was treated under Mao's justice system. From the perspective of class there were "five black elements"—landlords, rich peasants, counterrevolutionaries, rightists, and other bad elements (Leng & Chiu). When crimes were committed by persons so identified as "enemies," they were given longer sentences. Individuals who supported equality before the law were attacked by Maoists. During the entire period in which Mao led the Communist Party, the party played the predominant role in the criminal justice system. Judicial independence was strongly discouraged and the system of having cases approved by a Communist Party committee became a permanent fixture of the People's justice. It became utterly futile for a defendant to challenge a court ruling. Under the principle of "leniency to those who confess and severity to those who don't confess," an appeal or a refusal to confess was viewed as an aggravating factor leading to a longer sentence (Leng & Chiu, 1985).

Mass campaigns and mobilization campaigns characterized the early 1950s and along with attacks on landlords and rich peasants, there was a "Movement Against the Three Evils and Five Evils" (Chen, 2004). The "Three Evils" referred to corruption, waste, and bureaucracy within the Communist Party, while the "Five Evils" focused on bribery, tax evasion, theft of state property, cheating on government contracts, and stealing state economic information. Another step in the evolution of the Chinese legal system was the creation of the National People's Congress in 1954 and the first constitution, which will be discussed in greater detail in a later chapter.

# The Cultural Revolution

The next major stage in the development of the Chinese legal system was the Cultural Revolution, in which Mao unleashed millions of young people, called Red Guards, to challenge the bureaucracy and "maintain the revolution." Many years of chaos followed and even public security bureau offices were closed during this reign of terror. Some scholars claim that hundreds of thousands of peoples, perhaps even millions were arrested, persecuted, and even killed. One of Mao's ideas was to rid the nation of counter-revolutionaries and as a consequence ideology and revolutionary zeal prevailed. Mao Zedong relied on his cult of personality to allow this sweeping and powerful force to envelop the nation from around 1966 to 1978 (the time span varies, differing among historians). His authorization went unchallenged and was embraced. Virtually all semblance of order was destroyed, and any evidence of possession or interest in Western things—books, films, musical recordings, etc.—made one vulnerable to attack. Scholars with no experience in farming were forced to retreat to remote parts of China and engage in agricultural pursuits or other hard labor.

By way of a personal note, an esteemed Fulbright Scholar, Hou Wei Rei, who I became friends with, shared the following experience. He came from Shanghai International Studies University and was a visiting scholar at Yale University during the 1988–1989 academic year. He recounted his own experience in the Cultural Revolution. He and his wife were both forced out of their scholarly jobs and banished to the countryside from Shanghai. Both struggled with menial farm labor for several years. Years later, after this period of turmoil ended, they were able to go to Australia on academic fellowships. At that time, Hou Wei Rei's wife told him that she would never risk going back to China. He did return to Shanghai and for many years sent funds to her to support their adolescent son, but eventually, having been separated for more than 15 years, they agreed upon an amicable divorce.

Many high-ranking "cadres" were subjected to "struggle sessions" during the Cultural Revolution in which they were verbally abused and sometimes physically assaulted. Ideological purity was demanded, and those identified as counter-revolutionaries were subjected to interrogation, torture, imprisonment, and labor camps. Houses were invaded by Red Guards and many people lost prized personal possessions.

After Mao died, the Cultural Revolution finally came to an end with its own final chapter of violence. The so-called Gang of Four were top Chinese leaders who were targeted for blame for the Cultural Revolution. The four were Jiang Qing (Mao's widow), Zhang Chunqiao, Wang Hongwen, and Yao Wenyuan (MacFarquhar & Schoenhals, 2006). In the end, the Gang of Four were put on trial and imprisoned for long stretches. Two died in prison.

At the outset of the Cultural Revolution, Mao had been able to manipulate his Communist Party colleagues, but by the end the political system was so fractured by factions at the top that only the armed forces could impact the leadership. After the Gang of Four had been arrested, and eventually executed, Deng Xiaoping emerged as the new leader. He had also been disgraced earlier and forced to sweep a broom on a factory floor during the Cultural Revolution. Nonetheless, he emerged from the rubble of long years of destruction and mayhem to lead the government forward, and eventually to the enormous economic growth starting in the late 1970s. The massive transformation from state-owned enterprises to private capitalistic endeavors began to take hold at this time. "China had to jump on the bandwagon of successful Western-style modernization that had proved so effective on Taiwan and elsewhere in East Asia. The Cultural Revolution became the economic and social watershed of modern Chinese history" (MacFarquhar & Schoenhals, 2006). Deng Xiaoping, China's new leader at that time gave his full blessing to market forces. In 1983, he was quoted as saying "some people in rural areas and cities should be allowed to get rich before others." "Profit" was no longer a dirty word and private ownership of businesses and dwellings started to take hold. Deng's bitter memories of the Cultural Revolution resulted in policies that emphasized *stability* and that would attempt to minimize *disorder*.

It was around 1978 when Deng Xiaoping developed his "Open Policy" that actively encouraged modernization and what has now become the economic powerhouse (Cohen, 2005). The Soviet model, originally adopted by the PRC, had been battered by the Cultural Revolution and was basically dead. The new model provided for order, which had been completely lacking in the horrors of the Cultural Revolution. The new approach facilitated commercial and economic development and it did not tolerate lawlessness. Up until that point there was nothing resembling a legal system and the administration of justice (Cohen, 2005). The National People's Congress emerged as a force. Many of the criminal justice institutions that are essential to providing justice and fairness, such as prosecution and courts, had been non-functioning during that 12-year period. Chinese lawyers had been absent from society for a longer period.

The next chapter will flesh out the developments of the criminal justice system and trace its evolution along with the problem of crime in Chinese society.

# 8

# The Criminal Justice System in China

## The Post-Cultural Revolution Period

On the surface, today China has the appearance of a full-fledged legal system, but appearances can be deceiving. There have been many laws and regulations promulgated and there is today a wide-ranging system of courts, judges, lawyers, and a large public security (police) system. In comparison with 1978, and the end of the Cultural Revolution, the nation has over 180,000 judges, 150,000 procurators (prosecutors), 120,000 lawyers, 620 law schools and programs that graduate around 100,000 law students a year. Many law-related journals and periodicals are now published (Cohen, 2007). In addition to 3,100 basic courts, there are 400 intermediate courts, and 31 provincial level-high courts under the aegis of the Supreme People's Court. At all levels recruitment provides staffing for the expanding legal system. Historically, the court system was staffed, not by professional, legally trained individuals, but by former military and police officers. Currently, the ranks of the legal functionaries are being staffed by well-trained law graduates. Openings for judges and prosecutors now require applicants to pass a tough bar exam. Cohen (2005) stated that only a little more than 11 percent plus of applicants passed. There are now over 400 law schools in China and additional ones continue to be added annually. Scholarly articles are now being published and the Internet has contributed to the professional legal literature.

Foreign investment and China's decision to join the World Trade Organization (W.T.O.) in 2001 has created an additional need for lawyers to handle corporate and civil matters. There are hundreds of cities in China that have arbitration commissions that handle both domestic and foreign-linked disputes. All of this activity has contributed to a legal awareness on the part of a growing number of citizens.

An enormous gap of incomes exist between those who have benefitted from the growth of market forces or the capitalistic thrust of China's economy and the large number of those who have been left behind. Ross Terrill (2006), the Harvard Research Associate at the Fairbank Center, asked the question, "why has there been no revolution?" His answer as to why there hasn't been greater social instability is that the government has made compromises. One was the government's compromise on market forces that was required to get into the W.T.O. A second reason is that the regime wanted to maintain a peaceful environment on their borders. Terrill believes that the emerging economy will produce a new politics, but he believes the government may be able to hold on to power. Some scholars believe that the main goal of Chinese leaders is to hold on to power and that they will use almost any means to achieve this end. Many members of the Communist Party get special breaks and support for their activities, including sweetheart deals on the acquisition of businesses and the purchase of property. This is a form of corruption in the sense that those who don't have friends in high places don't have these opportunities. Terrill (2006) points to the simple fact that the government has retained control for 35 years as proof of their ability to cling to power. By deftly meeting some of the demands of those engaged in civil disobedience and protests, the government has been able to tamp down some of the dissident voices and thereby keep the protestors at bay. One report claimed over 87,000 demonstrations in 2005 alone. Since there has yet to be an established rule of law, the market reforms will not succeed in the long run according to Gordon Chang (2006). Chang's lecture at Yale went on to note that the future will be determined by economic reform and that it will in turn determine political reform. If that occurs many Communist Party members will quit the party, according to Chang.

The Chinese criminal justice system suffers from significant weaknesses that I will identify later. There is both the Criminal Procedure Law and the Criminal Law that were passed by the National People's Congress in 1979. Those laws reflect the legacy of the Soviet system during the time period when both nations were collaborating with each other on a variety of fronts.

The Public Security Ministry is in charge of investigation, detention, and the initial review of cases. Most cases start with the Public Security Ministry, but exceptions include cases of corruption, dereliction of duty by government officials, torture to extract confessions, and other cases involved with the abuse of power by officials (Chen, 2004). The procuratorate (prosecutor) approves an arrest and conducts the investigation. The courts are then responsible for adjudicating cases. Curiously, perhaps to a Westerner, the decision to detain a suspect may be authorized by law enforcement (Public Security) without prior approval of the procuratorate. The police are supposed to obtain a warrant from the procuratorate, and they are also supposed to inform the suspect's family. Often they do not strictly adhere to this policy. In addition, the police are expected to interrogate the suspect within 24 hours and the suspect has no right to remain silent. The policy on detention is that a party may be held during the investigatory period for up to two months, but an additional 30-day extension may be granted with the approval of the prosecutor (Terrill, 2007). Additional extensions beyond the 30-day period depend on some additional conditions now on the books.

Haibo He (2007), in a paper presented at the Yale University China-Law Workshop, noted that within the Chinese legal tradition the idea of due process was lacking and that the procedural code was rudimentary. Even as late as 1980, when the study of administrative law was resumed, China's legal scholars were unfamiliar with the concept of due process. Article 34 of the Public Security Administrative Penalty Law of 1986 promulgated by the People's Congress stated that four procedures were required: summons, interrogation, evidence collection, and ruling.

Returning to the basic steps that typically unfold in the prosecution of a case, when Public Security has a suspect a variety of measures may be applied: (1) attendance for examination, (2) bail, (3) surveillance of residence, (4) arrest, and (5) detention. Again, to reiterate, the Public Security Bureau has the power to detain a suspect without prior approval of the procuratorate (prosecutor) (Chen, 2004). A person may be detained if the individual is believed to be preparing to commit a crime or is in the process of committing a crime. After a person has been detained, and if Public Security believes it is necessary to arrest the party, the agency is supposed to apply to the procuratorate for approval. After a person is arrested, in addition to the family or work unit being notified within 24 hours, the location of the arrest and reasons for the arrest are supposed to be provided. However, a giant loophole exists that Chinese authorities often take advantage of, namely the clause: "except in circumstances where notification would hinder the investigation or there was no way to notify the family or work unit." A change in the legal system around 1996 stipulated that after the suspect has undergone the first interrogation, the individual may hire a lawyer for legal advice or for applying for bail (Chen, 2004). In many cases the suspect is denied "release under guaranty pending trial." Investigators do not need prior approval from another authority to search the suspects residence, office, or car (Cohen, 2005). In theory, the defense lawyer is allowed to inquire about the charge and meet with the suspect, but again the lawyer may be denied access to his client for the entire investigatory period, which may last for months.

Cohen (2005), among other scholars, has observed that the Criminal Procedure Law has too few protections for the individual and that they are ineffectual. There are many exceptions to the protections that prevent an adequate defense for the client.

The lawyer for the accused cannot begin his or her own inquiry as to the facts and evidence until the official investigation has ended. A genuine risk for the defense lawyer is that a witness, perhaps pressured by the government, will recant his testimony and thereby expose the defense lawyer to a charge of falsifying evidence (Cohen, 2005). The law is broad enough that it is not rare that defense lawyers have been charged and convicted under this vague statute. Rarely do witnesses appear in court, and prosecutors typically read the written statements, depriving the lawyer of the accused from an opportunity to cross examine witnesses.

Trials are typically conducted by a collegial panel of three to five judges, and decisions are based on majority rule. In a report of the National People's Congress in 1995, 99.65 percent of people tried in Chinese courts were found guilty (Lawyers Committee for Human Rights, 1996). Often, judges conducting pretrial examinations have submitted their conclusion to the court leadership for approval. Obviously this stacks the deck against the accused and can heavily bias the outcome. In China, there is an expression "decision first, trial later." Of course, this policy has led to the criticism that the role of the trial court is limited and that the courts are merely announcing a decision made by other parties. In 1996, the National People's Congress tried to address this problem by introducing more common law adversarial elements into a previously inquisitorial system, but this revision was also designed to separate the judge's function from that of the prosecutor and defense lawyer (Lawyers Committee for Human Rights, 1996). Technically, the law does not provide for either the presumption of innocence or presumption of guilt, but critics claim that it should explicitly state the presumption of innocence. There are no provisions against the gathering of illegal evidence, and indeed it appears that illegal evidence is not infrequently introduced.

In general, a key factor in the PRC criminal justice process is that it is almost impossible to mount a challenge to the criminal justice system's investigation and prosecution of a person. Attempts to appeal on the part of attorneys or friends of the accused have no administrative vehicle to draw upon. As Cohen (2005) has pointed out, the procurate has no incentive to monitor or evaluate its own investigations and is unlikely to intrude into the Public Security's or the State Security's areas of operation. Both rank higher than the prosecution office. Judicial review is mostly declined. As noted earlier, defense lawyers have to be careful about being charged with Section 306 of the Criminal Law which has a provision that they can be prosecuted for falsifying evidence. As of 2005, that provision has been exercised over 200 times, and defense lawyers have occasionally been jailed as a result.

One new development in 2012 is very encouraging if the government follows through. In 2012, the National People's Congress appeared ready to adopt hard-fought amendments to the Criminal Procedure Law (LaFraniere, 2012). The new language would curb the power of the police and prosecutors to detain suspects without notifying relatives, use evidence extracted by torture, and allow better access by defense attorneys. Given the power of the state in criminal proceedings, most legal experts question whether the new protection would be enforced or exist only on paper.

# Judges

The role of judges in the Chinese system is vastly different than their American counterparts. Judges often consult Communist Party members in making decisions. Chinese judges have a limited ability and power to interpret laws and they are also limited in their ability to rule on the policies of other governmental agencies. Local Communist Party officials control appointments, salaries, etc., and they can lose their jobs if they do not make decisions consistent with the government's policies and attitudes. The judiciary is a highly politicized office and judges historically have been reluctant to innovate and establish new legal ground in their decision-making from the bench. On the other hand, the People's Supreme Court has engaged in decision-making that is comparable to what legislative bodies do in other countries. Only a modest number of the roughly 250,000 judges have a university or legal education. However, this situation is now changing with many law school graduates entering the criminal justice system and some are being appointed to be judges. Still, as several scholars and researchers have pointed out, the quality of law schools provides a great deal of variability. Many are viewed as sub-average in quality. As Xin He (2011), a law professor at the City University of Hong Kong has pointed out, local politics is a crucial factor in determining the behavior of judges and that legal reform has been lacking for several decades, due to the inability of the courts to break free from the power of the Chinese Communist Party. Lacking independence, the courts find it difficult to rule on the merits of the cases that come before them. Therefore, many scholars view the courts as a tool of the state. Notwithstanding these views, Professor Xin He argued that there is some evidence based on his research that while the policymaking of courts is limited, there is still some innovation and creative activism that has occurred. Of course, given the size of China there is a great deal of variation in how different courts operate. In general, the Basic People's Courts are responsible for regions that include cities, towns, and counties. Around 3,000 of these courts exist throughout the nation, and they handle both civil and criminal matters (Terrill, 2007).

An extensive report that exposed flaws in the legal and court system was published by Kahn (2005). An example was the case of Mr. Qin Yanhong. He recalled his brutal treatment at the hands of his interrogators in Henan Province. Public Security officials raised his arms high above his back, jammed his knees into a sharp metal frame and kicked him in the gut whenever he fell asleep. After four days he broke down and confessed. The 35-year-old steel mill worker admitted to a rape and murder. On the strength of this coerced confession, a panel of judges sentenced him to death. As a result of a lucky break, he lived when another person's confession allowed him to go free. As previously noted, most prosecutions end up in convictions. Later, after being released, Mr. Qin commented in a letter to his family written while on death row—"Police use dictatorial measures on anyone who resists them" (Kahn, 2005). Although Deng Xiaoping had 30 years earlier stated that the nation "must rely on law," the case of Qin Yanhong is a rather common example of how justice is often denied in the Chinese legal system. To their credit, some police officers, prosecutors, and judges strive to be independent of the government's oversight, but it is a long struggle. Criminal law still poses a major challenge as the courts often rely on pre-trial confessions and perfunctory court proceedings. Forced confessions and torture are still widespread despite the fact the law explicably forbids coerced confessions and torture. Mr. Qin's family and friends showed how his case involved political motives and how difficult the problem is for a person who lacks power and money. Court documents did not provide any documentation of physical evidence—fingerprints, blood, semen, or clothing that would have allowed forensic analysis. Rather, police relied on the accounts of three children who were playing outdoors in the area. They had spotted Mr. Qin walking in the direction of the farm, where the peasant woman Jia Haironx had been raped and murdered. After the police took him into custody, they did not tell him why he was being detained. Later in prison he tutored himself in criminal law and received help from his family, and he cited passages in his court hearing regarding the Chinese constitution that forbids confessions by torture and "frame-ups." Sadly, he exhausted his family savings in his attempt to rally support and petition legal officials. When the trial opened, 50 relatives and villagers showed up to testify and/or provide support. The three-judge panel ordered the trial closed and all were excluded from the courtroom. The prosecution offered no witnesses and the judges prevented Mr. Qin from calling any. The trial was over within a few hours—the case relying completely on the coerced confession. Six months later the verdict of death was delivered and he was scheduled to be executed, and there was no right of appeal granted. Before he was executed he received a stroke of luck, not due to DNA evidence, but because a retired soldier by the name of Yuan Quifu walked into a police station in a nearly town and confessed.

# Crime in China

Crime rates that are reported to the police and then passed on to government agencies in most countries have to be treated with caution. A number of decades ago, in part to remedy this problem, the United States created the Bureau of Justice Statistics, whose role was to conduct direct household surveys of crime. That data revealed a lot more crime than that which was reported by police departments. This was not surprising considering the fact that for a variety of reasons some people do not report crimes to their local police departments. In turn, police departments sometimes want to look good and occasionally massage their statistics before passing them onto the F.B.I., which annually issues its national *Uniform Crime Reports*.

In China this situation is even more problematic, and with the exception of a survey in Beijing in 1993, they do not have the equivalent of a direct national household survey of crime. Data reported by Chinese police departments must be treated with great caution as local governments and police agencies act very autonomously from the central government in Beijing. Furthermore, many citizens are suspicious of the police, and lack respect for police, as is found in Japan. The quality of relationships between police and citizens in the United States probably falls somewhere in the middle when compared with those found in China and Japan. There are many reports, including some published and found on the Internet, of police misbehavior and outright corruption among Chinese police. In addition, some citizens have contempt and outright hostility toward Public Security officers. However the training and education of police have improved substantially since the Cultural Revolution, though most officers still lack a college degree. In my first visit to China, when I lectured at the Police Officers University outside of Beijing in 1986, I was very impressed with the quality and depth of education offered, but it was one of just two elite institutions offering police education at that time. Many faculty were non-Public Security personnel and held graduate degrees. Impressively, a great variety of subjects were offered by these well-trained civilian lecturers. Subjects included foreign languages, engineering, traffic management, and technical courses.

Returning to crime statistics, a central problem that runs through all the Chinese criminal justice institutions is that they are vulnerable to the highly politicized Communist Party policies and interventions. Notwithstanding the above mentioned concern, there have been some crime reports issued by the government since the post-Cultural Revolution period. Statistical information has been patchy, but some data have also been offered by the United Nations and other sources. One other issue needs to be recognized—namely, that authoritarian governments, by their nature, have been able to control crime to greater extent than their more democratic counterparts. Therefore it is not surprising that crime rates have gone up starting in the 1980s, when Deng Xiaoping initiated the market forces that yielded the wide open flowering of business and economic entrepreneurial activity. This transition correlated with the move to private property and from state-owned enterprises to private ones. Enormous economic growth and prosperity have resulted for a considerable numbers of individuals, but many millions more are mired in poverty, particularly in the countryside. Many scholars and outsiders realistically call it capitalistic, but the Chinese prefer terms such as "market forces." In this wide-open economic development, some kinds of criminal activity, such as prostitution and drug dealing, have returned. These kinds of crimes had mostly been eradicated after the Communist takeover of the 1950s.

Rapid change has contributed to the rise in crime rates that were observed in the 1980s. First, let's look at some historical crime statistics and trends over the past 25 years, up until around 2001, and then let's have a look at more recent data. From crime rates as low as 20 per 100,000 population in the 1950s, the rates started soaring and more than quadrupled to over 360 per 100,000 in 2001 (Bakken, 2005). Robbery was one crime that noticeably increased, from 22,266 in 1981 to 352,216 in 2001. Assault cases did not change much during that 20-year period. Rape rose from around 30,000 cases in 1981 to 50,000 in 1991, but declined to 35,000 in 2001. As Bakken (2005) has noted, crime trends reflect bureaucratic and political processing by Party operatives and raises the question of the accuracy of the reports. As in the United States, the "hidden figure" of crime is due to the fact that people frequently do not report crime. In 1996, the United Nations reported the overall crime rate in China was the lowest, or 67th out of 67 nations surveyed.

Homicide is a good measure of comparison between most countries because it tends to represent a more accurate number than those for theft, robbery, rape, etc. From 1981 to 2001, homicides tripled, from 9,576 to 27,501 (Bakken, 2005). For 2001, the United Nations data revealed a rate of 2.0 per 100,000 in China, compared to 6.0 per 100,000 in the United States. For the same year, South Africa was at the top with approximately 60 homicides per 100,000 population. For a more general picture of crime, from a 2000 Crime

Table 8.1  Homicide Rates, 2002–2009 per 100,000

|  | 2002 | 2003 | 2004 | 2005 | 2006 | 2007 | 2008 | 2009 |
|---|---|---|---|---|---|---|---|---|
| China | 2.0 | 1.89 | 1.90 | 1.59 | 1.37 | 1.22 | 1.12 | 1.12 |
| Japan | 0.62 | 0.60 | 0.56 | 0.50 | 0.49 | 0.44 | 0.46 | 0.46 |
| United States | 5.6 | 5.7 | 5.5 | 5.6 | 5.7 | 5.6 | 5.4 | 5.0 |

*Source:* Wikipedia: List of Countries by Intentional Homicide Rates, 2011.

Victimization Survey of "persons victimized once or more in twelve months," the following information was offered: United States 21 percent, Japan 15 percent, and China 13 percent. Therefore the recent historical picture for China shows that while crime has risen significantly from a low base rate, commencing with the Communist takeover in the 1950s, it is still relatively low compared to many nations around the world.

In examining some more recent crime statistics beginning around the year 2000, the following information emerges. Wikipedia's (2011) data on homicide reveals that China's rate is 1.12, Japan's 0.46, and the United States' is 5.0 for 2002. While the U.S. rate declined from 5.6 in 2002, it is still higher than its Asian counterparts for 2009 (see Table 8.1). Terrill (2007) reports that the actual numbers of homicides in China were 24,711 for the year 2004.

Additional information on the crime picture in China comes from the Institute of Public Security, a research arm under China's Ministry of Public Security. That source stated that for the year 2000, there were 3,637,307 total crimes reported to the police, and those numbers increased to 4,337,036 by 2002. They jumped further to 4,718,122 by 2004. Property theft was high, at 3,212,822 cases, burglary at1,257,253, auto theft at 663,933, and robbery at 341,908 (Terrill, 2007).

The United Nations Office on Drugs and Crime (2011) offered the following data on homicides in the three nations being compared: United States 15,241 (a rate of 5 per 100,000), China 14,811 (a rate of 1.1 per 100,000), and Japan 646 (a rate of 0.5 per 100,000). NationMaster.com (2009) provided some additional statistics on China that drew on various sources, such as Amnesty International, Transparency International, the Eighth United Nations Survey on Crime Trends, and the Operations of Criminal Justice Systems.

Trevaskes (2010) has made the case that political ideology in the current Hu Jintao era has impacted criminal justice policy and the way criminal sentencing has been implemented. In the last few years there is evidence that the courts are trying to balance the harsh punishment meted out for a minority of very serious crimes with reduced sentences for less serious offenses. The author notes that earlier "strike hard" campaigns (with swift punishment) from around the early 1980s until 2003 ended up by resulting in many harsh sentences and executions. The most recent policy, called "Balancing Leniency and Severity," is that a range of minor offenses have been decriminalized and lesser penalties offered. The author argues that there have been restrictions imposed on what are identified as "serious crime" and "minor crime." The new approach emphasizes the concept of mitigating and aggravating circumstances that already exist in the Criminal Law. Furthermore, this policy change has the weight of the Supreme People's Court behind it when it issued its "Opinion" on February 8, 2010 (Trevaskes, 2010). The goal, at least in part, seems designed to prevent or weaken the "social instability" or disharmony created by the history of harsh punishment that has been so typical of sentencing and punishment in the past few decades. In other words, the Communist Party fears that some of its draconian punishments will be recognized for what they are—unreasonable and unjust. While the death penalty will be discussed in greater detail in a later chapter, suffice it to say that there are 68 offenses in the Criminal Law that allow for the death penalty. Therefore within the context of the rapid economic reforms and market developments, the government, given its goal of harmony and social stability, has come to recognize the pragmatic value of a fairer treatment of the accused. At least implicitly it acknowledges the negative impact of its harsh and sometimes brutal treatment of offenders. As identified by the Supreme People's Court's "Opinion" on "Balancing Leniency and Severity," the focus on punishing crimes states:

- handing down the most severe custodial punishment or the death penalty *only* for cases in which the social dangerousness of the criminal act is extremely severe; and for extremely serious crimes that would normally attract a heavy custodial punishment or the death penalty; or
- punishing with relative severity (but not necessary the death penalty or the most severe custodial punishment) crimes in which the criminal offense is serious; or
- by punishing with relative severity in cases that comply with circumstances described in the Criminal Law for which aggravated circumstances can be attributed; for crimes which demonstrate malicious intent; and for crimes which can be considered dangerous to the person. (Trevaskes, 2010, p. 336)

The "Opinion" also indicates that relatively lenient treatment be offered for those convicted of crimes:

- of passion, domestic-related offenses, or crimes resulting from neighborhood disputes and other similar circumstances;
- for which the motive has its origins in labor disputes or other disputes relating to the workplace or company management where there is little malicious intent evident;
- in which the court determines that victim has partial responsibility for the consequences of the criminal's actions;
- in which there is to some degree self-defense involved in the motive of the crime;
- that do not involve premeditation. (p. 338)

Overall the framework attempts to present a balance that gives lower-level courts the freedom to weigh the merits of individual cases rather than relying on a broad brush of severe and harsh punishment. Furthermore, it attempts to limit the number of crimes in which the death penalty is applied.

The following chapter will explore in greater detail the role of public security and the earlier "strike hard" campaigns that were designed to reduce crime. In addition, the "reform through labor" policy, which allows police to directly imprison individuals while by-passing the courts, will be examined.

# 9

# Policing, State Security, Reform through Labor, and Drug Trafficking in China

The policing function in China is primarily through the Public Security Ministry but the State Security Agency also plays a role that would be similar to a merged F.B.I. and C.I.A., according to Chen (1998). Also, the People's Armed Police Force, a type of paramilitary unit, plays a role and its members are armed, unlike their counterparts in public security. The People's Armed Police Force, which was created in 1983, includes border guards, and units assigned to protect government buildings, embassies, and the residences of foreigners.

In general, the role of the public security bureaus is to maintain law and order like most police forces anywhere in the world. Some of the principal duties include investigation of crime and illegal activity, traffic safety, fire prevention, and the monitoring of the household registration systems. Included in the role of maintaining public order are functions such as preventing the disturbing of the peace, gang fights, the carrying of a weapon or explosives, assaults, thefts, prostitution, and gambling offenses (Terrill, 2007). Similar to Japan in one respect, Chinese often sort out disputes informally or through village heads, avoiding the formal criminal justice system. Neighborhood committees, although not as active as in the pre-reform era, also play a role. Members often serve as the eyes and ears of local Communist Party town or county officials.

While the ratio of police officers to citizens has gradually increased—they were around 14 for every 10,000 citizens in 2006—they are just one quarter of the ratio in the United States. In addition, Tanner (2006) reported that according to official reports the total personnel for public security was around 1,800,000 individuals. A major issue in understanding the role of police in China is the interlocking and overlapping system between local party officials and the public security forces within their communities. Theoretically, the Ministry of Public Security at the national level controls local public security bureaus throughout the nation, but the picture is more complicated. In reality, the local authorities expect significant influence over the police within their realms (Tanner, 2006).

During the 1950s, the Stalin model and the influence of the Soviet Union was evident in the way police were organized and undertook their duties, but the professionalization of police after the Cultural Revolution has included police universities, police academics, and an overall effort to improve the training of law enforcement personnel. The Stalin model was vertical or top-down like that found in the K.G.B., but the model in China gives a lot of power to local government officials. Local rule has meant giving control over police training, budgets, leadership, and promotions for many decades. Given the formal national structure of the Ministry of Public Security, along with the powerful influence of local government officials, the police find themselves caught between these sources of influence. Tanner (2006) maintains that the national influence pales compared to the local influence.

While the ratio of police to citizens nationwide is very modest compared to the United States, there is enormous variability across the county. For example, in Hunan Province the ratio is just 7 to 10,000, while in Beijing and the large cities the ratio is much higher. Also, it is not surprising that the quality of training varies enormously in China due to the variation of provincial and county budgets. As a consequence, the training and education of police is still a work in progress.

It is important to keep in mind that it has just been 40 years since the end of the upheavals of the Cultural Revolution in which many police departments were not ever operational. In the present period, the goals or mission of public security are still vague and need clarification. In turn, this has weakened the effectiveness of police and even indirectly contributed to the abuse of their powers. Weak oversight of public security operations have also created problems in Chinese law enforcement. Tanner (2006) notes that police activities are often confidential and lack transparency. The media in China are censored so they may or may not expose police abuse or corruption. At the local grassroots level, police misbehavior may escape the scrutiny of supervisors. To be an effective supervisor requires excellent training and incentives.

The Chinese State Security agency operates with even less transparency than the Public Security Agency. Massive funding has gone into internal security and Anderlini and Hille (2011) claim that the budget of 624.4 billion yuan exceeds the country's announced military budget. Major security operations included the 2008 Olympics, the 1989 Tiananmen Square Massacre, the Shanghai World Expo of 2010, and the security linked to the jailed 2010 Noble Peace Prize winner Liu Xiaobo, among other concerns. Kristof (1991), in describing the State Security Ministry, stated that it represented the acme of secrecy in an already secretive bureaucracy. It is located in a facility next to Tiananmen Square in a large walled compound. Although State Security sends spies abroad, its main task is to identify foreign spies in China. Staff in all the major cities of China monitor political troublemakers, religious figures, applicants for foreign travel, and almost every type of foreigner. Many of the staff members are younger and better educated than their colleagues in the Public Security Ministry.

The *Wall Street Journal* reporter Kathy Chen's encounters with State Security personnel in the late 1990s are illustrative (Chen, 1998). She described a variety of incidents including an attempt to interview students at Beijing University at the time of the anniversary of the 1989 Tiananmen Square Massacre. Dressed like a coed, she managed to interview two students concerning their feelings toward the anniversary. She sensed she was being watched and saw the "winking infrared eye" of an agent's camera behind her. One agent circled in a motorcycle and a dozen men moved in, herding the students in a different direction. She never saw the students again and the agents detained her over a lengthy evening. Other foreign reporters have been frequently detained and the State Security Agency cites laws that can make it illegal to interview any Chinese without permission, travel outside of certain prescribed areas or to take pictures of an airport or certain government buildings. Chen (1998) commented that the State Security's harassment of foreigners, reporters, dissidents, and perceived troublemakers was a constant reminder of the paranoia of China's authoritarian leadership.

In recent years, thousands of surveillance cameras have been installed in cities across China. Bradsher (2007) reported that 20,000 had been installed along the streets of the booming city of Shenzen. In the larger picture of surveillance security, experts claim that the overall endeavor represented the world's largest computer technology effort to date to track a population. In an article in 2010 by Michael Wines, he gave a breakdown of surveillance security in cities and cited that over 7 million security cameras had been installed nationwide, with over 470,000 in Beijing alone. Turmoil in cities where the government has experienced unrest have been targeted for surveillance. For example, Urumqi, despite its modest size, had over 47,000 cameras installed. Informants have been hired and added to security payrolls. The "Great Firewall" of China, a filtering system that helps block websites, has disrupted and shut down many electronic communicators, including cell phone communications. Many cybercops are employed by the government (Anderlini and Hille, 2011). The *New York Times* reported that many email accounts had been hit by hackers in China (Jacobs, 2010).

On a personal note, when I arrived in Beijing in 1986 for my month-long series of lectures at the People's Police Officers University, I was quietly informed by my contact, the Chinese woman scholar who had contacted me after reading one of my books, that everything I said to anyone would be fed back to the top administrator at the university. I was told that it was standard practice and to not take it personally.

# Strike Hard Campaigns

The Chinese government has reined in some of its more dramatic attempts to fight crime such as the *yanda* (which means "harsh"), known as "strike hard" campaigns, along with the "shame parades." In the latter, offenders are transported around in cities in open flatbed trucks with giant placards around their necks noting their offenses. The government's high profile effort was designed to deter future offenders.

For many years, public shaming has been a time-honored tool of Chinese law enforcement. In 2010, the Ministry of Public Security finally ordered an end to this widespread practice and gave orders to enforce laws in a "rational, calm and civilized manner" (Jacobs, 2010). In addition to parading alleged offenders publicly in streets and in sports stadiums, police in Hunan Province posted photographs of suspected prostitutes on the Internet. In other cities, names and addresses of convicted sex workers (along with their clients' names) were posted. The public response was outrage and took the form of questioning why corrupt officials weren't being posted. Directives against the humiliation of suspects have been passed down for years, but local authorities often ignore them (Jacobs, 2010).

"Strike hard" policing began in the 1970s and it identifies crimes for intensive, focused, fixed-term, and special targeting (Tanner, 2005). These campaigns involved large numbers of arrests, swift trials, weak procedural safeguards, and severe punishments, including executions. An individual arrested in a strike hard campaign could count on a more severe penalty than during a different period of time. These endeavors have been associated with Mao's mass mobilization campaigns—a hallmark of his ongoing revolutionary fervor. Shame parades were only recently discontinued. Typically, after the offenders had been transported openly on trucks through a city, they were brought into giant sports stadiums where their misdeeds were recounted. Then they were promptly taken outside and, not infrequently, shot to death. Photography and billboards offered photos of the offenders listing their crimes and punishment. Tanner (2005) argued that the use of these campaigns was in response to the low ratio of police officers to citizens and required the police to rely on the active support of "nonprofessional citizen security activists" to help maintain order. Another factor appears to have been the attempt to enlist the support of the law-abiding public to cooperate with the government against criminals. In addition, these campaigns have been organized under the theory that they were a deterrent to crime and disorder. This assumption appears to have adopted the rational theory of deterrence, which claims that offenders and prospective criminals calculate their actions in response to the severity of punishment they would face if caught (Tanner, 2005). Many criminologists are doubtful of the validity of this theory. The large-scale use of the death penalty during these campaigns has been justified by the government despite worldwide criticism from organizations such as Amnesty International. But death penalty cases have declined in the last few years.

A different, perhaps complimentary, view of these campaigns has been offered by Trevaskes (2010). In her view, the police have been hobbled in fighting crime in the transitional economy by the overarching political importance attached to this policy of punishing crime "severely and swiftly." The frequent employment of "strike hard" created a mentality that employs "political struggle" as its basic characteristic. Some of the campaigns ran up to three years and many crimes were subjected to this ideologically shaped strategy. Included were robbery, rape, homicide, assault, gambling, kidnapping, arson, crimes committed by crime syndicates, drug manufacturing and trafficking, and even lesser crimes such as property crime and major theft. Unquestionably, crime rates have risen since the opening up of the market economy. Trevaskes (2010) reported that a confidential document of the Party Central Committee stated that there were 64,000 cases of serious crime in 1982 but that number had risen to over 1,000,000 by 1999, a 1,460 percent increase. For example, in two provinces, Yunan and Sichuan, significant increases of crime were recorded in police files. In Yunan, the increase from 1979 to 2001 was 690 percent. In Sichuan, there were 3,000 persons murdered between 1980 and 1983, but in the year 2000, 3,845 were murdered in Sichuan Province for that year alone. These numbers are all in the context of the fact that police routinely underreport crime (Trevaskes, 2010). Over the past 25 years, using a variety of estimates, it appears that around 250,000 people have been sentenced to death. A number of authorities and scholars have pointed out that many high-ranking police officials have been critical of the strike hard or campaign-style policing tactics. Senior police, some who had been strong supporters of strike hard, became severe critics following the 2001–2003 campaign, which failed to improve public order (Trevaskes, 2010). Furthermore, the professionalization of policing has contributed to the decline of strike hard campaigns. Publicly, other Chinese criminal justice practitioners in recent years have begun to express their disillusionment with these campaigns. Trevaskes (2010) quoted from *Peoples Daily*, the Communist Party's own media vehicle:

> Strike hard is a vicious cycle, it's a treadmill that we can't get off—
> the more we attack the busier we get, the harder it is to keep up with
> the attacks, and the harder it is to prevent further crimes from oc-
> curring. (p.123)

One colleague of a police officer killed in the line of duty blamed the strike
hard policy for his fellow officer's death (Smith, 2001). The spirit of strike hard
had caused him to overextend himself. Lacking access to the police station's
only gun, Chang Dongqing picked up a long iron rod and less than an hour later
he was killed by a shotgun blast. In 2001, he was one of hundreds of officers
who died in that year's campaign of frenzied police activity. The percentage of
police killed during the early years of the twenty-first century was more than
ten times as many as during the Mao era. Tanner (2006) stated that from 1990
to 2006, 7,000 died on duty and 30,000 were injured in deliberate attacks.

Police are mostly unarmed and lack sizeable numbers, struggling against increasingly armed criminals. With police a officer to citizen ratio of just 6 to 10,000
(as noted earlier), and with shoestring budgets, the strike hard campaigns were
designed to offset these weaknesses in law enforcement. Government leaders have
been reluctant to arm their poorly paid and poorly trained police forces, fearing
that more guns in their hands would lead to a rise in extrajudicial killings and
crimes by police who may be tied to local organized crime groups (Smith, 2001).
Now, scholars like Trevaskes (2010) believe that the government and the Ministry of Public Security is trying to rebalance sentencing and punishment policies
by treating some offenses with greater leniency and retaining severe sentences for
a more restricted group of offenses. In the process there appears to be a reduction or perhaps integration of the strike hard policy into everyday policing. The
growth of professionalism and better training of police may be allowing this to occur.

Another challenge for public security officials in China are the huge numbers of activist gatherings, riots, and the large numbers of Chinese citizens
taking to the streets to express their resentments (Tanner, 2006). The number
of protests have continued to surge over the past 20 years. Police statistics
showed what they refer to as "mass incidents" as increasing from 8,700 in 1993
to 74,000 by 2004. Furious at lost jobs, unpaid wages, confiscated land, and
corrupt officials, these large-scale demonstrations have sometimes resulted in
officials caving into demands, and this has prompted even greater protests
(Tanner, 2006). In the last few years, police have been instructed to use force
reluctantly and cordon off non-violent protests in an effort to avoid inflaming
situations involving protesters. In 2005, in the province of Zhejiang, police
tried to control older demonstrators who were trying to shut down chemical
factories that they claimed were destroying their crops, causing still births, and

severely polluting the water. Police actions backfired, creating a riot, and 50 police were wounded.

In an incident back in 1999, public security police took four farmers deemed trouble-makers and drove them in a van to an isolated rice field hidden by trees and riddled them with bullets (Rosenthal, 1999). The bodies were cremated and the police believed that was the end of it. It was not that unusual, according to villagers in Zhanlong, that the police had acted illegally in engaging in harassment and summary executions in this rural town in Guangdong Province. At that point in history, citizens in this region had understood that police were supported by their superiors for such "swift" justice and that they even received $1,200 bonuses. Despite the frequency of such abuse of police power, on this occasion the matter did not go away. With a high-powered Beijing lawyer, the relatives, mostly illiterate, waged a year-long campaign for justice and an aggressive reporter exposed the heinous crime. In all, seven police officers were tried and convicted of murder—a rare spotlight at the time on criminal behavior on the part of police (Rosenthal, 1999).

Another practice at the time, in the same county, involved officers confiscating property, firing workers, and detaining or even physically punishing local citizens for the slightest provocation. Taxi drivers often refused to enter cities like Puning, the county seat of Zhanlong, citing examples of police stopping taxis, holding licenses, or even confiscating cars if they felt the drivers had no business being in the city.

# Re-education Reform through Labor and Incarceration

Longstanding policies of "reeducation through labor" and "reform through labor" have come under strong criticism from international critics for their fundamental abuses of due process. They are devices or tools of the Ministry of Public Security in which the individual is sent directly to a labor prison without the benefit of a judicial hearing. Re-education through labor needs to be distinguished from reform through labor. Re-education through labor's history goes back to 1957. The policy allows for deprivation of freedom and being sent to a labor prison camp for between one and three years under seven circumstances (Chen, 2004). For example, a person might be identified as a "counter-revolutionary" or "anti-party element." Another example would be if an individual refused to work with his work unit or disrupted production at a factory. In recent years, the person has the right to appeal for judicial review.

It represents the most severe form of punishment in China, without the person passing through the judicial system or any trial.

One major critic of the policy of reform through labor has been Harry Wu, who compared the Chinese penal system to the Soviet Gulag. Wu claimed that the only difference was that the Chinese system combined labor with brutality. He argued in well-publicized writings and lectures that the products of a prisoner's labor were sold in domestic and foreign markets and were a critical component of China's national economy (Dutton & Zhangrun, 2005). Although the government continues to promise the rule of law, the case of Mr. Li is a reminder of how the system works (Yardley, 2005). Forty years of age and well dressed, Mr. Li spent two years in Shandong No. 2 Labor Re-education Camp. He was one of the followers of Falun Gong, many of whom were jailed without trial. The government considers Falun Gong a dangerous cult, but has never provided evidence to back up its claim. Shandong No. 2 is a vast penal system and locked inside its various prisons are over 300,000 prostitutes, drug users, petty criminals, and political prisoners—all stripped of any legal rights. As previously noted, the Communist Party is under intense international pressure to abandon this endeavor, yet it is apparently reluctant to give up this weapon of security and political control (Yardley, 2005). Falun Gong made the headlines in April of 1999 when 10,000 followers held an unannounced protest in Beijing, surprising the authorities. Immediately the government cracked down. Officially an anti-cult law was approved months later, well after thousands of Falun Gong were sentenced to reform through labor. John Kamm, the executive director of the Dui Hua Foundation of Human Rights, was quoted as saying "pigs will fly" before the Chinese government will ratify the United Nation's International Covenant on Civil and Political Rights, given both the reform through labor and re-education through labor policies. Both policies give police the arbitrary power of placing a person in a labor camp without filing criminal charges and without having the person pass through the judicial system.

All inmates are expected to do manual labor in the more than 300 prisons. Some inmates have described mild conditions, but others have reported harsh conditions inside these institutions.

# Imprisonment

In addition to reform through labor, the Chinese also have a more traditional imprisonment. NationMaster.com (2011) estimated that, overall,

1,549,000 persons were in confinement of some type in China—this included individuals in prisons and in reform through labor camps.

A fuller analysis by Seymour (2005) estimated the size of the prison population over recent years as follows: in 1998 a publication claimed that there were about 1,250 prisons—including both reform through labor institutions and other prisons. If one included jails and other institutions, this would mean a grand total of around 3,000 units. As Seymour (2005) observed, it is difficult to come up with a number for the total size of those incarcerated. Officially the total number that entered the system of both prison and reform through labor camps was reported to be around 5.92 million individuals for the period of 1979 to 1998. The ratio of staff to prisoners, assuming a one to five ratio, means that there were about 300,000 corrections personnel for the entire country in 2003. Overall, Seymour gave the rate of imprisonment as approximately 160 per 100,000 population for 2003. From this early period of the twenty-first century, the prison population has been leveling off for a number of years. The number of women offenders, however, has been increasing over the past decade. For 2002, it was reported that less than 5 percent of women were in correctional institutions (Seymour, 2005). A significant number of the women were incarcerated for drug offenses. It is clear that while those incarcerated are primarily criminals in the usual meaning, there are significant numbers that are probably imprisoned due to political and religious reasons. The politically active regions of Tibet and Xinjiang, discussed earlier, have resulted in crackdowns by Chinese police, and unknown numbers have been imprisoned there.

Historically in China, the prison was viewed as a vehicle for pursuing a traditional idea of an "ordered and cohesive social body governed by the rule of virtue" (Dikotter, 2005). Confucian ideas have permeated the Chinese approach to corrections. Punishment should be a tool for educating people and whether it is the reform through labor device or straight improvement, the underlying Confucian idea is theoretically included. Punishment is supposed to educate and reform the person, and the norms of society were to be internalized by the offender. Practice was seen as more important than belief, and it was the responsibility of the state to provide a clear set of rules for proper conduct (Dikotter, 2005). All this was theoretical and the reality for Chinese prisons has been recidivism rates not unlike those of other countries including Japan and the United States, i.e., rates above 50 percent. Prisoners who were skilled at practicing, and sometimes faking, contrition were given earlier release, and some of those same inmates were among the most skilled criminals and returned to a life of crime upon release.

In 1994, a new law was created that changed the reform through labor laws framework. This law continues in some form to the present day despite worldwide criticism. The law essentially provided a "widening of the net" (Dutton & Zhargrun, 2005). Dutton and Zhargrun argue that attempts to change the reform through labor law were basically important in their impact on subsequently released inmates. In general, incarceration in China takes two forms— detention and prison. Detention is under the auspices of the Ministry of Public Security, while the prison sector falls under the Ministry of Justice. Chinese detention centers, unlike those in the United States, hold suspects and convicts. The Chinese law has two types of detention. One type is administrative detention, where the person receives labor education at a "reform through reeducation" institution, and the other is labor reform in a prison under the control of the Ministry of Justice. Ostensibly they are quite different (Dutton & Zhargrun, 2005). Earlier in history, at the time of Mao, imprisonment was used as a device to safeguard the political power of the Communist Party leadership (Seymour, 2005).

Another controversial prison issue that has gathered worldwide criticism is the donation and harvesting of organs from executed prisoners (Wong, 2009). The government was trying to change the system whereby organs taken from executed offenders sometimes ended up with black market sellers. As in other countries, there have been shortages of donors; 1.5 million Chinese need transplants annually but only 10,000 are performed due to shortages. The *Wall Street Journal* (Wang, 2009) estimated that 65 percent of organs come from executed prisoners. In concluding the discussion on imprisonment, I will point to a case of a former prison officer who exposed brutality and corruption within the system (SOH Network, 2010). Mr. Hu offered this account to SOH Radio: he claimed there was systematic corruption and he became disenchanted with illegal and marginal practices. He had also been a Communist Party member as a teacher and a Party cadre. In explaining his experience working in the prison system, he offered that "anyone with a hint of humanity would struggle to work for reform in the penal system." There was bribery, corruption, and beatings. In addition, some prison officials had the power to reduce prison terms, and they took advantage of it. They sometimes deceived the wives of prisoners and hinted that if the wife slept with the official, the husband's prison term would be shortened. Mr. Hu went on to describe a flawed training system that encouraged unfit and violent prison guards (SOH Network, 2010). Many who entered were unqualified and cheating was widespread on entrance exams. Some prison guards were former soldiers and brought brutality to the institutions. Hu gave up his job in exchange for "freedom and decency."

# Drug Trafficking

Hays (2011) noted that when Mao emerged in 1949 to lead the communists, there were about 20 million drug users in China. Instituting a harsh crackdown, including executions, he virtually eradicated the problem overnight. However, when the opening up or the reform period started in the 1980s under Deng Xiaping, border controls weakened and the drug trade began to flourish. Wikipedia (2011) stated that China offered a huge route for Southeast Asian heroin headed for various international markets. Heroin frequently crossed borders between Afghanistan, Pakistan, Tajikistan, and Myanmar (Burma). Drug traffickers have taken advantage of the many large ports of Qingdao, Shanghai, Tianjin, and Guangdong to move heroin along maritime routes.

One can break down the various drugs, such as cannabis, ephedra, opium, and synthetic drugs, and help illustrate the problem. Cannabis grows naturally throughout southwestern China, and in 2002, approximately 1.3 metric tons were seized by Chinese authorities—much of it cultivated for domestic use in Xinjiang and Yunan provinces. Hays (2011) stated that marijuana grows wild everywhere. Some Turkic speakers in Xinjiang (Uighurs) smoke hash. Ephedra farms are operated by the government and are under strict government control. Active alkaloids such as pseudoephedrine are chemically extracted for pharmaceutical purposes, but it also grows wild in northern areas of China. Opium cultivation is now negligible in China, and where it is grown, it is grown illicitly in remote areas of Yunan, Ningxia, and Inner Mongolia. Some historians state that opium first came to China by returning sailors or Tibetan priests from Africa or India as early as the first century B.C.E. The British supplied opium in China and actively marketed it, and it was popular with rich and poor.

Synthetic drugs such as crystal methamphetamine are made available from chemicals such as pseudoephedrine and ephedrine. There is an unrestricted availability of it and a large-trade exists. Organized crime groups in Hong Kong, Taiwan, and Japan have contributed to the problem. These synthetic drugs have been popular in the big cities of Beijing, Shanghai, Nanjing, and Guangzhou. From 1991 to 2003, the Chinese government reported that arrests increased from 5,285 to 25,879. Officially there are 900,000 registered drug addicts in China, but of course the actual number of addicts is far higher—some estimates go as high as 12 million.

In the region near the border of Myanmar (formerly Burma) the confluence of poverty, drugs, and HIV was reported on by Rosenthal (2001). An impoverished Yi minority, living in mud houses and using donkey carts for work and transportation, sat directly on a major drug route that connected Myanmar with China's northern city of Butuo. Public security officers claimed that in this small community of 10,000 individuals, poorly educated youth used heroin in response to their boredom, but also sold it as a way to make money as traffickers. Not only were there significant annual deaths from overdoses (around 20), but hundreds were carrying HIV, the virus that causes AIDS. Initially officials denied the problem but the numbers increased rapidly and Doctors Without Borders helped publicize the plight of the infected and those addicted.

As in many parts of the world, the enormous sums of money to be gained from the drug trade seduced Chinese into the illegal activity. French (2004) described the problem in Banlao, an impoverished rural area, again near the Myanmar border. Authorities stated that 10 percent of China's illegal narcotics traffic entered through the nearby Lancang Prefecture, and 85 percent of the arrests were in this village bordering Yunan Province. Local residents reported that perhaps 70 percent of the shops (many upscale) had been built by people who made their money from the illegal heroin trade (French, 2004). Locals claimed that around 1 million Chinese yuan (around $120,000) was not an uncommon payment for those willing to risk the 20-mile venture across the border into Myanmar and then arrange the sale to crime syndicates for export. Another perspective on the scale of the drug problem was offered by Trevaskes (2010). She stated that the drug lords enjoyed outstanding success in controlling the heroin market from the 1990s. One drug kingpin in Yunan Province was convicted for bringing 100 tons of heroin into China over a period of years. During the period from 1982 until 2005, public security officers cracked 166,500 major drug cases involving over 220,000 persons. Due to Thailand's success in limiting the flow of heroin in the 1990s, much of Myanmar's heroin was rerouted through China (Trevaskes, 2010).

One of the campaign style policing efforts during the 2005–2007 period was named "the people's war on drugs" (Trevaskes, 2010). The model was described as "comprehensive management of public order" (CMPO), an interagency cooperative effort that focused on both prevention and punishment. The CMPO focused on a combination of "moral, material, and coercive" approaches. It drew on an historical framework for identification and control of social deviance at a local level with formal intervention kicking in when matters worsened (Trevaskes, 2010). As the first line of defense, it focused on strengthening basic local community organization along with local public security bureaus. It involved maintaining the household register and education, particularly for juveniles. At the second line of defense, the framework called for use of administrating detention, investigation of offenders, and repatriation of juvenile delinquents, prostitutes, transients, and vagrants suspected of criminal activity. The CMPO concept has been a mainstay since the early 1980s.

Around 2006, the Chinese began international cooperation and in that year extradited 37 Chinese drug kingpins from nearby countries. In summary, despite the Chinese governments aggressive attack on the illegal drug trade, the scale of the problem has increased and has presented a major obstacle to the country's economic and social well being (Trevaskes, 2010).

# High-Profile Cases and the Role of Defense Lawyers in China

## High-Profile Cases

Jerome Cohen's (2005) article on "barefoot lawyers" brought to my attention the now celebrated case of lawyer Chen Guangcheng, a self-trained lawyer in the impoverished Yinan county in Shandong Province. *Newsweek* focused on him in an article on rural activists who struggled against the illegal activities of local officials. As Cohen noted in his article, "high officials speak beautiful words, but local officials do whatever they wish." Philip Pan (2008) in his wonderful book on the lives of individuals' struggles in the post-Mao period offered a summary of lawyer Chen's struggle for justice:

> Even before graduating, Chen began to develop a reputation back home as someone who understood the law and wasn't afraid to stand up to the government. The fact that he was blind only enhanced people's respect for him. They understood the difficulties faced by the disabled, especially in backward and impoverished villages like Dongshigu, and they admired Chen for making something of himself despite these challenges. At first he was known as a legal advocate for people with disabilities. If officials could not provide better services for the disabled, he argued in court again and again, they should at least stop collecting taxes from them. Judges sympathized with his cause, handing him victories in three cases. But then the party bosses instructed the courts to stop accepting any more of his lawsuits; apparently, they were worried about the loss of tax revenues.

> Word of Chen's success spread, though, and residents began seeking his legal advice on other matters. In 2002, he helped organize dozens of villages in a petition campaign to shut down a paper mill that was dumping black noxious wastewater into a local river, destroying crops, killing fish and turtles, and making residents sick. When the government refused to act, because a party official owned the mill, Chen found another solution, persuading a British aid agency to fund the construction of a new well, complete with pipelines for irrigation and drinking water. (p. 297)

As his career unfolded, Chen continued to anger and embarrass local officials. A problem arose when a man from Dongshigu called and told him that couples in the village with more than one child were being contacted by village officials, they were taking either the mother or father away to be sterilized. Lawyer Chen knew that the government had outlawed forced sterilization and abortion years earlier, but local officials in various parts of China had continued to defy the law. Chen decided to generate a mass legal challenge to the state's power to compel sterilization and abortion (Pan, 2008). He helped many local victims bring lawsuits against offending officials. In addition, given the slowness of the legal process, he went to Beijing as a petitioner—a practice that had gone on for centuries (Cohen, 2005). He drew on the Internet and foreign correspondents in his quest for justice. Linyi County officials fought back, and without legal authority, a mob of around 200 (supported by city, county, and town officials and their hoodlums) surrounded his poor farmhouse. They confined him and his wife around the clock. Their phone was disconnected and their cell phones were confiscated. The blind lawyer's specially adapted IBM computer was removed. In addition, an eight-hour search of his farmhouse took place, but no search warrant or any legal documents were ever presented. Outsiders were not allowed to visit and supporters were detained or beaten by local police and organized mobs (Cohen, 2005). Even though Chen Guangcheng himself was beaten and bloodied, no doctor was allowed to administer treatment.

In 2006, in what experts called a sham trial, the blind lawyer was convicted of destroying property and organizing a crowd to block traffic while he was under house arrest. After being released from jail and a 51-month sentence, he and his wife were confined to their home with no telephone or Internet access. The details of his mistreatment continued to generate widespread support for him. Some courageous citizens continued to try to visit him knowing that they risked being physically attacked by thugs (Jacobs, 2011).

While local authorities continued to prevent physical contact with Chen or his family, an online campaign generated a lot of support and shook officials beyond the county and Shandong Province. Some government-controlled media have responded, and in one instance *Global Times* noted that Chen's human rights were being abused. The *Oriental Morning News* went beyond the *Global Times'* comments and mentioned that a reporter for a publication owned by the Xinhua News Agency had been beaten while trying to visit Dong-shigu, where Chen lives. Despite the plight of Chen, government officials at the national level refused to intervene.

In a later development, near the end of 2011, the blind lawyer's struggle continued (*The Economist*, 2011). Chen escaped his house arrest, and managed to get to the American Embassy in Beijing. An uproar ensued, and after a tense standoff in which Chen wanted the Beijing authorities to protect him and his family but allow him to stay in the country, he changed his mind. He feared the Chinese would go back on any agreement and punish him. A face-saving device allowed him and his family to go to the United States as a "law student." The latter was arranged through the assistance of the prominent American-China law scholar Jerome Cohen, who arranged a scholarship at New York University law school.

A second high-profile case that attracted very wide attention in China involved a young man who killed a number of police officers in apparent retaliation for the abuse he suffered at the hands of the Public Security Bureau officers, "Confessed Police Killer Lionized by Thousands in China" read the headline story in the *Washington Post* (Fan, 2008). The account was roughly as follows:

Yang Jia slipped into the Zhabei Police Station in north Shanghai through the service entrance. A knife in his right hand and a mask over his face, he fatally stabbed four police officers on the first floor and one each on the ninth and the eleventh before finally being subdued.

Yang, 28, has confessed to the crime and is destined for execution. But in a bizarre twist that reveals the fissures that run beneath China's elaborately constructed social order, he is also an unlikely hero. Thousands of Chinese have lionized him for standing up to the security forces that are increasingly seen as a blunt instrument of the Communist Party's chief aim: to ensure its authority by maintaining stability and stifling dissent.

At one of Yang's hearings last month, hundreds of protesters descended on the Shanghai Higher People's Court, carrying signs that read "Long Live the Killer" and shouting "Down with the Communist Party" and "Down with Fascists." Many of the protesters were educated and middle-aged.

More than 4,000 people have signed an open letter posted online urging that Yang's life be spared. The letter has been erased from many

Web sites by government censors, and coverage of the case in the state-run media has been strictly controlled.

As heinous as the July 1 crime reportedly was, and despite Yang's confession, many Chinese still doubt the government's findings. Public support for Yang has been bolstered by reports that he had been mistreated by police on at least two occasions and may have been seeking revenge.

"There are many citizens who have suffered similar treatment but are too afraid to speak out," said Liu Xiaoyuan, the family's attorney. "They feel that if someone stands up to the police, he or she is fighting for justice on their behalf." (p. A13)

Many thousands of protests occur every year in China, but this case attracted particular attention as there is a widespread perception that average citizens are taken advantage of by wealthy and heavy-handed government officials. Yang was an unemployed supermarket clerk in Beijing who loved biking, hiking, and photography. In addition, he enjoyed reading, according to his MySpace blog, generated before his killing spree.

It appears that previous confrontations played into the event at the police station. Two years prior to the incident he sustained a concussion and three broken teeth in a confrontation with public security when the officers beat him for cutting in line at a train station, according to his lawyer Liu (Fan, 2008). In the previous year he was falsely accused of stealing a bicycle he had rented in Shanghai and was insulted and beaten by police. He asked for a written explanation and $30 compensation. The police offered to pay $210, but would not provide a written explanation. He refused the case, but wanted the police to acknowledge their mistake. Yang filed multiple complaints after he was harassed and claimed the offending officer should have been fired. Police claimed they "educated" him, but Yang experienced it as harassment and abuse. One online blogger stated, "Yang did what we dare not do."

Later, after the death of the police officers, he was arrested, found guilty, and sentenced to death. The case moved to the Shanghai Higher People's Court, where authorities relented to an open hearing after strong public opinion was aroused from a closed first trial. Hundreds of protestors gathered outside along with his father. In a bizarre side incident, Yang's mother, who had been absent from the outset of the legal process, turned up in a mental hospital on the outskirts of Beijing where she claimed the police had locked her up and forced her to hire a lawyer (Fan, 2008). A lawyer familiar with the case noted that although Yang was legally entitled to a psychiatric review, none was provided prior to his execution a short time later.

A third high-profile case involved Zhao Yan, a talented Chinese staff member of the Beijing Bureau of the *New York Times* (Cohen, 2006). He was detained by the Ministry of State Security on September 17, 2004, for supposedly leaking state secrets to a foreign organization, a charge that could result in a long prison sentence or possibly a death sentence. Zhao was accused of informing the *New York Times* that former President Jiang Zemin was about to leave his post as leader of the Military Affairs Commission. The report turned out to be true and this deeply angered another Chinese leader. The *New York Times* denied these allegations. While the case ostensibly involved state secrets (like many others), the process lacked transparency and Zhao was denied a lawyer. Although the police apparently lacked evidence they did not release him, but employed another tactic, which was to charge him with defrauding a friend — a crime outside the normal work of the secret police (Cohen, 2006). As the time went on, and after enormous foreign criticism, the prosecution proceeded with charges on both matters — fraud and exposing state secrets. Late in the process, on March 17, and the last day before the deadline for a trial, the Beijing Intermediate Court issued a surprising ruling — it allowed the prosecutor to withdraw the indictment on the grounds that it needed more time to investigate the fraud charge, but it made no comment concerning the state secrets matter. The judge responded to a defense inquiry as to whether or not both charges were effectively withdrawn. When the answer was yes, Mr. Zhao should have been released or at least offered a more relaxed house arrest or bail. Amazingly, nothing happened, and he was not released.

Finally, on August 25, 2006, the court acted and dismissed the state secrets charge, but sentenced him to three years in jail on the fraud charge (Yardley & Kahn, 2006). The Beijing Intermediate Court rejected the state secrets charge with strong language, stating that "the evidence is insufficient" and that "the charge for this crime cannot stand, and this court does not accept it." The defense lawyer, Mo Shaoping, commented that "this is the way they proclaim someone innocent." The international attention included lobbying on behalf of the correspondent by the Bush administration. Another defense attorney proceeded to appeal the fraud charge, which he claimed had no basis. Under Chinese law, the time served since 2004 was to count against the three-year sentence, and he was on track to be released in September of 2007.

A fourth high-profile case involved the Chinese Noble Peace Prize winner Liu Xiaobo, who was in jail at the time of the award. He was awarded the prize in Oslo, Norway, but the government did not allow him to attend, and his words at the ceremony were spoken by the actress Liv Ullman (Welgaren, Richburg, and Richards, 2010). He was honored for his campaign to bring democracy to China. Ullman read from his statement prior to commencing his jail sentence of 11 years for "political incitement." The statement read, "I have once again been shoved into the dock by the enemy mentality of the regime." "I still want to say to this regime, which is depriving me of my freedom, that I stand by my convictions—I have no enemies and no hatred." His jail term began in 2009, but his writings were published in the West in November 2011 while he was still jailed on his 11-year sentence. The author was not even aware of his English language 345-page volume, published by Harvard University Press (Alberge, 2011). The jailed dissident has been unable to communicate with his wife, and friends have been unable to reach him or his wife despite the fact that she has been charged with nothing. At the funeral of his father he was forbidden to talk with anyone. His book is said to offer a full range of his views and a penetrating analysis of Chinese culture, politics, and society. He came to the attention of authorities in 1989 during the Tiananmen Square upheaval and was sent to prison for 19 months. In 1995, he was put behind bars for seven months with no explanation offered, although it occurred after he released a petition entitled "Learn from the lesson written in blood and push democracy." Later, in 1996, he was charged with "disturbing the public order" and put in a "re-education labor camp" for three more years. During his time in the labor facility, he wrote a number of poems including one dedicated to his wife entitled "Your Lifelong Prisoner." Perry Link, the editor of the new book, commented that it was during the period of confinement in the prison camp during the late 1990s that Xiaobo's humane values emerged when he and Liu Xia, a poet, fell in love and married. His wife was allowed to visit once a month, and she recounted how there were numerous instances of his descriptions of police brutality and the persecution of individuals for their "words" (Alberge, 2011).

The fifth case that is highlighted in this chapter is that of the Chinese artist and dissident Ai Weiwei (Wines, 2010). He has been an outspoken critic of Chinese political and social restrictions on citizens, and famous during the Chinese Olympics for being one of the designers of the Birds Nest Stadium. Also known as a filmmaker, architect, and performance artist, he was arrested as he attempted to leave his home and fly to Shanghai. He was placed under house arrest and, typical of many Chinese arrests, nothing was disclosed by the authorities as to why he was arrested. Mr. Ai himself speculated that he had offended high-ranking officials in Shanghai over a million dollar studio that they had asked him to create and then later demolished. The artist had been subjected to previous difficult encounters with the authorities over his artistic endeavors, alternating between being tolerated and hectored by high officials (Wines, 2010). The previous year, 2010, he had gone to Munich to stage a major exhibit which blamed the Chinese government for the deaths of children in the 2008 Sichuan earthquake. At the time of the earthquake incident, parents had charged local officials with shoddy construction of schoolhouses. In another incident, he blogged on the case of Yang Jia (mentioned earlier in this chapter). In an interview, he stated: "They put you under house arrest or they make you disappear, that's all they can do. There's no facing the issue and discussing it—it's all a very simple treatment" (Wines, 2010).

After being held for over 80 days without being charged, he was released in June 2010 from detention, but said he could not talk about his case. Although released on bail, they imposed a year-long restriction on his movements and he was prohibited from interfering with an investigation against him on tax evasion (Jacobs, 2011). It appeared that he had been instructed that his freedom was dependent on his ability to censor himself. Supporters and admirers were concerned that this outspoken critic had been silenced. The government had reportedly gained a confession of his "crimes."

In a report by Gladstone in August 2011, the artist broke his silence on political matters for the first time since he had been released from prison, but tax evasion charges against him were still pending. In a Twitter post, Mr. Ai claimed "four business colleagues had been illegally detained because of me" (Gladstone, 2011). The artist went on to write that the colleagues had experienced serious suffering in the form of "huge mental devastation and physical torture." One of the four, a Mr. Liu, had suffered a heart attack during detention and had come close to death. Ai Weiwei was offered a lectureship at the Berlin University of the Arts for 2012, but he was unsure if the authorities would let him leave the country. A later report in the *Guardian* indicated that the artist was facing a 15 million yuan tax bill as a result of tax evasion charges. Supporters found creative ways to provide 8 million yuan in support of his tax bill. In a newer charge that jeopardized his liberty, he was being investigated for spreading pornography—for a photo entitled "one tiger eight breasts," which revealed him naked with four women. It was observed on the Internet (Watts, 2011).

The next case I wish to explore, the sixth, involves a well-known Chinese democracy activist who was sentenced to ten years in jail (Jacobs, 2011). Liu Xianbin, from Sichuan Province, had earlier spent nine years in jail for "organizing an illegal political party," and he was imprisoned for "writing subversion of state power"—a typically vague Chinese law. The basis for these charges were articles he wrote for overseas Chinese-language publications that focus on human rights and democracy. During the spring of 2011, more than two dozen writers, lawyers, and political advocates were detained (Jacobs, 2011). Some of those detained may have been inspired by the uprisings in the Middle East, the so-called "Arab Spring." Mr. Liu himself was arrested after the Tiananmen Square Massacre in 1989 for "counter-revolutionary propaganda and incitement" linked to posters he created calling for an end of repression.

During one of the periods that he was out of jail he signed Charter 08, an online petition calling for expanded liberties and universal suffrage. Some of his writings criticized the Communist Party. A defense lawyer argued that his writings were guaranteed under the constitution, which guarantees free speech. His wife, Chen Mingxian, stated that in his brief trial that his comments in the courtroom were frequently cut off by the judge. While out of jail for 13 months, he was often harassed by public security officers. For example, if he found work, the prospective employer was pressured into rejecting the offer to Mr. Liu. The Laogai Research Foundation (2011), founded by Harry Wu, the former prisoner of a labor camp prison, mentioned that Liu Xianbin and two fellow dissidents had filed a lawsuit in federal court in the state of Maryland. They charged that Cisco Systems had illegally cooperated with the Chinese government through its use of sophisticated surveillance technology that was used to track dissidents. Furthermore, the suit argued, the Communist Party lacked the tools to conduct these searches on its own.

The seventh high profile case is that of Liao Yiwu (2011), who has written extensively of individuals struggling to survive in the underground economy or of other accounts from the underbelly of China. He is the author of *The Corpse Walker* and *God is Red*. His eloquent writing in *The Corpse Walker* provided tales from prostitutes, narcotics addicts, and individuals hired to bury the dead. He literally walked out of China in mid-2011, and managing to slip out of the country through the vast wilderness of Yunan Province and making his way eventually to Germany. The author claimed he had resisted the temptation to leave for many years. As he stated in his essay, "I chose to stay in China, continuing to document the lives of those occupying the bottom rung of society." A more extensive quote follows from his translated article that appeared in the *New York Times* (Yiwu, 2011):

An old-fashioned writer, I seldom surf the Web, and the Arab Spring simply passed me by. Staying on the sidelines did not spare me police harassment, though. When public security officers learned that my books would be published in Germany, Taiwan and the United States, they began phoning and visiting me frequently.

In March, my police handlers stationed themselves outside by apartment to monitor my daily activities. "Publishing in the West is a violation of Chinese law," they told me. "The prison memoir tarnishes the reputation of China's prison system and 'God Is Red' distorts the party's policy on religion and promotes underground churches." If I refused to cancel my contract with Western publishers, they said, I'd face legal consequences.

Then an invitation from Salman Rushdie arrived, asking me to attend the PEN World Voices Festival in New York. I immediately contacted the local authorities to apply for permission to leave China, and booked my plane ticket. However, the day before my scheduled departure, a police officer called me to "have tea," informing me that my request had been denied. If I insisted on going to the airport, the officer told me, they would make me disappear, just like Ai Weiwei.

For a writer, especially one who aspires to bear witness to what is happening in China, freedom of speech and publication mean more than life itself. (p. A35)

In summary, he stated that he had to escape the "colossal and invisible prison called China" so that he could publish freely. In his escape, he walked through a remote border post and first traveled to Hanoi before going on to Germany. In an emotional encounter, he was greeted on July 6, 2011, by his German editor Peter Sillem. Not surprisingly, Liao Yiwu's family and girlfriend were questioned by Chinese authorities as news of his escape circulated rapidly.

The eighth case to be explored, and offered as an example of Chinese citizens' attempts to seek justice, is the case of Li Jian (Zhiqiang, 2007). It was included as part of a presentation offered by the law activist Pu Zhiqiang at the Yale University China Law Workshop. The scholar discussed the general role of the media, and the case of a man who suffered the demolition of his tiny property.

First, Pu's comments on the media observed that the Chinese constitution does guarantee freedom of expression, but that it does not work out that way in realty. Only "approved publications" can move forward, and only government agencies can receive the green light. Even when they are established, they are still subjected to oversight, so in reality there is no freedom of expression. Authorities reviewing materials for publication give greater leeway compared with earlier historical periods, but anything that questions the wisdom of the Communist Party will be censored. Some writers and journalists take risks and try to publish books and articles that they think will pass muster.

The second matter raised by Mr. Pu Zhiqiang during his Yale lecture concerned Li Jian. His small property was demolished in less than a day. He had developed a business with this property over several years, but he was unable to obtain legal relief when it was destroyed. Knowing that others shared his plight, he established a network of individuals that was appropriately titled "Network of Upholding Citizens' Rights." It was designed to serve as a vehicle for sharing views about the unlawful infringement of citizens' rights and relevant legal information. Without notice, the government shut it down. Lawyer Pu Zhiqiang was retained to bring a lawsuit in Xuanwu Court in Beijing, but without an explanation that court rejected his suit. At the next level, the Beijing No. 1 Intermediate Court was almost identical in noting "the suit does not meet the condition for the bringing of an administrative law suit." Attorney Zhiqiang (2007) stated in his article:

> The significance of these judgments is that in the name of the law, the courts have declared the reality of utter lawlessness to the public. They have told the people that court judgments can ignore the law, that when there is a conflict between power and law, there may be absolutely no room for law to exist—even if it's the so-called law that they [the powerholders] wielded the sword to make themselves!
>
> It cannot be denied that after acknowledging and accepting the corruption and arbitrariness of government organs, thinking people put their hopes for the rebuilding of social justice in the courts only on the basis of reason and there being no other alternative. They fervently hoped that courts could, in an era of social transition, lead China to realize the rule of law and constitutionalism. They wishfully believed that only the judiciary could undertake this great mission of national resurgence. (p. 61)

# Defense Lawyers

As already noted in previous chapters on China, a portrait has begun to emerge of the struggles of defense lawyers in China. The picture is evolving somewhat with China's amendment to the Law on Lawyers, but defense lawyers still run a significant risk of crossing vague boundaries as they attempt to defend their clients.

Jerome Cohen (2002), in an article for the *South China Morning Post,* offered both the strengths and weaknesses in the Chinese system. As described earlier, there has been a huge growth in the numbers of legal professionals, including thousands of new judges, prosecutors, and attorneys over the last 25 years. Many are "transforming themselves from state legal workers to increasingly recognized prosperous and semi-independent professionals" (Cohen, 2002). In addition, they are promoting international trade and foreign investment, and others are supporting the rights of women and children. Taking a significant risk, some have sought to protect workers' rights.

By 2000, some of the government's legal agencies that hire prosecutors, judges, and law professors were struggling to retain top talent as many sought independent practices. Of course, along the way, and continuing to the present time, many lawyers have had to suffer the politics, corruption, and personal influence that impacts their practices. One significant change occurred in 1996 with the Criminal Procedure Law, which conferred the right of a detained suspect to meet with his lawyers after the first interrogation or from the first day of detention. In 1998, a further revision to the law gave the family the right to retain counsel on behalf of the suspect. Later, in 2007, China amended the Law on Lawyers approved by the National People's Congress. It appeared to have made it even easier for lawyers to meet suspects and obtain evidence, and it came into effect on June 1 in 2008. At the time of the announcement, Secretary General of the Jiangxi Lawyers Association in Jiangxi Province commented that it was "big progress" (Jianhua, 2007).

Looking back to 2000, Western scholars and journalists were pointing to very serious problems for defense lawyers in China (Rosenthal, 2000). Here is how Elizabeth Rosenthal described the plight of a new idealistic attorney, Liu Jian, at that time: the firm that employed him in Nanjing sent him to a rural location to defend a local official accused of taking bribes. The attorney worked round the clock to prepare, and interviewed witnesses and reviewed documents, along with brainstorming the issues with his client. However, when the court met almost none of the 37 witnesses showed up. The prosecutor ranted at him and called him a criminal. At the end of the trial, outside the Binhai Courthouse, Liu Jian was in police custody and charged with illegally obtaining evidence. Although legal experts claimed he was innocent, he spent a hellish five months in jail. He endured beatings, day-long interrogations without food or rest. Later he stated, "I've tried not to have any contact with the criminal law since." Rosenthal (2000) summarized the problems confronted by attorneys in 2000:

> The police often refuse to let lawyers meet their clients in private or in a timely manner, despite a law giving them access within 48 hours.
>
> Lawyers are often not provided with legally guaranteed access to court material, like transcripts of confessions, medical examinations, and witness lists.
>
> Intimidation of witnesses by the local police and prosecutors often leave lawyers with few people willing to testify.
>
> "Because of these problems, it's sometimes hard to find a lawyer for criminal cases," Professor Li said, adding that the work can be dangerous. "Many lawyers are scared they could become implicated in the case and lose their livelihood." Business law is more lucrative, and safer.
>
> Gu Yongzhong, a former criminal law specialist in Beijing who now takes on criminal cases only occasionally, said: "For the amount of time it takes to prepare the case, it doesn't pay. And it's very hard to get a not guilty verdict."

Lawyers agree that the obstacles are far greater in the rural areas, where the legal training of judges and the police is often poorest. But some problems are more widespread, like the difficulty in meeting defendants, lawyers said.

Defendants in cases that are politically sensitive are rarely granted their legally guaranteed rights.

One lawyer said he had recently spent two weeks trying to meet a client detained by the Beijing Public Security Bureau, which repeatedly deflected requests and turned him away from the detention center before finally allowing the meeting.

One technique used by authorities during the new millennium, according to Cohen (2002), was to inform the family and defense lawyer that the suspect was not really detained, but was being held at a guest house run by the agency. As I commented earlier, a person might not even move through the formal judicial system, but instead be subjected to a punishment in a re-education labor camp. In bypassing the formal judicial system, the detention notice is not offered, as it is defined as a non-criminal punishment. Another device that has even been used against Communist Party members is called *shuanggui,* and can result in a form of house arrest and/or a period of incommunicable detention (Cohen, 2002).

The following is another example of a problem that is typical of the struggles faced by defense lawyers. In the late fall of 2005, the Beijing Judicial Bureau convened a hearing on a matter related to one of China's most prominent law firms (Kahn, 2005). The matter under consideration was whether the law firm would have to shut down because it failed to file a change of address form when it moved its offices. The firm's founder, Gao Zhisheng, was almost 2,000 miles away in Xinjiang at the time of the hearing. Commenting on the matter, he called it "absurd and corrupt," and he chose to spend his time with an underground Christian church group in their consideration of a case to sue the secret police. His advice was that the church group might not win, but if the group was too timid to confront the "barbaric behavior" of the police, they would be completely defeated. A strong and brusque figure, Mr. Gao traveled the nation as one of a modest number of "rights defenders" in filing lawsuits over corruption, land seizures, police abuses, and religious freedom. The Communist Party informed him to cease and desist, and the firm's suspension of their license included his personal permit to practice law. Secret police then monitored his home and followed him extensively. Mr. Gao exclaimed, "you cannot be a rights lawyer without becoming a rights case yourself" (Kahn, 2005). In a more sinister development in 2011, Hutzler reported on the torture of Mr. Zhisheng and his disappearance. His account read, "police stripped

Gao Zhisheng bare and pummeled him with handguns in holsters. For two days and nights they took turns beating him and did things he refused to describe." The victim went on to state, "that degree of cruelty—there is no way to recount it—for forty-eight hours my life hung by a thread." Gao spoke to the Associated Press much later when he seized a moment, in a nearly empty Beijing teahouse, watched by plainclothes police. Looking weary, he told the AP that over the previous 14 months police had stashed him in hostels, farm houses, apartments, and prisons in Beijing and in his native province of Shaanxi. There were periods of time in which he was not abused, followed by periods in which he was viciously attacked (Hutzler, 2011). In the early part of 2011, he disappeared and 20 months went by before he resurfaced. On December 16, 2011, La Franiere (2011) reported that he will serve three years in prison because he repeatedly violated his probation. Other rights advocates say in light of the Arab Spring, the Chinese government has increasingly used secret detentions to suppress dissidents.

This is the final high profile case. Coverage was extensive for weeks in major media outlets including the *Financial Times*, the *New York Times*, and *The Economist*, during the spring of 2012. A powerful and charismatic political leader and provincial governor, Bo Xilai was ousted from office and was under investigation by the Communist Party. He had been scheduled to rise to the highest governing body of the Chinese government, the Standing Committee of the Politburo, during the fall of 2012. Bo Xilai was faced with charges of corruption and abuse of power, but his wife, Gu Kailaj, had been charged with the murder of a British businessman, Neil Heywood. The latter event was initially covered up by police in the city of Chongqing. Reuters reported that a disagreement over money had erupted between Ms. Gu and Mr. Heywood. The British businessman had been instrumental in arranging for the couple's son to enter the prestigious private school of Harrow. Later, the son, Bo Guagua, attended Harvard for graduate school. The son, much to the disapproval of the Communist Party hierarchy, received extensive publicity for his partying and flamboyant lifestyle. As one official noted, if one is discreet Communist Party members look the other way, but Bo was often in the news. His father Bo Xilai had become highly popular as a prominent governor who supported peasants and those at the lower economic level. He developed a reputation for cracking down on organized crime, but critics pointed out that he abused his authority and imprisoned and tortured opponents. Furthermore, he resurrected the far left wing of the early Communist Party of the Mao era, much to the consternation of high ranking officials in Beijing. He arranged large scale demonstrations to encourage the Mao era propaganda. One of his top supporters had been Zhou Yongkang, head of the Ministry of Public Security and leader of China's repressive internal security and surveillance apparatus. This supporter, a sitting member of the Politburo in 2012 was scheduled to step down from this high ranking body in the fall of 2012 but there were rumors he might be removed earlier due to his support of Bo Xilai.

The next chapter provides a certain continuity in the examination of human rights, forced psychiatric hospitalizations, and the death penalty.

# Human Rights, Forced Psychiatric Hospitalizations, and the Death Penalty in China

In some respects this chapter can be viewed as an extension of earlier chapters on China, as matters of human rights and the struggles Chinese have encountered in seeking justice have already been explored to some degree. This chapter will explicitly identify issues raised by human rights organizations such as Amnesty International, Human Rights Watch, and the Dui Hua Foundation. It will then examine China's forced use of psychiatric facilities as a vehicle for repression and imprisonment. Finally, it will explore China's history and the contemporary use of the death penalty.

## Human Rights

Kristof has written eloquently about the repression and exploitation of people in various parts of the world, including Africa and Asia. Sometimes he has focused on governmental organizations. While still working as a journalist in China in 2002, he wrote about the beating of a woman, Ma Yuqin, who refused to give the authorities the names of her Christian congregation or sign a statement renouncing her faith (Kristof, 2002). Her worst memory was to hear her son being tortured in the room next to where she was being beaten, and each could hear the other's screams. A woman of great strength, she claimed she was close to death, but she was brave enough to tell her story to the *New York Times* and risk identifying herself. Other members of her church were still in prison at the time she recounted her tale. The interview took place after several church members sneaked into an unwatched farmhouse near Zhongxiang, a city 650 miles south of Beijing. Police can arrest and torture people with impunity, as previous examples in this book have demonstrated. One book, *China's New Rulers*, noted that Communist Party documents willingly identified 60,000 Chinese killed, either executed or shot by police while fleeing, between the years 1998 and 2001. Strangely, in some areas of China, Christians are free to worship, but in other areas authorities brutally crush those practicing Christianity. In the group that was initially arrested with Ms. Ma, five were sentenced to death. There is solid documentation of the many Christians and Falun Gong members that have died while imprisoned.

The Dui Hua Foundation and its director, John Kamm, investigate human rights issues all over the world. In China they sometimes investigate selected prisoners and bring those individuals to the attention of prison authorities. The organization, based in San Francisco, has been able through its network of contacts to work on an unexplored and unpublished list of various detainees who have been identified and who are imprisoned in various locations around China. These lists, generated by the database, are the foundation for pursuing inquiries. The Dui Hua Foundation has found that those detainees who were asked about tended to receive better treatment. The process has enhanced transparency and helped to secure the early release of some. A key feature, according to John Kamm (2009), is developing a dialogue with the authorities about the imprisoned parties.

One example cited by the Foundation involved parole granted to an American businessman, Jude Shao (Dui Hua News, 2008). He had been arrested in April 1998 and sentenced in March 2000 by the Shanghai Number One Intermediate People's Court. His sentence is scheduled to expire in May 2013, but he was allowed to live with his family in Shanghai after leaving Qingpu Prison on parole. He had already served 10 years in prison, more than half his sentence, and had been released on good behavior. The fact that he was willing to reside in the city where he was born was a factor in his parole offer. Stanford University classmates and former President George W. Bush weighed in on his behalf through raising the issue repeatedly with President Hu Jintao. John Kamm noted that he started working on the case in 2002 when Stanford Business School classmates persistently raised the matter. However, Kamm said the case also illustrated the perils of doing business in China, particularly if one is an ethnic Chinese. The case illustrated the arbitrariness of being convicted on economic crimes as well as political crimes. Jude Shao did not have access to a lawyer until he was brought to trial over 26 months after being incarcerated, and after being kept in solitary confinement for many months. His trial was very brief—just one day (Kamm, 2008). Even though he was able to locate the documentation of taxes paid, the appeal court ruled that the evidence was inadmissible. He had originally been charged with tax evasion. Some Chinese lawyers came to his support, but a retrial was denied and the Chinese Supreme Court eventually rejected Mr. Shao's petition. With his situation appearing dark, classmates mounted a campaign, along with Secretary of State Condoleeza Rice, President Bush, and members of Congress. Finally, just prior to the opening of the Olympics he was granted parole.

Hu Jia, a well-known human rights activist, was arrested for "inciting subversion" on December 27, 2007 (Dui Hua Foundation, 2008). Family members were notified on January 30, 2008. Historically, he had been active on behalf of victims of injustice, working with petitioners and rights lawyers, and employing the Internet to report on rights abuses throughout China. It had resulted in various confrontations with the Security Police and he had spent 200 days incommunicado in house arrest during 2006. In addition, he and his activist wife had been prevented from traveling to Europe in 2007 on the grounds of endangering state security. Hu's case became classified as a "state secret," effectively barring him from meeting with a defense lawyer (Dui Hua Foundation, 2008). This classification also meant that at trial the court was required to bar all members of the public. A few months later, Hu Jia was sentenced to three-and-a-half years in prison by the Beijing Number One Intermediate People's Court (Dui Hu Foundation, 2008). The official China news agency, Xinhua, stated, "Hu published articles on overseas-run websites, made comments in interviews with foreign media, and reportedly instigated other people to subvert the state's political power and socialist system." The Dui Hua Foundation criticized the conviction on several grounds. First, they noted it took only 98 days from the point of being jailed to the court's verdict— an unusually short time given China's Criminal Proceeding Law with its numerous provisions that allow for extensions. Secondly, the government press, Xinhua, argued that he was given a light sentence, but China's law for "inciting subversion" states the maximum sentence is five years. In comparison with 48 other comparable cases, in a database generated by the Dui Hua Foundation, the median punishment was three-and-one-half years. However, the difficulty in comparing cases is tied to the fact that Chinese courts don't reveal the considerations or analysis that go into sentencing practices. In closing, the Dui Hua Foundation believes the case was handled rapidly and the sentence was not lenient.

Not surprisingly, the United Nations investigation conducted by Manfred Nowak in 2005 into the treatment of offenders in China found "widespread" use of torture by Chinese law enforcement (Kahn, 2005). Nowak (Kahn, 2005) commented in his report that:

> "obtaining confessions" and fighting "deviant behavior" continued to be central goals of China's criminal justice system. The police and prison guards are pushed to extract admissions of guilt and are rarely

punished for using electric shock, sleep deprivation and submersion in water or sewage. (p. A1)

Human Rights Watch has been active in China for 30 years, and Nicholas Bequelin (2010) has been focusing on China for the organization. In a lecture at Yale University he offered some observations concerning his work. He stated, "political change comes from the bottom up" in response to the question "how much effort does China put into legal reform?" In addition, he noted that Human Rights Watch did have empirical data in the form of first-hand interviews with citizens to address these issues and that in general there was a large gap between what the government states and what is happening on the ground. Overall, there is a lot of flux in the system, but in views shared by other scholars he commented that the "goal of the Communist Party is to stay in power." Controlling the media is critical for the government, and occasionally when it feels it can give ground it does, as in the case of the Sichuan earthquake disaster when many died. Mr. Bequelin's sense of the situation was that the 2010 time period represented a crossroads for legal reform, but he was doubtful that the government would move forward. Essentially, the Communist Party leadership was worried about risking additional reforms. In most respects legal reform was not in the interests of the Party. Subsequent developments in 2011 and 2012 and the heavy repression and imprisonment of dissidents have supported his views as voiced in 2010. Deng Xiaoping, in the 1980s, took a huge gamble in modernizing China, and later when China joined the World Trade Organization, and there was a general recognition that this increased the risk of active dissent since and that workers would want better treatment. Consequently, leaders in the past 20 years appear to want to preserve the status quo. Under the guise of "social harmony" the government suppresses a lot of things, but despite crackdowns in high-profile cases, some very modest improvement has taken place in China over the past several decades, according to Bequelin. The future, however, in this context has not unfolded in a promising manner. The newly identified Chinese leaders scheduled to take over from Hu Jintao are "consensus" candidates, not reform-minded. The upshot of Bequelin's comments was that the future leaders would have limited power within the ranks of the top. Governing members of the Politboro have a security focus and will not allow reforms to advance.

Pu Zhiqiang (2006), in a comment for the *New York Review of Books*, described his encounter with police in Beijing in an article entitled "Deputy Chief Sun Di of Department #1 of the Beijing Public Security Bureau": "He ordered me, 'controlled' in police lingo, to go to the Fanjiacun police station in the Feng Tai District of Beijing. This practical action, although it violated basic human rights, was taken in support of the 'stability' that the violent suppression at Tiananmen had brought about." Legal activist Pu Zhiqiang (2006) provided this historical background to his being ordered to the police station:

> I recall the early hours of June 4, 1989. The few thousand students and other citizens who refused to disperse remained huddled at the north face of the Martyrs' Monument in Tiananmen Square. The glare of fires leaped skyward and gunfire crackled. The pine hedges that lined the square had been set ablaze while loudspeakers screeched their mordant warnings. The bloodbath on outlying roads had already exceeded anyone's counting. Martial law troops had taken up their staging positions around the square, awaiting final orders, largely invisible except for the steely green glint that their helmets reflected from the light of the fires. It was then that I turned to a friend and commented that the Martyrs' Monument might soon be witness to our deaths, but that if not, I would come back to this place every year on this date to remember the victims. (p. 1)

Pu Zhiqiang recounted his difficulties in keeping his promise to go to Tiananmen on the anniversary of the massacre, as public security repeatedly interrogated him and accompanied him "for his own safety"—effectively preventing him from joining others at the site of the Tiananmen Square bloodshed. His trouble with police was precipitated by his sharing text messages sent to friends concerning the anniversary with the police. He pointedly noted during one of his verbal exchanges with the police that he wanted to be aboveboard and that since he had been under surveillance for some period of time he didn't want any misunderstandings concerning his text messages. In addition, he commented that text messaging was legal in China and that it was legal to go to Tiananmen Square on June 3, and therefore the police demanding his presence was superfluous. Furthermore, for the police to come to his residence in the middle of the night, without legal documents, asking for a "chat" was an illegal use of police power. He was told to lower his profile and stop sending text messages. He was briefly free to go, but hours later the police showed up again and prevented him from leaving his residence to go to Tiananmen Square for the anniversary gathering. Only a day later was he free to leave his residence.

An interesting issue concerning how various legal activists approach cases in China was offered by Pils (2006) in a lecture at Yale University. The Cornell University scholar noted that some activists who might be called radical would take on cases of political persecution that had virtually no hope of being successfully litigated through the courts. But from that perspective, it would be wrong not to defend these individuals who were in need of strong support. In other words, it would border on dishonesty not to defend them. A more conservative approach to those who needed defense counsel would be focus on violations of people's rights, but be able to cite the appropriate articles within the Chinese constitution to argue for justice. The latter approach has not been without risk, and many lawyers have paid the price for vigorously defending their clients even though the law appeared to be on their side (Pils, 2006). Of course, some elements of Chinese law and the constitution have contradictions and elements that do not offer a basis for the protection of individual rights within the legal system. These contradictions offer another pitfall for lawyers seeking relief for their clients. In conclusion, these different strategies concerning the best way to defend clients and choosing which ones to defend have created a division among activist lawyers.

An example of an attorney who strived to work within the system in his defense of clients is Xu Zhiyong, a soft-spoken and savvy lawyer who was arrested in early August of 2009 (Jacobs, 2009). He had developed a reputation while representing migrant workers, death row inmates, and the parents of babies poisoned by tainted milk. Although he was released a couple of weeks later, perhaps in response to a strong backlash from organizations and individuals both in China and internationally, he was detained again in May 2011. It appears that a back tax bill of 1.4 million yuan (about $200,000) was the basis for the authorities pursuit of Xu Zhiyong. Rights activists claim that his now shuttered office, called the *Open Constitution Initiative* and the tax issue were a pretext for going after him.

The exploitation of children and their entry into slavery has not been a headline story in China, but French (2007) several years ago discussed the problem. One example cited concerned many teenagers or younger adolescents being forced to work in the brick kilns of Shanxi Province. News reports and editorials shocked readers in a story that identified Heng Tinghan, the manager of the brick works, who was arrested. He inflamed his reputation by declaring that it was a "fairly small thing" to beat and abuse underage workers and deprive them of pay. This account is by no means unique, as the press often reports on the injuries and deaths of child workers. Factory zones, infamous for their sweatshops, and kitchens and brothels in major cities are often cited for the abuse of young people. Scholars and experts state that China's emphasis on rapid growth has played a role in the exploitation of children (French, 2007). The government stepped in, somewhat late in the game, by creating a major revision of laws governing the rights of children in June 2007. Labor experts remained unconvinced that the legislation would have much of an impact. Like many laws in China, enforcement is always a question mark.

Amnesty International (2007) has been reporting extensively on rights abuses in China. Below are excerpts from their report in 2007:

An increased number of lawyers and journalists were harassed, detained, and jailed. Thousands of people who pursued their faith outside officially sanctioned churches were subjected to harassment and many to detention and imprisonment. Thousands of people were sentenced to death or executed. Migrants from rural areas were deprived of basic rights. Severe repression of Uighurs in the Xinjiang Uighur Autonomous Region continued, and freedom of expression and religion continued to be severely restricted in Tibet and among Tibetans elsewhere.

## INTERNATIONAL COMMUNITY

Before China's election to the new UN Human Rights Council, it made a number of human rights-related pledges, including ratification of the International Covenant on Civil and Political Rights and active co-operation with the UN on human rights. Chinese companies continued to export arms to countries where they were likely to be used for serious human rights abuses, including Sudan and Myanmar.

## HUMAN RIGHTS DEFENDERS

The government crackdown on lawyers and housing rights activists intensified. Many human rights defenders were subjected to lengthy periods of arbitrary detention without charge, as well as harassment by the police or by local gangs apparently condoned by the police. Many lived under near constant surveillance or house arrest and members of their families were increasingly targeted. New regulations restricted the ability of lawyers to represent groups of victims and to participate in collective petitions.

Gao Zhisheng, an outspoken human rights lawyer, had his law practice suspended in November 2005. He was detained in August 2006 and remained in incommunicado detention at an unknown location until his trial in December 2006. In October he was formally arrested on charges of "inciting subversion," and in December he was sentenced to three years' imprisonment, suspended for five years.

## JOURNALISTS AND INTERNET USERS

The government's crackdown on journalists, writers, and Internet users intensified. Numerous popular newspapers and journals were shut down. Hundreds of international websites remained blocked and thousands of Chinese websites were shut down. Dozens of journalists were detained for reporting on sensitive issues.

The government strengthened systems for blocking, filtering, and monitoring the flow of information. New regulations came into effect requiring foreign news agencies to gain approval from China's official news agency in order to publish any news. Many foreign journalists were detained for short periods.

DISCRIMINATION AGAINST RURAL MIGRANTS

Rural migrant workers in China's cities faced wide-ranging discrimination. Despite official commitment to resolve the problem, millions of migrant workers were still owed back pay. The vast majority were excluded from urban health insurance schemes and could not afford private health care. Access to public education remained tenuous for millions of migrant children, in contrast to other urban residents. An estimated 20 million children were unable to live with their parents in the cities in part because of insecure schooling.

Beijing municipal authorities closed dozens of migrant schools in September, affecting thousands of migrant children.

The Dui Hua Foundation's (2009) report on prison conditions in China compared the overcrowding with conditions in the United States, and noted that the two countries have the largest prison populations in the world. Both nations have enacted strict laws to imprison criminals more easily and for longer periods of time. A brief summary would note "three strikes" in the United States (California being primarily noted for this policy) and strike hard campaigns in China. Despite the prison laws on the books in China, which addressed overcrowding, the reality has been quite different. The Criminal Life Sanitation Management Measure requires that, in order to maintain safety and airflow, a certain minimum amount of space per inmate is required. Each prisoner should be guaranteed five square meters of personal space (Dui Hua, 2009). However, in a study of 24 prisons in six Chinese provinces published in 1998, 42.2 percent of prisoners had less than three square meters and only 13.1 percent had five square meters. In a separate research study, the findings stated that Chinese prisons were 30 percent over capacity and 100 percent over capacity in Guangdong Province. Unlike in the United States, where federal courts not infrequently intervene to improve prison conditions, the legal recourse is very limited in China. In 2009, China was estimated to have over 2 million prisoners or detainees, with each inmate costing the government around 10,000 yuan per year, or almost double the average worker's annual wage. As the Dui Hua (2009) Foundation on human rights properly observed, China could improve the overcrowding problem by expanding its use of early release, parole, and sentence reduction policies.

# Psychiatric Hospitals as Prisons

There have been many reports over the years by human rights organizations and the press—both foreign and domestic—concerning China's use of mental hospitals for effectively incarcerating citizens. One report in 2001 by Erik Eckholm provided an overview of the problem at that time. The government has taken the position that Falun Gong members are mentally disturbed in order to justify the large-scale rounding up of individuals, placing them in closed psychiatric hospitals—effectively imprisoning them. Hundreds of defiant followers have been forcibly medicated. Historically, unlike the former Soviet Union, China did not have a record of using hospitals to imprison individuals for their beliefs. One example cited by Eckholm involved the case of Cao Maobing, a worker in a state-owned silk factory in Jiangsu Province:

> Last year, Mr. Cao was in trouble with authorities after he protested against corruption and tried to organize fellow workers into an independent trade union. Then in December, one day after he spoke with foreign reporters about his complaints, the police took him to a psychiatric hospital, where he has been medicated and forced to undergo electroshock therapy, said relatives and friends who insist he is not insane but a determined advocate.
>
> The hospital director says a committee of 17 experts has declared Mr. Cao to suffer "paranoid psychosis." (p. A1)

Robin Munro, a British author and researcher (Eckholm, 2001), claimed that China operated a secret police-controlled system of 20 centers for the criminally insane. In his report, Munro estimated that from 1980 to 2000, over 3,000 people were arrested for political crimes and given psychiatric evaluations and then confined for various periods of time.

*Amnesty International*, in its 2001 annual report on China, offered the following report on the abuse of individuals in China's psychiatric hospitals. The excerpt was entitled "Torture of the Mentally Ill and Misuse of Psychiatric Hospitals":

> In spite of regulations prohibiting the detention of the mentally ill in penal institutions, former prisoners have testified to being detained with mentally-ill prisoners. Such prisoners are among the most vulnerable to attack and bullying by "cell bosses" and other prisoners. Several recent reports have revealed gross ill-treatment of the mentally ill within the public security system.

On 28–29 March 1998, the *Yangcheng Evening News* exposed the case of Deng Qilu, a 43 year old man who had been imprisoned without charge for nearly ten years, and kept in a steel cage 2m length and little more than 1m in height and width since June 1995. Deng Qilu had reportedly been imprisoned for 3 years in 1984 for assault. On his release he had been diagnosed as suffering from "periodic mental illness," and had been involved in several violent incidents. In May 1989 he was arrested, accused of stabbing a public security official, but never charged. Two months later Zhanjiang City Psychiatric Hospital and judicial psychiatric evaluation organs reportedly determined that Deng had "suffered from schizophrenia for 16 years which had not been effectively treated, becoming chronic, especially as he had been violent many times, seriously threatening the public's life and safety, long-term forcible detention (*jiaqiang jianguan*) is recommended to avoid future violence and injury." Deng had since been detained at the Xuwen County Detention Centre. Reportedly, after assaulting fellow prisoners he was held in solitary confinement where he continued to attack those bringing him food. In June 1995, when the detention centre was being repaired, the cage was constructed and thereafter Deng was confined in it, outside the gates. In August 1997, during a visit to the county to resolve other cases, higher-level government representatives reportedly instructed staff to resolve the case and send Deng home. Public security officials simply moved the cage to a yard in Beitan, Deng's home village. They reportedly returned later to put Deng in shackles, warning his 81 year-old father not to release him. Once the newspapers exposed the case, local officials moved swiftly to release Deng into a local hospital. Subsequent reports claimed that the police had few options faced with the villagers' opposition to his release. (p. 20)

In a further example of the use of psychiatric hospitals to confine citizens, local authorities in Shandong Province removed a variety of "muckraking citizens who dare to challenge authorities" (Jacobs, 2008). Interestingly, a government owned press, *Xintai*, blew the whistle on abuse, and an investigative report exposed a widespread process of confining and forcibly medicating citizens who had campaigned against corruption, and the unfair seizure of property. Under duress, many were released from the psychiatric facility after agreeing to give up their causes. Here is an account of one citizen in a report by Andrew Jacobs (2008):

Sun Fawu, 57, a farmer seeking compensation for land spoiled by a coal-mining operation, said he was seized by local authorities on his way to petition the central government in Beijing and taken to the Xintai Mental Health Center in October.

During a 20-day stay, he said, he was lashed to a bed, forced to take pills and given injections that made him numb and woozy. According to the paper, when he told the doctor he was a petitioner, not mentally ill, the doctor said: "I don't care if you're sick or not. As long as you are sent by the township government, I'll treat you as a mental patient."

In an interview with the newspaper, the hospital's director, Wu Yuzhu, acknowledged that some of the 18 patients brought there by the police in recent years were not deranged, but he said that he had no choice but to take them in. "The hospital also had its misgivings," he said.

Xintai officials do not see any shame in the tactic, and they boasted that hospitalizing people they characterized as trouble-makers saved money that would have been spent chasing them to Beijing. There is another reason to stop petitioners who seek re-dress from higher levels of government: they can prove embarrassing to local officials, especially if they make it to Beijing. (p. A13)

An interview by Shannon Van Sant (2009) for *PBS NewsHour* entitled "Chinese Dissidents Committed to Mental Hospitals" revealed additional abuses of the psychiatric system in China. One interviewee, Qin Xinair, described repeated forced hospitalizations. He, in the long tradition of "petitioners," had gone to Beijing to report on corruption. Petitioners have had a system that goes back to the Ming Dynasty 700 years ago when individuals appealed to the imperial court if they had problems with local officials. A former officer in the People's Liberation Army, Qin had been hospitalized six times. The first time it was "acute stress disorder"; the second time, "paranoid schizophrenia"; and the third time "paranoid psychosis."

His problem began when he went to Beijing to complain about corruption in his factory. Like many others who arrive in Beijing, he sought shelter in a makeshift village with other petitioners seeking justice. Security personnel spotted him and removed him from this community of fellow petitioners. The local officials who may be the target of petitioners often seek retribution by locating the complainants and then attempting to stop them before they can reach officials at the national government in Beijing. Local officials worry that their jobs and salaries will be hurt if petitioners complain about them at the national level.

Zheng Ran believed he had been unfairly denied a promotion at a branch of the Bank of Beijing and decided to respond (Ford, 2008). He did not imagine that his Internet postings of financial misdeeds at the bank would create serious problems for him. When, however, he expanded his criticisms of the

Chinese government, the authorities identified him as a troublemaker. Individuals viewed as troublemakers at the time of the 2008 Olympics in China were particularly vulnerable to a crackdown, and Zheng Ran was forcibly detained at a mental hospital. Doctors diagnosed him as suffering "paranoid disorders." He spent five months in confinement at the psychiatric facility. In another case that gained national attention, Xu Wu, a former security guard, was dragged from a TV station in Guangzhou where he had described his plight—he had escaped from a mental hospital managed by his employer (Ford, 2011). He claimed he had been incarcerated for four years after petitioning local and national government authorities to resolve a wage dispute with his employer.

One additional case that reveals the Chinese government's use of psychiatric hospitals to quash dissent is that of Xu Lindong, a poor village farmer with a fourth-grade education (La Franiere & Levin, 2010). The farmer had been a hardworking, physically fit person whose physique reflected years of plowing and harvesting in the fields of Louhe. However, after four years of psychiatric hospitalization he was barely recognizable in his pajamas, his face marked with the abuse he had suffered. His family described the radical change in his appearance from his earlier robust appearance. A brother denied he had been emotionally ill; he said Xu had run afoul of authorities. Apparently this occurred when Xu became involved in a land dispute and filed a series of complaints against the local government. The local government then filed an order to commit him to a mental hospital, forging his brother's name. After six-and-one-half years of confinement he was released from Zhumadian Psychiatric Hospital. Mr. Xu's painful experience had included 54 electro-shock treatments, and he was frequently injected with powerful drugs. Worrying that he would be permanently disabled, he tried several times to commit suicide.

Overall this case, along with the other cases of forced psychiatric hospitalization in China, illustrates a number of problems. There are significant loopholes in legal remedies and protections for people who are treated in this fashion and confined in mental hospitals. Questionable medical ethics and poorly trained psychiatrists compound the problem (La Franiere & Levin, 2010). Furthermore, hospital administrators often feel obligated to go along with government officials who sometimes accompany the person being hospitalized. Additionally, there are reports that local government officials are under pressure to nip social unrest before it expands to include larger numbers of citizens. One lawyer, Huang Xuetao, an expert on mental health law, stated that governmental authorities recognized a gap in the law and have taken full advantage of the opportunity to take away a person's freedom. Only six of China's 283 cities have a local mental health ordinance, and a report from attorney Xuetao stated that "there is no way for patients who are committed for treatment to complain, appeal, or prosecute" (La Franiere & Levin, 2010).

# The Death Penalty

There have been references earlier in this book to the large-scale use of the death penalty in China, but in this section a more detailed examination will follow. Perhaps curiously to Westerners, a large portion of Chinese surveys claimed that 90 percent were in favor of the death penalty, according to Professor Zhu Suli (2011), a professor from the prestigious Peking University Law School. Furthermore, he added, perhaps less than 1 percent were advocates for banning the death penalty. While the death penalty is still active in some states in the United States, it has been abolished in most European countries. Zhu Suli informed his audience at Yale University that much earlier in Chinese history an emperor tried unsuccessfully to abolish the death penalty.

As I have noted earlier on China's crackdown on offenders during strike hard campaigns, the authorities often act quickly and that includes executions of those deemed to have committed serious crimes. Here are reports of two executions that took place in mid 2001 (Smith, 2001):

> BEIBAISHA, China—Nothing in Hao Fengqin's abbreviated life suggested that she would end her days on an execution ground.
>
> The 45-year-old Ms. Hao lived a hard life in this village of low brick houses, set in wheat fields 200 miles south of Beijing. She was born poor and married poor, and she bore two daughters, considered a misfortune in rural China because girls traditionally leave the family after they marry and offer little support to their parents later on.
>
> But Ms. Hao unwittingly sold explosives for a mass murder: a man named Jin Ruobao was found guilty of killing 108 people with some of Ms. Hao's homemade ammonium nitrate, which she sold to nearby quarries and which was the type of explosive that brought down the federal building in Oklahoma City in 1995, killing 168 people.
>
> Like Timothy J. McVeigh, Mr. Jin was executed, though his death was swifter and less gentle: he was shot in the back of the head, the usual method of capital punishment here, just 37 days after his arrest and less than seven weeks after the crime.
>
> For her unintentional role in the bombing, Ms. Hao was shot in the head too, one month after the police took her away from her home.

> Typically, someone found guilty of making and selling unlicensed ex-
> plosives would have been fined. (p. A1)

The ancient Chinese saying "killing a chicken to scare the monkeys" is sometimes cited by Chinese Communist Party officials in its published comments
on its dealing with criminals. Smith's (2001) comments on the randomness of
executions during strike hard campaigns, echo those offered earlier in the section of this book on police tactics used during the periodic harsh crackdowns.
Amnesty International claimed there were 4,367 executions in 1996, or about
a dozen a day. There have been numerous reports in the press that China for
many years has executed more individuals annually then the rest of the world
combined. A dozen years later in 2008 Amnesty estimated that there were 1,718
executions or about three fourths of those worldwide (MacDonald, 2010).

Outsiders have persistently asked the Chinese government as to why the authorities do not reveal the numbers executed if, as the government claims, the
numbers are declining. In 2009 in Europe there were no executions while 388
were executed in Iran for the same year. For 2009 there were 52 executions in
the United States. There were seven other countries in Asia that exercised the
death penalty in 2009, including Bangladesh, North Korea, Maylasia, Singapore, Thailand, Vietnam, India, Pakistan, Afghanistan, Indonesia, and Japan,
for a total of 26. In the case of Japan there are some years with no executions,
but in other years just a few or less. Here is an excerpt from Amnesty International's
report on China for 2007 (Amnesty International, 2007):

> The death penalty continued to be used extensively to punish around
> 68 crimes, including economic and non-violent crimes. Based on pub-
> lic reports, AI estimated that at least 1,010 people were executed and
> 2,790 sentenced to death during 2006, although the true figures were
> believed to be much higher.
>
> The National People's Congress passed a law reinstating a final re-
> view of all death penalty cases by the Supreme People's Court from
> 2007. Commentators believed this would lead to a reduction in mis-
> carriages of justice and use of the death penalty.
>
> Executions by lethal injection rose, facilitating the extraction of or-
> gans from executed prisoners, a lucrative business. In November a
> deputy minister announced that the majority of transplanted organs
> came from executed prisoners. In July new regulations banned the
> buying and selling of organs and required written consent from donors
> for organ removal.
>
> Xu Shuangfu, the leader of an unofficial Protestant group called
> "Three Grades of Servants," was executed along with 11 others in No-

vember after being convicted of murdering 20 members of another group, "Eastern Lightning," in 2003–4. Xu Shuangfu reportedly claimed that he had confessed under torture during police interrogation and that the torture had included beatings with heavy chains and sticks, electric shocks to the toes, fingers and genitals and forced injection of hot pepper, gasoline and ginger into the nose. Both the first instance and appeal courts reportedly refused to allow his lawyers to introduce these allegations as evidence in his defence.

In returning to Professor Zhu Soli's (2011) lecture on the death penalty, he stated that defense lawyers might be expected to rally against the death penalty but they do not. His claim was that, ironically, defense lawyers pretend to be against the death penalty but that they support it because they can't make money otherwise. In addition, he commented that some defense lawyers genuinely believed it was useful and necessary to keep it on the books. The scholar is known for his controversial views on this and other legal matters.

Scientist Wo Weihan was executed by the Chinese government after authorities had been told that they would be granted an additional opportunity to meet with him (Dui Hua Foundation, 2008). He was accused of gathering military and political intelligence for Taiwan. He was a 60-year-old biomedical researcher and businessman. A Dui Hua representative had hoped that since death penalty cases were required to be reviewed by the Supreme People's Court the justices would decide that such a severe penalty wasn't required. He had been denied access to a lawyer for ten months and may have been abused during his confinement. Due to poor health he had been locked up in a prison hospital. He was sentenced to death for the crime of espionage in a closed trial on May 27, 2007.

As previously mentioned, the governments retention of the death penalty has been supposedly tied to popular support, but a survey in 2010 by the Max Planck Institute for Foreign and International Criminal Law (Dui Hua Foundation, 2010) offered a more nuanced picture. Although a majority of the 4,500 adults surveyed in Beijing, Hunan, and Guangdong supported the death penalty in a general way, when respondents were asked about applying it for specific offenses and varied scenarios, there was less support. In the survey conducted in 2007–2008, 63.8 percent stated the Chinese government should publish the annual number of executions. Critics of the death penalty believe that if citizens were better informed they would offer less support for executions, and that greater transparency would have a significant impact on public opinion.

In 2011, the National People's Congress Standing Committee review of a draft amendment to the criminal law concerning the limitations of the death penalty generated a lot of debate, but ultimately the resolution passed (Dui Hua Foundation, 2011). An earlier draft indicated the government was considering removing 13 non-violent criminal offenses from the death penalty, but Dui Hua officials did not believe this would reduce the large number of annual executions—it would be a more symbolic step toward a gradual reduction of executions. One issue that was focused on was exempting the elderly—75 years and older. Opponents argued that this might result in corrupt officials being spared death. Tsinghua University professor Zhou Guangquan offered his views reported from a newspaper interview in China (*Southern Weekend News*, 2010). He stated that most of the 13 crimes occur infrequently, and that the government believed that its decision would not shock the public's concern about public safety. Of the 13, many were crimes where the penalty had rarely been applied, according to Zhou Guangquan. In response to another question from a newspaper reporter, Zhou Guangquan stated that although serious cases of corruption could involve the death penalty, there were thousands of cases of corruption every year and that capital punishment had a limited deterrent effect.

As mentioned earlier, thousands of security cameras now are in place across China. The government calls it the Safe Cities program. According to Jacobs & Bullock (2012), "The Uniview Company produces what it calls 'infrared antiriot' cameras and software that enable police officials in different jurisdictions to share images in real time through the Internet." Chinese cities are rushing to construct these systems. Chongqing is spending $4.2 billion on 500,000 cameras. Guangdong Province, the manufacturing hub, is installing 500,000 cameras, 1 million cameras in Hong Kong, and Beijing is seeking to place cameras in all entertainment venues. For the 2008 Olympics, 300,000 were installed. Nicholas Bequelin, of Human Rights Watch, stated, "when it comes to surveillance, China is pretty upfront about its totalitarian ambitions" (Jacobs & Bullock, 2012).

# 12

# Market Forces, Social Unrest, Pollution, and Healthcare Problems in China

## Social Disturbances and the Market Economy

The powerful and rapid economic developments in China have impacted many. Social unrest continues to relentlessly increase in communities and cities across China. It has taken various forms, from small groups to large-scale uprisings involving entire communities. Materialism and demand for economic fairness have underlined social unrest.

This is what took place in Wukan near the end of 2011 (Wines, 2011): Virtually an entire community of around 13,000 people barricaded access to the village and chased local officials out of town. Police were unable to penetrate for a week until villagers relented. There are estimated to be 625,000 potential uprisings in similar communities, given the way many citizens and entire communities have been treated. Lack of accountability, secret sales of land by village heads, and the lack of transparency in transactions have contributed. Wines has noted that in theory these wholesale uprisings should have been unlikely. Since Chinese village committees are elected, unlike government officials at other levels. These committees are charged with delivering many services such as sanitation and social welfare (including public health). They also collect taxes. However, the raising of funds for economic development is supposed to be controlled by the central Communist Party in Beijing. But as noted throughout this discussion on China, local officials are powerful and they often ignore policy and legislative edicts from the national government. The relationship of local officials to those in Beijing have often contributed to corruption as officials sometimes use payoffs to accomplish their goals. The matter of land sales is where the big money lies, and there is corruption from different levels of government by officials who scheme to profit illegally (Wines, 2011). Applicants for official positions in local government sometimes pay vast sums to secure a post—one official for a committee chairmanship in Laojiqotou village allegedly paid 2 million yuan, or about $245,000. One of the incidents that contributed to the closing of Wukan involved the lack of an accounting ledger—it had been removed. Protest leaders claimed that the village committee had sales of long term leases for as much as 60 percent of the community's 11 square miles. Sales were supposed to have been approved by the villagers, but in a practice widespread in towns across China, local citizens are often bypassed. In Wukan, land was sold to hotels, factories, power companies, and a wealthy businessman who purchased an interest in a 50-year lease for land used as a pig farm. The proceeds of these sales were unaccounted for, and many villagers, according to protest leaders, had no idea of their rights. Monitoring the way local government officials operate appears to be a challenge that in the short term appears insurmountable.

A footnote to the Wukan uprising was noted in a different approach that belatedly was exercised by Wang Yang, a former rising star of the Communist Party. He was secretary for Guangdong Province, which included Wukan (La Franiere, 2011). Unlike other protests in China, Mr. Wang chose to use restraint and not have public security personnel storm the blocked-off community. Rather he chose to consider the merits of the villagers' complaints. The government's premium newspaper, *Peoples Daily*, applauded his approach. Within two months of the uprising, democratic elections were held in Wukan—a major development in China. To what extent this development will set a precedent remains to be seen.

An excellent overview of the sources for social unrest in the context of the rapid economic developments in China was offered by Minxin Pei (2007), a scholar at the China Program, Carnegie Foundation for International Peace. According to Pei, there have been a number of fundamental causes of the large-scale social disturbances. First, he identified high taxes in the countryside imposed by local officials. Officially they are not supposed to exceed 5 percent according to Beijing, but one study found that in the late 1990s about 10 percent was common in rural communities. Furthermore, often additional illegal fees were charged, and therefore the actual tax rate could be closer to 20 percent of rural gross domestic product (DGP). Adding insult to injury, local officials sometimes used heavy-handed, even brutal, methods to collect taxes.

A second issue, according to Minxin Pei, has been the large-scale shifting of state-owned enterprises (SOEs) to the private sector, or the actual closing of some. This has resulted in enormous pain and disruption of workers' lives. Many were left without jobs or suffered greatly reduced wages. Unlike the earlier years of the "Iron Rice Bowl," in which the government provided some safety net, many were left to fend for themselves. Unemployment benefits were practically non-existent and health insurance vanished until around 2010, when the government tried to make amends. As Pei noted, by the late 1990s, upwards of 35 to 40 million workers from state-owned enterprises lost their jobs. Minimal placement and retraining schemes further exacerbated the problem. Massive demonstrations and anger erupted in the wake of these developments. Corruption among the ranks of industrial managers and public officials were widely reported by China's state-owned media outlets.

A third factor, according to scholar Minxin Pei (2007), involved widespread land seizures from farmers, peasants, and some of the new middle class. Moving from a nation of great poverty to many citizens moving into the middle class exacted a price. The sale of land was one of the critical issues in the closing of the community of Wukan by its citizens. Takeovers by local town officials precipitated the citizen outrage. In general, across China, some of the disputes resulted in arrests and even deaths in clashes with public security officers. Typically, local officials sell user rights at low prices to developers and, in addition, the farmers whose land has been taken over are not informed. Local officials frequently receive kickbacks that play into the problems of land sales. Often the farmers demand higher compensation or refuse to give up their land, and physically attempt to block the purchaser from taking over. Part of the larger portrait of social unrest is the huge and growing gap between haves and have-nots—a problem that has also created tensions in the United States, as seen in Occupy Wall Street and similar protests. In China, many low-income citizens believe that the new rich have gained their wealth from corruption. Widespread corruption at many levels of business and government has been a repeated theme in my discussion of the Chinese criminal justice system. A major problem, according to Pei, is that the national government lacks a vehicle to allow remedies of the above-mentioned problems of high taxes, the transition from state-owned enterprises, land seizures, and gaps between rich and poor. As I have previously noted, petitioners have a long history in China of personal visits and letters to Beijing, but that system is defunct. Many receive no response or are locked in a bureaucratic maze. Others are intercepted by local authorities or thugs on their way to visiting national government officials. An additional source of relief is appeal to a local official, but they have been largely unresponsive and often thwart efforts, sometimes bullying the person asking for redress. A third way is theoretically the legal system itself. A system of administrative law created in 1989 allowed for citizens to file lawsuits against government agencies, but the courts have adjudicated just 20 percent of plaintiff suits (Pei, 2007).

In summary, the government has beefed up its use of riot police to attempt to quickly and effectively quell protests. Some minor public policy changes have taken place under President Hu Jintao and Premier Wen Jiabao in the national government's efforts to hold onto the reins of power, but the larger problems remain unaddressed.

Another example of a large-scale social uprising occurred in Zhili, a town in Zhejiang Province (Tejada, 2011). Tax issues were in the forefront as authorities demanded that residents stay indoors after protests by the owners of small businesses and workers over increases in local taxes that were viewed as unreasonable. Protests, according to local media, were precipitated when a number of owners of local clothing companies (some who had come from neighboring Anhui Province) rebelled against the increased taxes. One owner spurred others on, and the protests reached riot proportions as police were assaulted and cars were overturned in the community 80 miles west of Shanghai.

# Pollution

Another problem that has exacerbated social tensions and which is tied to China's economic growth is the growing pollution across China. The environmental agency in China, which would roughly be the counterpart to the Environmental Protection Agency in the United States, has historically been weak and lacked the muscle to crack down on illegal polluters. When I arrived in Changsha, Hunan Province, on a brief visit around 2006, there were warnings to drink only bottled water and local media reported that some lakes were so loaded with pollutants and chemicals that one should not touch the water— never mind drink it. A major source of the darkened skies over Beijing and other major cities, like Shanghai and Guangzhou, has been the belching smoke from China's industrial juggernaut. Jacobs (2010) reported that China has become the largest emitter of greenhouse gas. The air in many cities has been plagued by coal-burning power plants and dust from construction sites during China's huge construction boom. One surprise, detailed in a government report (Jacobs, 2010), was that even in cities where officials have struggled to control air quality and limit auto emissions, inhalable particulates continued to foul the air. Up to ten industrial accidents per month exacerbated the problem. Citizen groups periodically complained and protesters across the nation charged that serious health effects had occurred in their families. Clashes with police were common, and in one case the state media reported that thousands of residents mobilized in the Guangxi Zhuang Autonomous Region and fought police over the unregulated emissions from an aluminum plant. The director of the Institute of Public and Environmental Affairs in Beijing commented that the government's efforts to cut pollution had been offset by construction projects. China continues to search all over the world, from Africa to North America, for energy sources to support their huge industrial enterprises. Many industries use coal, which is cheap and widely available but a huge source of pollution. In 2010, Beijing imposed restrictions on driving in the capital city and removed a fifth of private cars from roadways each weekday. Unfortunately this modest limitation on pollution was offset by the hundreds of thousands of new car sales (Jacobs, 2010). The government continues to grapple with problems associated with the huge volume of car sales. In one respect, it's an economic boost, but many of the poorly trained new drivers on crowded roadways cause numerous accidents. Spotty law enforcement and traffic regulation have worsened conditions.

As a result of heavy industrial and auto pollution, there are hundreds of thousands of deaths annually due to poor air quality. Cancer deaths have risen. In 2007, cancer was the leading cause of death in China (Kahn & Yardley, 2007). During that year there were approximately 500 million people reported to lack safe drinking water. Similar to my own experiences in Beijing and Changsha, there are citizen reports of sunny days in which heavy clouds of smoke and dust block out most of the sun's rays. Poor visibility on streets is the product of the dense pollution, which comes and goes depending on the atmospheric conditions. Ironically, China's greatest achievement has "become our greatest burden" according to Wang Jinnan, one of China's leading environmental researchers (Kahn & Yardley, 2007).

# Healthcare

Another major problem facing China moving forward has been the collapse of the healthcare system. Although the Communist Party, in its earlier days, offered broad-scale, but admittedly basic, health insurance for all its citizens, it abandoned the free healthcare plan when Deng Xiaping unleashed market forces in the 1980s. People had to pay for medical treatment, which has been extremely costly for many Chinese who do not enjoy middle-class incomes. Citizens often faced excruciating choices in which sometimes half their modest incomes had to go to medical treatment or to putting food on the table. If one were to compare the healthcare cost in the United States with China, the second largest economy in the world, the following picture emerges (Emanuel,

2011). In 2000, China's GDP was $5.9 trillion, compared to America's $14.6 trillion. The U.S. population, a quarter of China's, spends just on healthcare slightly less than half of what China spends on everything.

An historical perspective on China's healthcare system was offered by Blumenthal & Hsiao (2005). In 1949, when Mao and the Communist Party took control, the government owned and financially supported all hospitals, from specialized facilities in urban areas to small town clinics in the countryside. There was no private practice of medicine—medical doctors were employed by the state. The commune was the centerpiece of healthcare in rural areas and communes owned the land and supplied most services, including social services and healthcare. So-called "barefoot doctors" provided both Western and traditional Chinese medicine. From the early 1950s until the early 1980s, huge improvements took root in healthcare (Blumenthal & Hsiao, 2005). Infant mortality fell from 200 to 34 per 1,000 live births and life expectancy grew from 35 to 68 years. In addition, major strides were taken in controlling infectious diseases through immunizations and basic healthcare measures. However, by the early 1980s, the system was fundamentally terminated overnight. The central government changed the way it financed healthcare by reducing the government's contribution to the system, and it imposed price regulation—the latter had unanticipated consequences. In trying to ensure access to basic medicine, the government maintained tight control over what hospitals and clinics could charge for routine visits, surgery, standard diagnostic tests, and drugs. However, it allowed the hospitals and clinics to earn profits from new tests and technology with profit margins of 15 percent or higher. Bonuses were offered to doctors and revenues overall were tied to profitable sales of pharmaceutical products and high tech services.

The outcome up to 2005, before the government attempted to radically reboot the system in 2009, was disastrous. Only 29 percent of Chinese citizens had health insurance and out of pocket expenses accounted for 58 percent of healthcare spending in 2002, as compared to 20 percent in 1978. Many went without healthcare due to the cost. The income of the average Chinese person became directly correlated with whether or not the person received medical treatment. Quality varied from the thriving industrial areas as compared with the rural countryside (Blumenthal & Hsiao, 2005).

One dimension of the growing wealth in China has been the impact on the care of the elderly. With offspring heading to the cities from rural areas, many older people are left to fend for themselves. It has become common over the last two decades for older citizens in rural farmland communities to struggle at backbreaking labor in the fields to plant and harvest crops as younger offspring have left. As French (2006) quoted from the chief of a local village,

"Knock on ten doors and nine will be opened by old people." China has a rapidly aging population, and the economic growth has created a large-scale migration to the cities. As previously observed, hundreds of millions move back and forth across China's vast landscape. From the foregoing sketch, China's healthcare system has been one of ups and downs to the most recent period of around 2006. There are now intensive efforts on the part of the government to recover from the disaster of recent decades.

China's government announced a plan to pour $124 billion into overhauling the dysfunctional healthcare system (Fairclough, 2009). The goal has been to extend medical insurance to 90 percent of the population over the next five years, and provide "basic" healthcare to 1.3 billion people. The plan included the concept of putting in place a network of hospitals, clinics, and community healthcare centers covering both rural and urban regions. One aspect included providing subsidies for premiums. The pay-as-you-go approach of recent decades meant that many citizens decided to forgo treatment.

Unquestionably, the history of violence in hospitals and clinics contributed to the government belatedly deciding to reshape the system. The following are several noteworthy examples of the crisis: in 2006, a boy's death spurred a riot in southwestern China (Kahn, 2006). A three-year-old boy died in a hospital at Guang'an City No. 2 People's Hospital. He had been taken to the facility for emergency care after ingesting pesticides. The report was that care was denied until his grandfather, who was taking care of him, could pay. The youngster died after the grandfather was unable to raise the funds. A contrasting report from the *New China News Agency* confirmed the dispute, but said that doctors treated the boy even though the grandfather could not pay the $82 bill. Local residents, hearing of the problem, demonstrated outside the hospital. A riot ensued and windows were smashed and three police vans overturned. Ten people were injured when police broke up the demonstration. In the healthcare system at that time, hospitals were left to their own devices to cover the soaring costs of care—many even ceased providing emergency care. Not surprisingly, enormous frustration and anger spread across China in the wake of the lack of broad-scale health coverage.

Another example of the crisis prior to China's decision to reform healthcare was described by LaFraniere (2010). In a dramatic announcement, officials in Shenyang, a large northern city, exclaimed, "what this city's twenty-seven public hospitals really needed were police officers." The idea was that police—not just at the entrance—were required to assist in protecting doctors and medical staff. For the year 2006, published statistics on hospital violence revealed that attacks by patients or their relatives injured over 5,500 medical workers. In June 2010, a doctor was stabbed to death in Shandong Province by the son of a patient who had died of liver cancer. Three physicians were seriously burned in Shanxi Province when a patient set fire to a hospital office. In Fujian Province, a pediatrician was hurt after jumping out a fifth-floor window to escape enraged family members of a newborn who had died under his care. During 2010, families of deceased relatives forced doctors to don mourning clothes as a sign of atonement for poor healthcare. Occasionally, hospital entrances have been barred. As Sharon La Franiere noted in her article, protests over healthcare have been part of the broader picture of citizen unrest over the many years of frustration experienced by citizens since the reforms of the 1980s. In 2000, the World Health Organization ranked China's health system at 188 out of 191 countries in terms of being equitable—about two out of five sick people went untreated. Just one in ten had health insurance at the turn of the twenty-first century.

Since China launched its reform, investing the $124 billion in 2009, things have improved dramatically. By 2010, the World Bank claimed three out of four Chinese had health insurance for basic care. Furthermore, far more people were receiving care even in the outlying rural areas. Nonetheless, reports over recent years claim that care is low grade—some doctors never graduated beyond junior high school. Some patients are hospitalized for poor reasons— colds and the flu. Needless surgery is still common, and patients often get useless prescriptions. Sales of drugs are the second biggest source of income for hospitals. Incentives cause doctors to overprescribe medicine as doctors salaries are linked to the money they generate. In addition, some drug companies offer doctors under-the-table inducements to use their pharmaceutical products. In one outrageous example, a patient paid $95 for a checkup and received several injections and a dozen different drugs, including pills for liver disease. The individual had a cold! (La Franiere, 2010).

In summary, this chapter has described a series of inter-related problems that present a challenge for Chinese society in general, but to some extent these issues directly confront the criminal justice system. Pollution, corruption linked to the rapid development of the industrial engine, and healthcare crises have all resulted in large-scale social unrest in communities and cities across the vast Chinese landscape.

# 13

# Conclusion: Japan and China Going Forward

This book has covered a great variety of issues and problems faced by the Japanese and Chinese criminal justice systems. Some comparisons have been offered along the way with the United States' criminal justice system. While the two Asian giants share some things in common, they are vastly different in many respects. They are interesting to compare given their historically different backgrounds and political systems—Japan is democratic and China is communist (at least politically). Both economies outstrip not only their fellow Asian nations but countries around the world. China is on track to be a larger economy then the United States in the future, and based on some measures, it has already surpassed America.

Corruption in both government and business is far greater in China than in Japan, and while the rule of law in China may be growing at a snail's pace, and may help curb corruption someday, there is little evidence of it at the present time. In this modern era, from the period beyond World War II, Japan's criminal justice system is far more mature and there is a much greater respect for the rule of law. While the prosecutorial side seems to be heavily favored in Japan, by United States standards, it is far more evenhanded and fairer than China's. Notwithstanding the enormous increases in trained lawyers, prosecutors, and judges in China, there are enormous problems in the justice system. The Communist Party is in virtually every aspect of the government, and it regularly intrudes itself in many legal events. As mentioned throughout the portion of this book on China, it is not uncommon for the government to secretly remove a legal proceeding from public access. The court may simply announce a verdict after the fact with the defense attorney being totally blindsided. Overall, repression on the part of police, prosecution, the courts, and the prison system is widespread. While juries have returned in Japan, there is no discussion in China about implementing them. The death penalty, while legal in Japan, is rarely exercised, and occasionally there are years with no executions. On the other hand, China leads the world in capital cases.

A fundamental problem for China's legal system is the lack of independence of police, courts, and corrections, unlike in Japan and the United States. No reform of this critical problem is on the horizon. Linked to this issue is the power of local officials to manipulate legal matters despite the policy dictates of the central government in Beijing. Furthermore, the fact that local officials pay the salaries of most government officials—including criminal justice officials and judges—creates a serious impediment in their ability to mete out justice, and the entire process becomes tainted. Private lawyers, including law firms, can have their licenses pulled if their performance does not meet the expectations of the local village government officials. This gives sweeping power to these individual officials and stifles reform and the meritorious treatment of the legal problems the justice system confronts.

When it comes to broad relationships between Japan and China, there are positives and negatives. There are still ongoing tensions over territorial waters and islands that are in dispute, and there is a lingering resentment of Japan's World War II takeover and the atrocities on the China mainland. The latter may be gradually fading as older citizens die off, but hostility arises and demonstrations occasionally break out. On a more positive note, the two giants are economically strongly interconnected on many fronts. For Japan, China is its largest trading partner and Japan has made enormous investments in factories in China. While the hostilities from World War II still resonate with some Chinese, there are more Chinese now spending time and living in Japan compared with just 20 years ago. Neither country can afford to ignore the other for political as well as economic reasons, and both nations are actively involved with their Asian neighbors. North Korea continues to create great concern, given its dangerous and reclusive character, while South Korea, also a nation that suffered wartime atrocities and exploitation at the hands of Japan, has far stronger relations with its former enemy. China also has actively strengthened relations with South Korea, particularly on the economic front. One cannot ignore the fact that Vietnam has risen from the ashes of the Vietnam War period in which the United States destroyed much of the nation. It now trades actively with Japan, China, and the United States.

A major concern for Japan moving forward has to do with demographics. As noted earlier, the Japanese population is already not replacing itself and is shrinking. Japanese women, like their counterparts in other industrialized nations, are having fewer children and are employed in far greater numbers than they were 30 years ago. The population is aging, and the reluctance of Japan to allow foreign immigration has profound implications for its economic future. Without younger workers, the projection is for a receding economic future. It is still very difficult for foreigners to gain citizenship and many *gaijin* understand this before setting foot on Japanese soil. The relationship between Japan and the United States remains strong and there are still significant numbers of American armed forces stationed in Japan. That, along with the "nuclear umbrella" provided by the United States, has relieved Japan from the enormous economic burden of military expense, which continues to sap the treasury of the United States. While Japan's self-defense forces are among the most powerful armed forces in the world, they represent a much smaller part of Japan's national budget than is the case of the United States. China's military is growing rapidly, but it is still far less developed than in the United States, and China has not yet decided to spend a similar portion of its budget on military expansion.

In Chapter 7, when I introduced China, I commented on Cheng Li's future possible scenarios—the emergence of a democratic China, prolonged chaos, or a resilient authoritarian China. Projecting into the future is very risky, but it appears to me that the last scenario—at least for the next decade—seems most likely. As I mentioned in that chapter, the Chinese authoritarian collective leadership of the Communist Party—while rigid at times—usually finds a way to compromise when its survival is at stake. If the leadership, through the Politburo, needs to back off from its repressive tendencies to survive, it will back off somewhat. Some reforms in the legal system may prosper and a reduced use of the death penalty appears to be in the cards. "Children of the Revolution," or China's princelings (sons and daughters of prominent Communist Party officials), have attained enormous prominence in China—sometimes to their own detriment. Many have taken advantage of their connections and gained enormous wealth while others have advanced within the political system. Jeremy Page (2011) in a commentary on the role of princelings (and quoting Cheng Li) offered this statement: "Princelings were never popular, but now they've become so politically powerful, there's some serious concern about the legitimacy of the 'Red Nobility.' The Chinese public is particularly resentful about the princelings' control of political power and economic wealth." The present leadership includes several princelings, but they are mixed in with rival non-princelings. The future head of the nation, scheduled to replace Hu Jintao, is the son of a former revolutionary hero and by that definition is a princeling. Finally on the topic of the children of prominent party officials, some of them have become controversial as they have flaunted their wealth and position. One 15-year-old son of a general was in a BMW that crashed into another car in Beijing and then, with a friend, beat up the occupants of the struck vehicle, warning them not to call police (Page, 2011).

In conclusion, Japan's justice system is staffed by highly trained professionals and corruption is rare. While the system is stacked in favor of the prosecution, it is a system that does entertain reforms—the return of the jury system is an example. In contrast, China's system is deeply flawed. Corruption is widespread and defense attorneys are often abused or jailed. The government regularly controls and manipulates the outcome of cases. A silver lining is that a constitution has been created, and an army of young educated legal functionaries is starting to take over. If the Communist Party can allow these legal functionaries to properly do their jobs without constantly intervening, there is a ray of hope.

# References

Adelstein, J. *Tokyo Vice: An American Reporter on the Police Beat in Japan.* New York: Pantheon Books, 2009.

Alberge, D. "Liu Xiaobo: New Book Lifts China's Gag on Jailed Noble Peace Prizewinner," *The Guardian/The Observer*, November 12, 2011.

Allen, D. "Ex-Marine Decries Nature of Japan Prison Work," *Stars and Stripes*, July 18, 2004.

Ames, W. *Police and Community in Japan.* Berkeley: University of California Press, 1981.

Amnesty International. "Peoples Republic of China: Torture — A Growing Scourge in China — Time For Action," *Amnesty International*, February 12, 2001.

_____. "Annual Report — China," *Amnesty International Action for Human Rights*, 2007.

_____. "Japan — Prison Conditions," London: Amnesty International Press Office, 2009.

Anderlini, J., and K. Hille. "A Sharper Focus," *Financial Times*, May 11, 2011, p. 9.

Auerbach, J. "A Plague of Lawyers," *Harper's Magazine*, October,1976, p. 53.

Bayley, D. *Forces of Order: Policing Modern Japan*, Berkeley: University of California Press, 1991.

Bakken, B. "Comparative Perspectives on Crime in China," in Borge Bakken, *Crime, Punishment, and Policing in China.* Lanham, MD: Rowman & Littlefield Publishers Inc., 2005.

Banyan. "The Mongolian Sandwich," *The Economist*, October 8, 2011, p. 58.

Belson, K. "As Routines Falter, So Does National Confidence," *New York Times*, March 16, 2011, p. A1., 229–230.

Bequelin, N. "Human Rights in China," lecture presented at Yale-China Law Workshop, New Haven, CT, November 16, 2010.

Blumenthal, D., and W. Hsiao. "Privatization and Its Discontents—The Evolving Chinese Health-Care System," *The New England Journal of Medicine*, September 15, 2005, p. 1165.

Bradsher, K. "China Enacting High-Tech Plan to Track People," *New York Times*, August 12, 2007, p. A1.

Chang, G. "A Closer Look at China," lecture presented at Symposium, Yale University, New Haven, CT, April 19, 2006.

Chapman, L. "Tokyo's Bosozoku Battle," Culture Section, *Tokyo Times*, June 18, 2008.

Chen, A. *An Introduction to the Legal System of the People's Republic of China*, 3rd ed. Singapore: Lexis Nexus, 2004.

Chen, K. "Life in the Shadow of China's Police State," *Wall Street Journal*, September 16, 1998.

Chira, S. "Secrets of Police Cell: Woman's Grim Story," *New York Times*, September 20, 1988.

Chubu Connection. "Aichi Biker Gangs Up But Downsized," *Japan Times*, July 17, 2010.

Chwialkowski, B. "Japanese Policing—An American Invention," *Policing: An International Journal of Police Strategies and Management*, 21, no. 4, 1998.

Cohen, J. "China Needs Real Defense Lawyers," *South China Post*, September 17, 2002.

_____ "China's Legal System in Transition," *New York University Journal of International Law and Politics*, U.S. Senate Commission Hearing on Law and Legal Institutions of the People's Republic of China, July 26, 2005.

_____ ."China Trips Up Its Barefoot Lawyers," *Far Eastern Economic Review*, November, 2005.

_____ ."The Great Stonewall of China," *Wall Street Journal*, April 15–16, 2006, Op-Ed page.

_____ . "Can, and Should, the Rule of Law Be Transplanted Outside the West: The Case of China," *American Chamber*, January 2007, 231.

Cohen, T., and H. Passin, eds. *Remaking Japan: The American Occupation as New Deal*. New York: Free Press, 1987.

Correction Bureau—Ministry of Justice. "Penal Institutions in Japan." Tokyo: Government of Japan, 2008.

Dickie, M. "Japan Murder Case Puts Focus on Criminal Justice System, *Financial Times*, June 20, 2009, p. 5.

_____. "Japan's Prosecutors on Trial as Critics Call for Limits to Their Powers," *Financial Times*, October 16, 2010, p. 5.

Dikotter, F. "Penology and Reformation in Modern China," chapter in Borge Bakken, *Crime, Punishment, and Policing in China*. New York: Rowman & Littlefield Publishers, Inc., 2005.

Dui Hua Foundation. "Hu Jia Formally Arrested: Human Rights in Olympic Spotlight," *Dui Hua News*, January 31, 2008.

_____. "Some Observation of the Conviction of Hu Jia," *Dui Hua News*, April 4, 2008.

_____. "Parole Granted for American Businessman Imprisoned in China," *Dui Hua News*, July 2, 2008.

_____. "China Executes Scientist for Alleged Spy Activity," *Dui Hua News*, November 28, 2008.

_____. "Practical, Humanitarian Means Can Help Relieve Crowded Chinese Prisons,"*Dui Hua News*, Spring 2009.

_____. "Study Forces Rethinking on Popular Support for Death Penalty in China," *Dui Hua News* (Dialogue: Issue 41), Fall 2010.

_____. "Update on Criminal Law Amendment's Proposed Limits on Death Penalty," *Dui Hua News* (Dialogue: Issue 42), Winter 2011.

Dutton, M., and X. Zhangrun. "A Question of Difference: The Theory and Practice of the Chinese Prison," chapter in Borge Bakken, *Crimes, Punishment, and Policing in China*. New York: Rowman & Littlefied Publishers, Inc., 2005.

Eckholm, E. "China Said to Use Psychiatric Abuse in Repressing Sect," *New York Times*, February 18, 2001, p. A1.

Education in Japan Community Blog. "The Youth Drug Problem in Japan," *Education in Japan Community Blog*, 2002.

Emanuel, E. "How Much Does Health Cost?" *New York Times*, October 30, 2011, p. 5.

Fackler, M. "Career Women in Japan Find Blocked Path, Despite Equal Opportunity Law," *New York Times*, August 5, 2006.

_____. "In Japan New Jobless May Lack Safety Net." *New York Times*, February 8, 2009, p. 6.

_____. "A Towering Japanese Cliff, a Campaign to Combat Suicide," *New York Times*, December 18, 2009, p. A6.

_____. "A Shaken Japan Faces Reality: Many of Its People are Poor," *New York Times*, April 22, 2010, p. A6.

_____. "Falsely Convicted, Freed, and No Longer Just," *New York Times*, August 14, 2010, p. A1.

Fairclough, G. "China Plans $124 Billion Overhaul of Health Care," *Wall Street Journal*, January 22, 2009, p. A8.

Fan, M. "Confessed Police Killer Lionized by Thousands in China," *Washington Post*, November 14, 2008, p. A13.

Ford, P. "China's Mental Hsopitals: A New Push to Quash Dissent," *Christian Science Monitor*, June 9, 2011.

French, H. "Japan Unsettles Returnees Who Yearn to Leave Again," *New York Times*, May 3, 2000, p. A1.

_____."Educators Try to Tame Japan's Blackboard Jungles," *New York Times*, September 23, 2002, p. A6.

_____."A Corner of China in the Grip of a Lucrative Heroin Habit," *New York Times*, December 23, 2004, p. A1.

_____. "Rush for Wealth in China's Cities Shatters the Ancient Assurance of Care in Old Age," *New York Times*, November 3, 2006.

_____. "Fast-Growing China Says Little of Child Slavery's Role," *New York Times*, June 21, 2007, p. A3.

Fuyuno, I. "Japan Grooms New Lawyers: Slew of Law Schools Open Up, as Deregulation Spurs Litigation," *Wall Street Journal*, April 13, 2004.

Gibney, F. *Japan: The Fragile Superpower.* New York: W.W. Norton, 1975, p. 82.

Gladstone, R. "Dissident In China Ends Silence on Politics," *New York Times*, August 10, 2011, p. A1.

Hays, J. "Opium and Illegal Drugs in China: Facts and Details," article from Yahoo.com, February 2011.

He, H. "The Dawn of Due Process Principle in China," paper presented at the Yale University China-Law Workshop, New Haven, CT, 2008.

He, X. "Judicial Innovation and Local Politico: Judicialization of Administrative Governance in East China," paper presented at the Yale-China Law Workshop, New Haven, CT, October 25, 2011.

Herbert, W. *Foreign Workers and Law Enforcement in Japan.* London and New York: Kegan Paul International, 1996.

Hill, P. *The Japanese Mafia.* Oxford: Oxford University Press, 2003.

Hirano, R. "The Accused and Society: Some Aspects of Japanese Criminal Law," in A. Von Mehren, ed. *Law in Japan: The Legal Order in a Changing Society*. Cambridge, MA: Harvard University Press, 1963, p. 290.

Hokkaido Prefectural Police. "Organizational Chart of Hokkaido Prefectural Police," *Hokkaido Prefectural Government* website, 2011.

Hoover Institution. "Lessons from Abroad: Japan's Parole Model," Hoover Institution Stanford University, Policy Review, no. 75, March 1, 1996.

Horiuchi, K. *Japan: Criminal Justice Profiles of Asia*. Fuchu, Japan: United Nations Far East Institute for the Prevention of Crime and Treatment of Offenders, 1995.

Hutzler, C. "Gao Zhisheng, Missing Chinese Lawyer, Described Torture before Disappearing," *Huff Post World: The Internet Newspaper*, January 10, 2011.

Ike, N. *Japanese Politics: Patron-Client Democracy*. New York: Alfred Knopf, 1972.

Jacobs, A. "China Stifles Dissenters With Pills, Paper Says," *New York Times*, December 9, 2008, p. A13.

_____. "Decades of Settlers Sweat Build Chinese Region at Uighurs Expense," *New York Times*, August 7, 2009.

_____. "Arrest In China Rattles Backers of Legal Rights," *New York Times*, August 10, 2009, p. A1.

_____. Mail Accounts of Activists, Scholars, and Journalists Hit by Hackers in China," *New York Times*, March 31, 2010.

_____. "China Seeks to End 'Shame Parades' of Suspects," *New York Times*, July 28, 2010, p. A2.

_____. "As China's Economy Grows, Pollution Worsens Despite New Efforts to Control It," *New York Times*, July 29, 2010, p. A4.

_____. "Chinese Democracy Activist Is Given 10-Year Sentence," *New York Times*, March 26, 2011, p. A6.

_____. "Anger Over Protesters' Deaths Leads to Intensified Demonstrations by Mongolians," *New York Times*, May 31, 2011, p. A8.

_____. "Now Free, A Chinese Dissident Muzzles Himself," *New York Times*, June 24, 2011, p. A6.

_____. "Taking Big Risks to See a Chinese Dissident Under House Arrest," *New York Times*, October 19, 2011, p. A1.

_____, and Bullock, P. "A U.S. Tie to Push on Surveillance in Chinese Cities," *New York Times*, March 16, 2012, p. A1.

Japan Inc. "Alcoholism in Japan," *Japan Inc. Newsletter*, November 7, 2007.

Japan Society. "The Role of Public Prosecutors in Criminal Justice: Prosecutorial Discretion in Japan and the United States," Seminar Report, *Public Affairs Series* 14, New York, September 15, 1980, p. 5.

*Japan Times.* "The Slow Road to Gender Equality," editorial page, August 28, 1999.

Jianhua, F. "Fixing Flaws in the Law," *Beijing Review*, December 1, 2007.

Johnston, E. "Alcoholism Remains a Taboo Issue," *Japan Times*, April 7, 2009.

Kahn, J. "Deep Flaws, and Little Justice, In China's Court System," *New York Times*, September 21, 2005, p. A1.

_____. "Torture is Widespread in China, U. N. Investigator Says," *New York Times*, December 3, 2005, p. A1.

_____. "Legal Gadfly Bites Hard, and Beijing Slaps Him," *New York Times*, December 13, 2005.

_____. Boy's Death at China Hospital Spurs Riot Over Care and Fees," *New York Times*, November 3, 2006, p. A1.

_____, and J. Yardley. "As China Roars, Pollution Reaches Deadly Fumes," *New York Times*, August 26, 2007, p. A1.

Kamiya, S. "Life Term Urged for Ichihashi," *Japan Times*, July 13, 2011, p. 1.

_____, and J. Hongo. "Ichihashi Gets Life For Hawker, Rape, Murder," *Japan Times*, July 21, 2011, p. 1.

Kamm, H. "In Tokyo, A Raucous Honky-Tonk Area That Has No Crime," *New York Times*, July 22, 1981.

Kamm, J. "Free on the Fourth of July," *Wall Street Journal*, July 4, 2008.

_____. "Issues and Cases: A Human Rights Dialogue with the Chinese Government," paper presented at the Yale-China Law Workshop, New Haven, CT, August 28, 2009.

Kanetake-Oura, B. *Fifty Years of New Japan.* London: Smith Elder, 1910.

Kawashima, T. "Dispute Resolution in Contemporary Japan," in A. Von Mehren ed. *Law in Japan: The Legal Order in a Changing Society.* Cambridge, MA: Harvard University Press, 1963, p. 43.

Kirk, D. "The Shame of Japanese Justice," *Asahi Evening News (London Observer Service)*, February 2, 1981.

Kristof, N. "For Chinese Spies, the Enemies are Everywhere," *New York Times*, October 18, 1991.

_____. "Japan's Invisible Minority: Better Off Than in Past, But Still Outcasts," *New York Times*, November 30, 1995, Op-Ed page.

_____. "God and China," *New York Times*, November 26, 2002, p. A.

Kuno, O. "The Meiji State, Minponshugi, and Ultranationalism," in J.Victor Koschmann,ed. *Authority and the Individual in Japan*. Tokyo: University of Tokyo Press, 1978, p. 61.

Kyodo News. "Rise in Elderly Shoplifters Due to Loneliness: Police Study," *Japan Times*, August 3, 2009.

_____. "Biker Gang Ranks Fall Below 10,000," *Japan Times*, February 11, 2011.

_____. "Poverty Rate Hit Record High in 09," *Japan Times*, July 13, 2011.

Lacey, M. "Teen-Age Birth Rate in U.S. Falls Again," *New York Times*, October 27, 1999, p. A16.

LaFraniere, S. "Discontent on Health Care Spurs Violence at Hospitals in China," *New York Times*, August 11, 2010.

_____, and D. Levin. "Assertive Chinese Held in Mental Wards," *New York Times*, November 11, 2010, p. A1.

_____. "China Revokes Probation of Missing Human Rights Lawyer," *New York Times*, December 16, 2011.

_____. "A Chinese Official Tests A New Political Approach," *New York Times*, December 31, 2011, p. A5.

_____. "China Acts to Bolster Defendants' Rights," *New York Times*, March 9, 2012,p. A6.

*Laogai Research Foundation*. "Lawsuit Filed by Liu Xianbin and Others," Newsletter (Founded in 1992), August 30, 2011.

Lawyers Committee For Human Rights. "Opening to Reform: An Analysis of China's Revised Criminal Procedure Law," Lawyers Committee on Human Rights, New York, 1996.

Lee, P. "Law Schools Get Practical," *Wall Street Journal*, July 11, 2011, p. B5.

Lehavot, K. "Mental Illness in Japan: A Need for Change," Japanese Civilization, Arts & Sciences, Washington University in St. Louis, MO, December 3, 2001.

Leng, S. and H. Chiu. *Criminal Justice in Post-Mao China*, Albany, NY: State University of New York Press, 1985.

Li, Chen. "China in the Year 2020: Three Political Scenarios," *Asia Policy*, no 4, July 2007, pg. 17–29.

MacDonald, M. "China Heads in Executions, Report by Amnesty Finds," *New York Times*, March 31, 2010, p. A1.

MacFarquhar, R. and M. Schoenhals. *Mao's Last Revolution*. Cambridge, MA: Harvard University Press, 2006.

Matsuda, R. "Review of Mental Health Care Reform," *Health Policy Monitor*, Kinugasa Research Institute, Ritsumeikan University, Kyoto, Survey No. 14, 2009.

McCurry, J. "Prisoner Driven Insane on Japan's Death Row, Says Amnesty," *The Guardian.*

Ministry of Justice, *White Paper on Crime*, 2008. Tokyo: Research and Training Institute, Ministry of Justice, 2008.

Mitchell, R. *Thought Control in Prewar Japan.* Ithaca, NY: Cornell University Press, 1976, p. 192.

Murphy, J. "Joblessness Spurs Shift in Japan's View on Poverty," *Wall Street Journal*, May 2, 2009, p. 2.

Nakatani, Y. "Treatment of Offenders with Mental Disorders: Focusing on Prison Psychiatry," Seishin Shinkeigaku Qashi (translated into English as an abstract in *Pub Med*), 113 (5), 2011.

*Nation Master.Com*, "Asia-China-Crime." On-line Facts and Statistics, 2011.

National Police Academy. "Community Policing in Japan," *Tokyo: International Research and Training Institute for Criminal Investigation, National Police Academy*. Japan: International Cooperation Agency, 1998.

National Police Agency of Japan. *The Police of Japan*. Tokyo: Government of Japan, 1998.

_____. *The Police of Japan*. Tokyo Government of Japan, 2011.

Office of Juvenile Justice and Delinquency Prevention. "Juvenile Justice Bulletin," United States Department of Justice, 2009.

Okudaira, Y. "Some Preparatory Notes for the Study of the Peace Preservation Law in Prewar Japan," Annals of the Institute of Human Relations.

Onishi, N. "For Japan's New Homeless, There's Disdain and Danger," *New York Times*, December 17, 2003, p. A2.

_____. "Never Lost, but Found Daily: Japanese Honesty," *New York Times*, January 8, 2004, p. A1.

_____. "Japan, Easygoing Till Now, Plans Sex Traffic Crackdown," *New York Times*, February 16, 2005.

_____. "Pressed By Police, Even the Innocent Confess in Japan," *New York Times*, May 11, 2007, p. A1.

_____. "Japan Learns Dreaded Tasks of Jury Duty," *New York Times*, July 16, 2007, p. A1.

_____. "Starving Man's Diary Suggests Harshness of Welfare in Japan," *New York Times*, October 12, 2007, p. A1.

_____. "As Japan Ages, Prison's Adapt To Going Gray," *New York Times*, November 3, 2007, p. A1.

_____. "As Its Work Force Ages and Shrinks, Japan Needs and Fears Chinese Labor," *New York Times*, August 15, 2008, p. A5.

_____. "In Japan, Hope Fades For Disposable Workers," *New York Times*, October, 11, 2008.

Page, T. "Children of the Revolution," *Wall Street Journal*, Saturday-Sunday, November 26–27, 2011, p. C1.

Pan, P. *Out of Mao's Shadow: The Struggle For the Soul of a New China.* New York: Simon & Schuster, 2008.

Parker, L. *The Japanese Police System Today: An American Perspective.* Tokyo: Kodansha International, 1984.

_____. *Parole and the Community Based Treatment of Offenders in Japan and the United States.* New Haven, CT: University of New Haven Press, 1986.

_____. *The Japanese Police System Today: A Comparative Study.* Armonk, NY: M.E. Sharpe, 2001.

Pei, M. "Social Unrest in China: Symptoms, Causes, and Implications," lecture presented at the Yale-China Law Workshop, New Haven, CT, 2007.

Pilling, D. "Tokyo Begins to Heed Nation's Cry For Help," *Financial Times*, June 23, 2007.

Pils, E. "Rights Activism in China." lecture presented at the Yale-China Law Workshop. New Haven,CT, November 10, 2006.

Rosen, E. "The Influence of Culture on Mental Health and Psychopathology in Japan," Japanese Civilization, Arts & Sciences, Washington University in St. Louis, MO, November 29, 2001.

Rosenthal, E. "Police Abuses Start to Get Attention in China," *New York Times*, March 8, 1999, p. A1.

_____. "In China's Legal Evolution, The Lawyers are Handcuffed," *New York Times*, January 6, 2000, p. A1.

_____. "A Poor Ethnic Enclave in China Is Shadowed By Drugs and H.I.V.," *New York Times*, December 21, 2001, p. A1.

_____. "Workers' Plight Brings New Military in China," *New York Times*, March 10, 2003, p. A8.

Savage, C. "Trend to Lighten Harsh Sentences Catches On in Conservative States," *New York Times*, August 13, 2011, p. A14.

Seymour, J. "Sizing Up Chinese Prisons," chapter in Borge Bakken, *Crime, Punishment, and Policing in China.* New York: Rowman & Littlefied Publishers, Inc., 2005.

Smith, C. "China Justice: Swift Passage to Execution," *New York Times,* June 19, 2001, p. A1.

_____. "China's Efforts Against Crime Make No Dent as Sparse Policing Belies Crackdowns," *New York Times,* September 9, 2001, p. A1.

SOH Network. "Former Prison Officer Exposes Brutality and Corruption in Chinese Prison System," *SOH Network—China Uncensored,* online, May 26, 2010.

*Southern Weekend* (Chinese Newspaper). Interview with Tsinghua University Professor and Member Legal Committee of the National People's Congress, August 26, 2010.

Stran, S. "Use of the Internet Quietly Transforms Way Japanese Live," *New York Times,* Sunday, May 14, 2000.

Sugai, S. "The Japanese Police System," in R. Ward ed. *Five Studies in Japanese Politics.* Center for Japanese Studies, Occasional Papers, no. 7. Ann Arbor: University of Michigan Press, 1957.

Suli, Z. "The Current Legal, Judicial, and Political Controversy Over the Death Penalty in China," lecture presented at the Yale-China Law Workshop, New Haven, CT, November 15, 2011.

Suo, Masayuki. *I Just Didn't Do It.* Feature Length Japanese Film (English subtitles), from the director of the highly acclaimed film *Shall We Dance,* 2008.

*Supreme Court of Japan.* "Guide to Judicial Proceedings," Tokyo: Supreme Court of Japan, 2009.

_____. "Overview of the Judicial System in Japan," Tokyo: Supreme Court of Japan, 2010.

Tabuchi, H. "Goodbye Honored Guest," *New York Times,* April 23, 2009, p. B.

_____ and M. McDonald, "Once Again, Trial by Jury in Japan," *New York Times,* August 7, 2009, p. A1.

_____. "Japan Gives Journalists a tour of the Execution Chambers," *New York Times,* August 28, 2010.

Takakashi, I. Personal communication to the author, August 12, 1999.

Tanabe, T. "The Processes of Litigation: An Experiment with the Adversary System," in A. Von Mehren, ed. *Law in Japan: The Legal Order in a Changing Society.* Cambridge, MA: Harvard University Press, 1963, p. 77.

Tanner, M. S. "Campaign-Style Policing in China and Its Critics," chapter in *Crime, Punishment, and Policing in China*. Lanham, MD: Rowman & Littlefied Publishers, Inc., 2005.

_____. "We the People (of China)," *Wall Street Journal*, February 2, 2006, Op-Ed page.

_____. "Policing in China and the Rule of Law," lecture presented at the Yale-China Law Workshop, New Haven, CT, March 2006.

Teague, M. "The Other Tibet," *National Geographic Magazine*, November 16, 2010, p. 1.

Tejada, C. "Outrage Over Taxes Rocks a Chinese Town," *Wall Street Journal*, October 28, 2011, p. A12.

Terrill, R. "A Closer Look at China," a lecture at the Yale University Symposium, New Haven, CT, April 19, 2006.

Terrill, R.J. *World Criminal Justice Systems: A Survey*, 6th ed. Newark, NJ., Lexis Nexus Group, 2007.

*The Economist*. "Mental Health Care in Japan—In the Dark Ages," November 22, 2001.

_____. "Suicide in Japan: Death Be Not Proud," May 1, 2008.

_____. "Japanese Immigration Policy: A Nation's Bouncers," May 15, 2010.

_____. "They All Came Home," April 23, 2011.

_____. *Pocket World in Figures*, London, 2011.

_____. "Japan's Post-Quake Economy: Casting About For A Future," May 21, 2011, p. 77.

_____. "Activism in China: Blind Man's Bluff," November 15, 2011, p. 51.

_____. "Welcome Home: Changing Migration Patterns," February 25, 2012, p. 53.

Tipton, E. *Japanese Police State: The Tokko in Interwar Japan*, Honolulu: University of Hawaii Press, 1990.

Trevaskes, S. "The Shifting Sands of Punishment in China in the Era of 'Harmonious Society,'" *Law & Policy*, vol. 32, no. 3, July 2010.

_____. *Policing Serious Crime in China*, New York: Routledge, 2010

UNAFEI (United Nations Far East Institute). Chapter 7: "Rehabilitation of Offenders," Criminal Justice in Japan, 2010.

United Nations. "Homicide Statistics—Latest Year Available," *United Nations Office on Drugs and Crime*, 2011.

United States Department of Justice. *Crime in the United States: Uniform Crime Reports*, 2009. Washington, D.C.: U.S. Government Printing Office, 2010

United States Department of Labor. "Labor Statistics for May 2008," U.S. Government, 2009.

Van Sant, S. "Chinese Dissidents Committed to Mental Hospitals," *PBS Newshour* interview, September 11, 2009.

Wang, S. "China's Organ Donation System and Executed Prisoner's as Donors," *Wall Street Journal*, August 27, 2009.

Watts, J. "A. Weiwei Investigated Over Nude Art," *The Guardian*, November 18, 2011.

Wheatley, A. "Why Japan Will Avert a Fiscal Crash," *Toronto Globe and Mail*, March 17, 2011. Op-Ed page.

Westney, E. "The Emulation of Western Organizations in Meiji Japan: The Case of Paris Prefecture Police and the Keishi-Cho." *Journal of Japanese Studies*, vol. 8, no. 2, 1982.

Whipp, L. "Long-Term Incentives Needed to Counter Population Decline," *Financial Times*, April 18, 2010, p. 2.

Wikipedia. List of Countries by Homicide Rate, *Wikipedia—The Free Encyclopedia*, 2011.

_____. "Judicial System of Japan," *Wikipedia—The Free Encyclopedia*, 2011.

_____. "Bosozoku," *Wikipedia—The Free Encyclopedia*, 2011.

_____. "Illegal Drug Trade in the Peoples Republic of China," *Wikipedia—The Free Encyclopedia*, 2011.

Wilgoren, D., K. Richburg, and C. Richards. "Liu Xiaobo, Jailed in China, Honored in Absentia by Nobel Committee," *Washington Post*, December 10, 2010.

Wilkinson, R., and K. Pickett. *The Spirit Level: Why Greater Equality Makes Societies Stronger*. New York: Bloomsbury Press, 2009.

Wines, M. "China Keeps 7 Million Tireless Eyes on Its People," *New York Times*, August 3, 2010, p. A1.

_____. "Chinese Police Confine Artist and Activist to His Beijing Home," *New York Times*, November 6, 2010, p. A4.

_____. "Amid the Chaos, Finding Reassurance in Order," *New York Times*, March 26, 2011, p. A1.

_____. "Vendors' Dispute in China Escalates Into Violent Melee," *New York Times*, June 13, 2011, p. A4.

_____. "A Village in Revolt Could Be A Harbinger," *New York Times*, December 26, 2011, p. A1.

Wong, E. "China Has Sentenced 55 Over Tibet Riot in March," *New York Times*, November 6, 2008, p. A18.

_____. "China: Unrest Follows an Increase in Security Budget, Group Reports," *New York Times*, October 13, 2011, p. A3.

Yamaguchi, M. "Prisons Trying to Cope With Swelling Elderly Population," *Japan Times*, December 9, 2010.

_____. "Japan Suicide Role Still Among The World's Highest Due To Low Job Prospects," *Huff Post World: The Internet Newspaper*, March 3, 2011.

Yardley, J. "Issue in China: Many in Jails Without Trial," *New York Times*, May 9, 2005, p. A1.

_____ and J. Kahn. "China Gives Times Researcher 3 Years," *New York Times*, August 25, 2006, p. A1.

Yiwu, L. "Walking Out on China," *New York Times*, September 15, 2011, p. A35.

Zhiqiang, P. "June Fourth Seventeen Years Later," *New York Review of Books*, vol. 53, November 13, August 10, 2006.

_____. "Freedom of Expression and The Law in China & the Media," lecture presented at the Yale-China Law Workshop. Accompanying article, "An Absurd Decision Reflects a Crisis of Confidence in the Judicial System: Written After Li Jian Lost His Lawsuit," New Haven, CT, December 3, 2007.

# Index